The Echo of Us

The Echo of Us

A Love Tethered
Through the Seasons of Life
and Beyond

Tammy Rébéré

For the children we've lost
May they be cherished and loved
Forevermore

TABLE OF CONTENTS

TABLE OF CONTENTS

TABLE OF CONTENTS

A NOTE TO READERS

*L*ife is a beautiful journey of happiness, pain, and growth. When it comes to happiness, life can be full of love, and bliss, and wonderful experiences. But when it comes to pain, life can be harsh and traumatic, and sometimes empty. I'm sure you're familiar the expression, "No pain, no gain," but the opposite is true as well, for if we've never had something we wouldn't know what it's like to lose it. The pain of losing something or someone that we treasure so much is the worst kind of pain because it leaves gaping holes in our lives and grief has a way of swallowing us up if we let it.

But does that mean we should never love? Not at all! We should love with all our might, and love fiercely, for we never know what the future might hold. I'm reminded of what C. S. Lewis wrote in his book, *A Grief Observed*, after the death of his wife. "The pain I feel now is the happiness I had before. That's the deal." Lewis understood the equation of happiness and pain, and he was willing to endure all future sorrow if it meant he could experience the love he would share with his dying wife.

We can't have one without the other. We can't escape the pain. There's no hurdling it. There's no bypassing it. We must journey through it, and therein lies the growth. *That's* the deal.

Do we need pain in order to grow? Not necessarily. However, when we experience pain, hindsight often comes into play. We ponder what could have been done differently, what could have changed. Or, in the absence of understanding the meaning of why things happened, we may attempt to make our suffering more meaningful by sharing it with others so that they, too, may experience catharsis.

The Echo of Us continues where *The Echo of You* left off—with a couple fated to be together. In this sequel, the couple begins their journey in a blissful state of matrimony. All their hopes and dreams are still in the future, yet to be realized. Unfortunately, their lives take a sharp turn and they encounter loss, and together they must learn to heal, and grow, and lean on each other if they are to face and overcome the tragedies still waiting on the horizon.

When writing this book, I pulled from much of my own life experiences. I can honestly say there were times when I didn't want to continue. I felt gutted. Sometimes the words flowed as freely as my tears. Other times, they were stuck in my throat and difficult to conjure. Pairing the photos with the poems was even harder because it made it all come to life. Painful memories I'd sooner forget came forward, but also blissful, happy memories. And through it all, I found growth. I grew to understand more about myself and to appreciate that the healing process happens over a lifetime of various stages.

It is my hope that the experiences of this fated couple who share millennia of lifetimes together—all their love, laughter, passion, and heartache—will resonate with you, and that you, too, may find happiness through them, and if need be, healing.

With love,
Tammy Rébéré
August 2024

LOVE

&

HOPE

Love, in it's purest form,

is patient and kind.

It always protects,

always trusts,

always hopes,

always perseveres.

It will never fail.

1 Corinthians 13

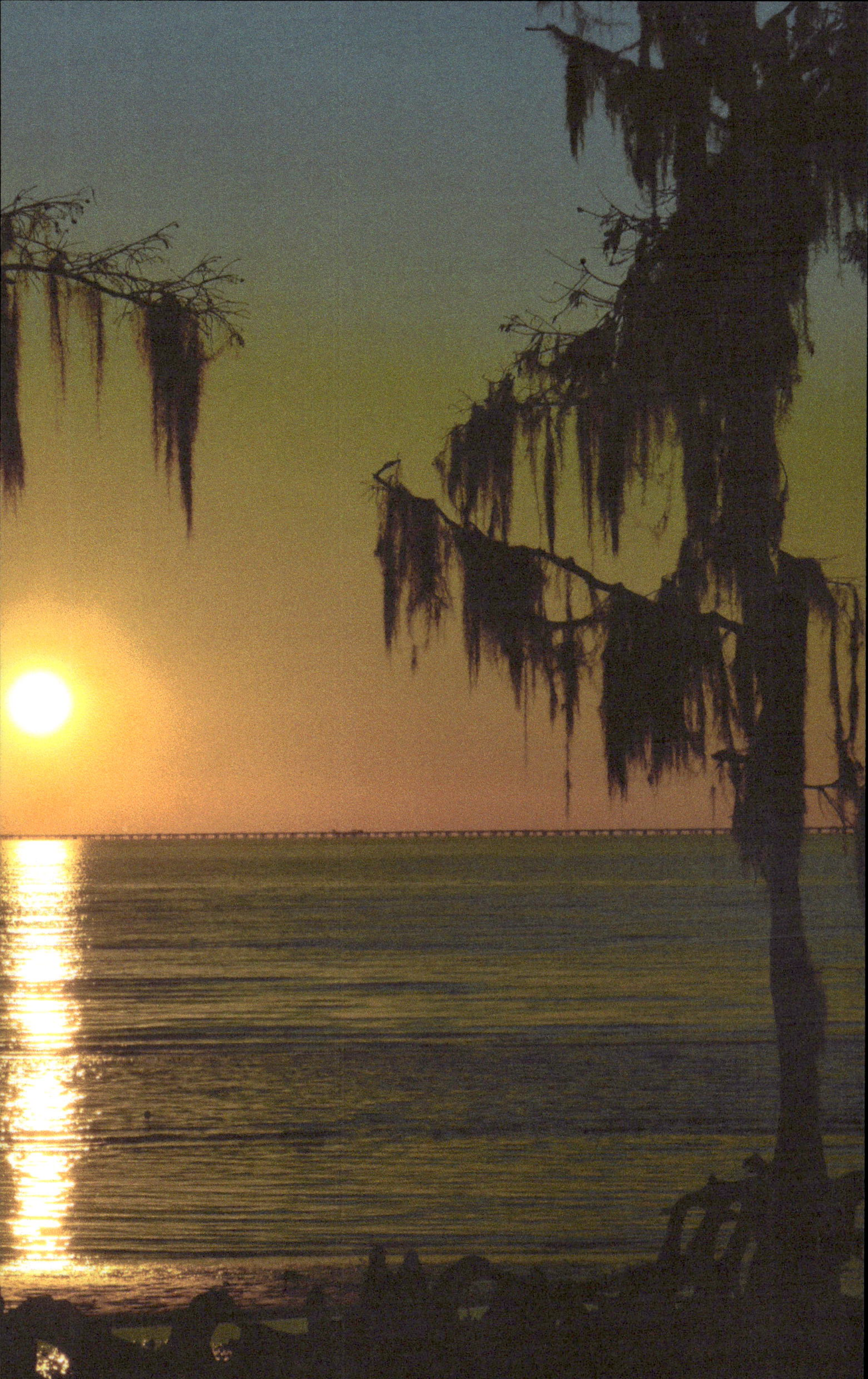

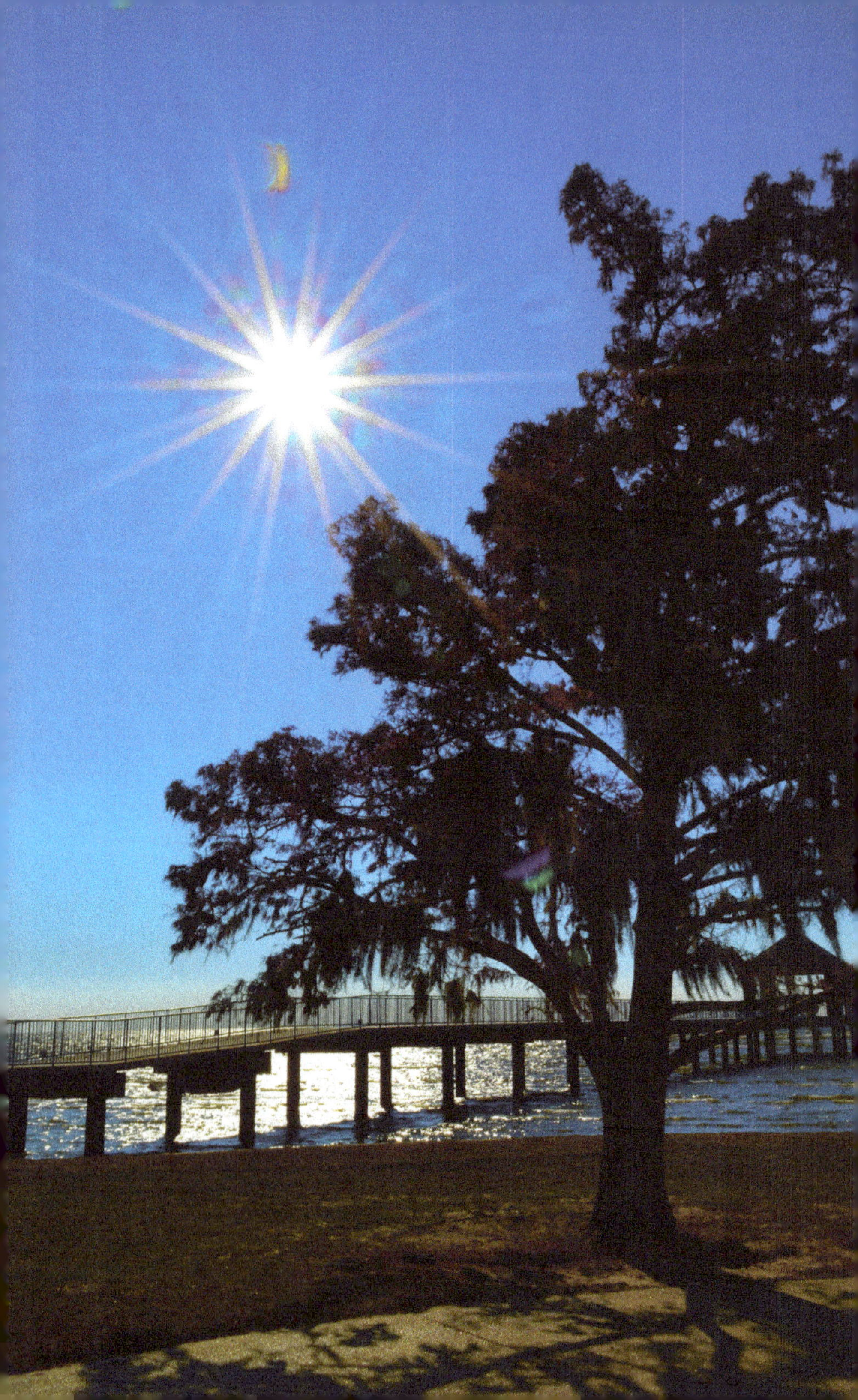

It's Only Ever Been You

From the dawn of time I searched
For the one that would complete me.
Faint echoes amidst the terrors of life
Kept my soul alive and free.

I knew your face and your heart
Before we had ever met.
Even upon my very essence
Your name was inscribed and set.

Loud and strong your echo found its way
Through the chaos and the dark.
It shone a brilliant beacon
With a new path to embark.

All my life I dreamed and waited
With a love that was pure and true.
And now, I pledge myself body and soul
Because darling, it's only ever been you.

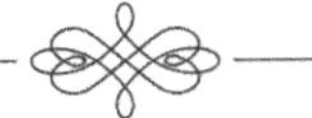

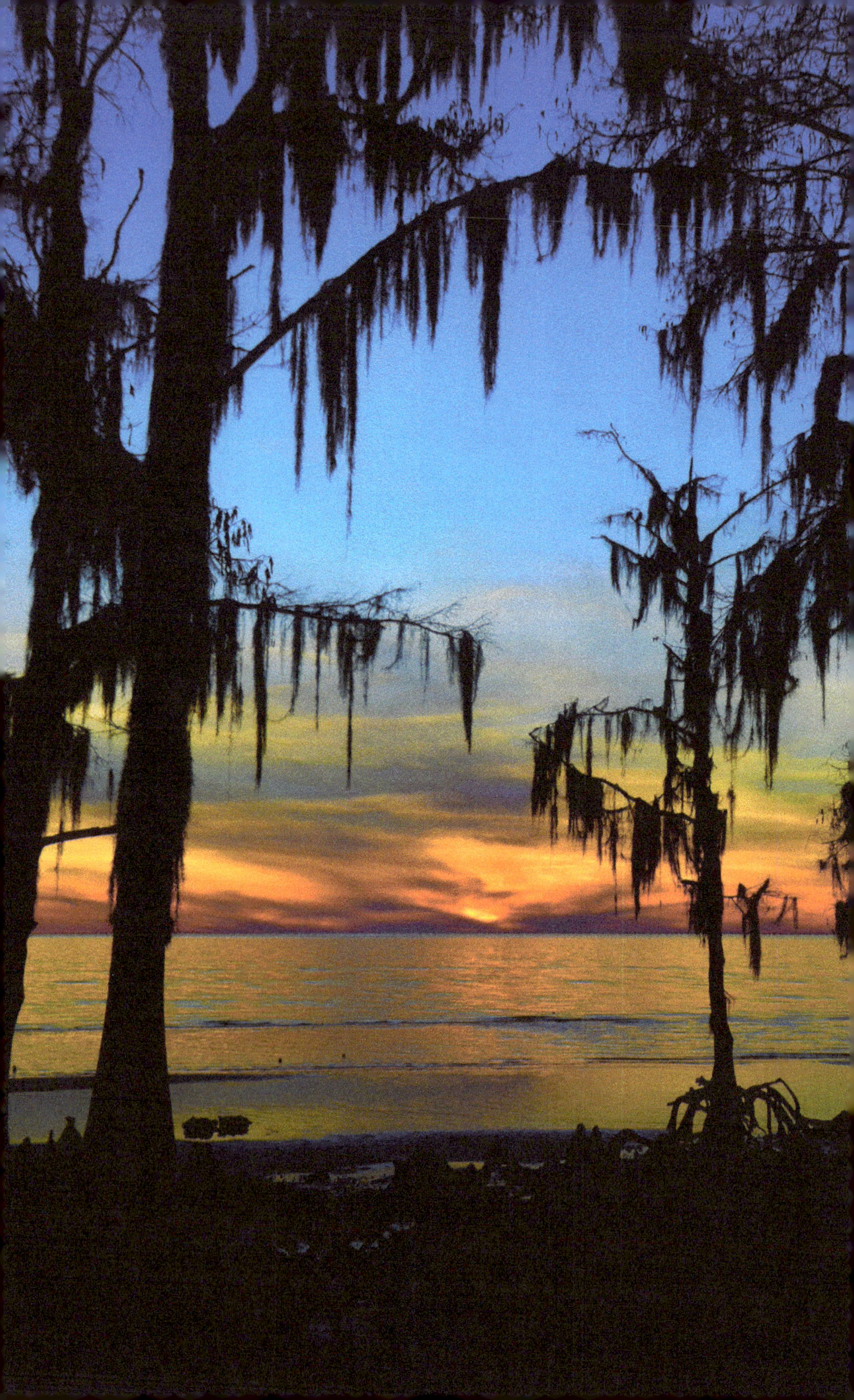

Kites of the Sky

For so long I searched for you
Without knowing who you were.
You infiltrated my dreams,
And you were the one. I was sure.

Night after blissful night,
We met on an abandoned beach,
Underneath a crescent moon
Far away and out of reach.

We declared our vows of love,
And promised to stay true.
But then, life got in the way,
And for a while, I lost you.

We became like kites in the wind
With our tether trailing behind,
Flying this way and that—
I was sure to lose my mind.

Once I learned to fly on my own,
I was stronger and free.
And when you were ready,
The tether led you back to me.

Now we soar through the clouds
And to the moon we fly.
The wonders of the world are ours
Because we are the kites of the sky.

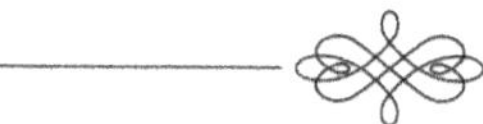

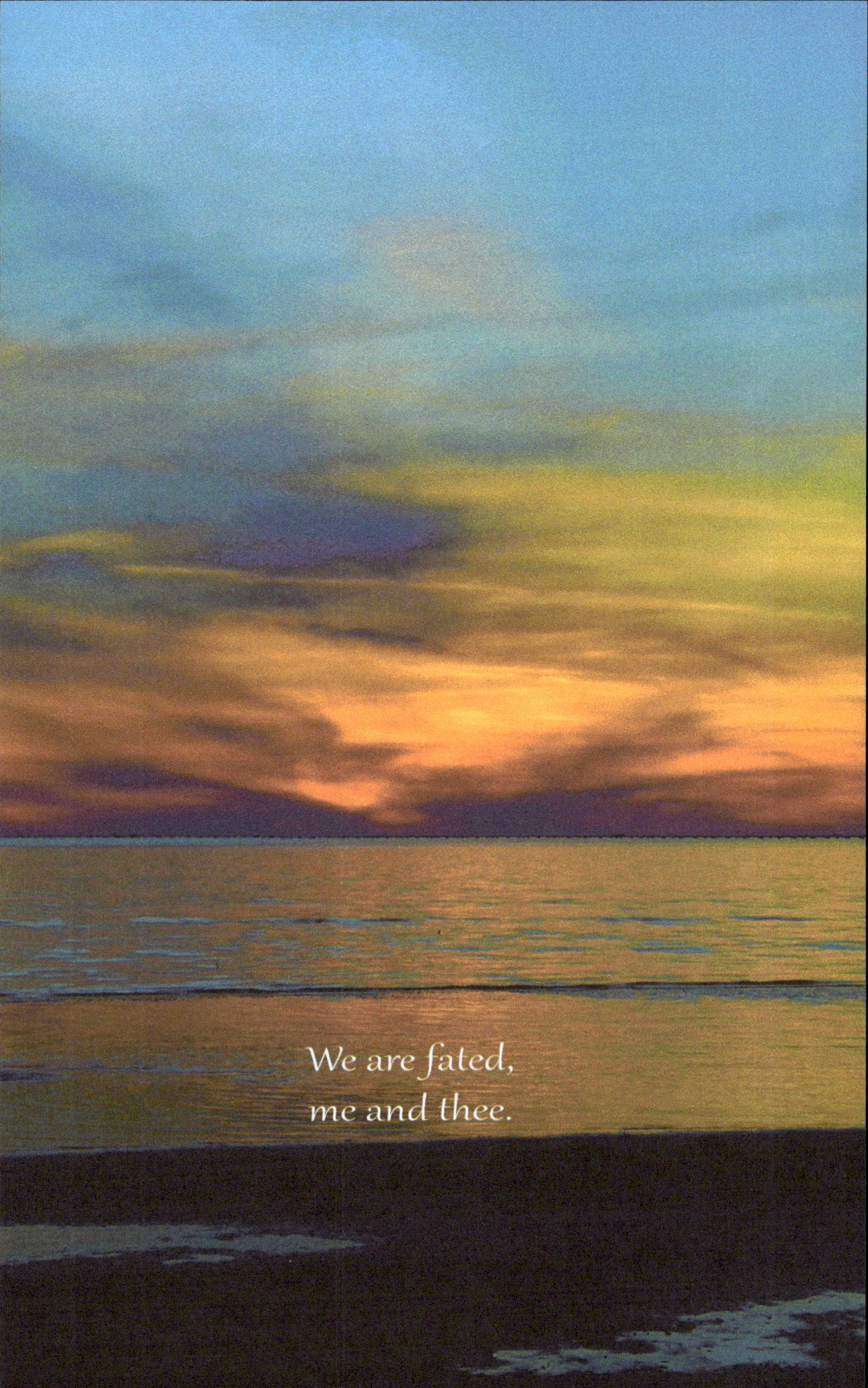
We are fated,
me and thee.

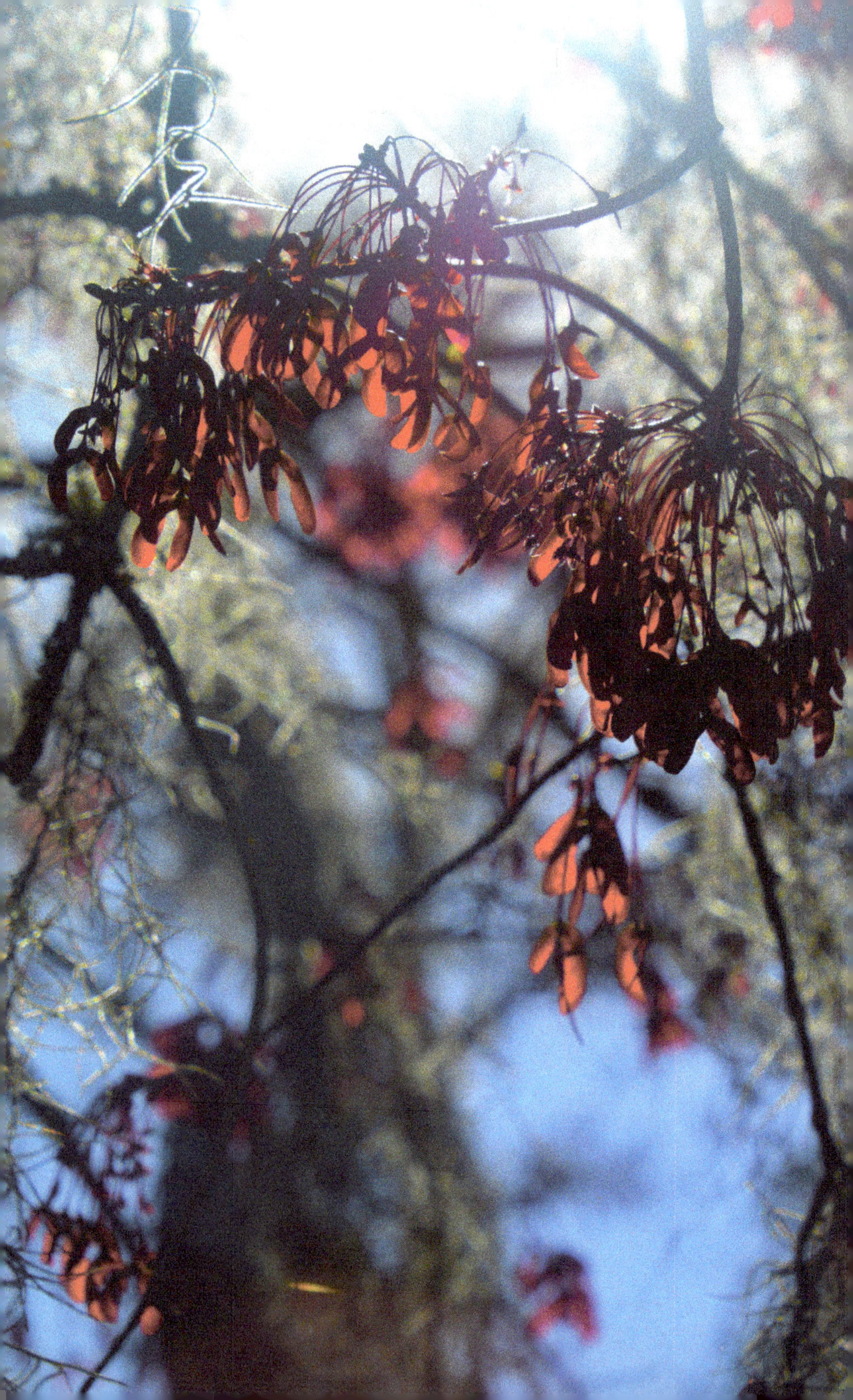

Eternity

How can it be?
That I, a speck of astral dust,
Should find in thee
Eternity?

A world exists
Behind your eyes,
A galaxy of no goodbyes,
Just bliss.
And this:

A crescent moon
That grins
Because it knows
It wins
Before it ends.

And so shall we.

And having won,
The cosmos comes undone.
Two planets merge as one—
Its shore and sea,
Forever fused
in victory.

A diamond oath,
a single ring,
Encircles this brave celestial thing.
A billion crystals
Licked by light,
The frozen, hot,
The wrong made right.

And so I kneel
Upon the grass,
And watch the universe
Collapse
Around the bride,
The bud, the bloom—
They both survive.
And more than that . . .

They thrive.

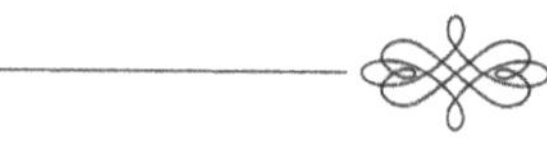

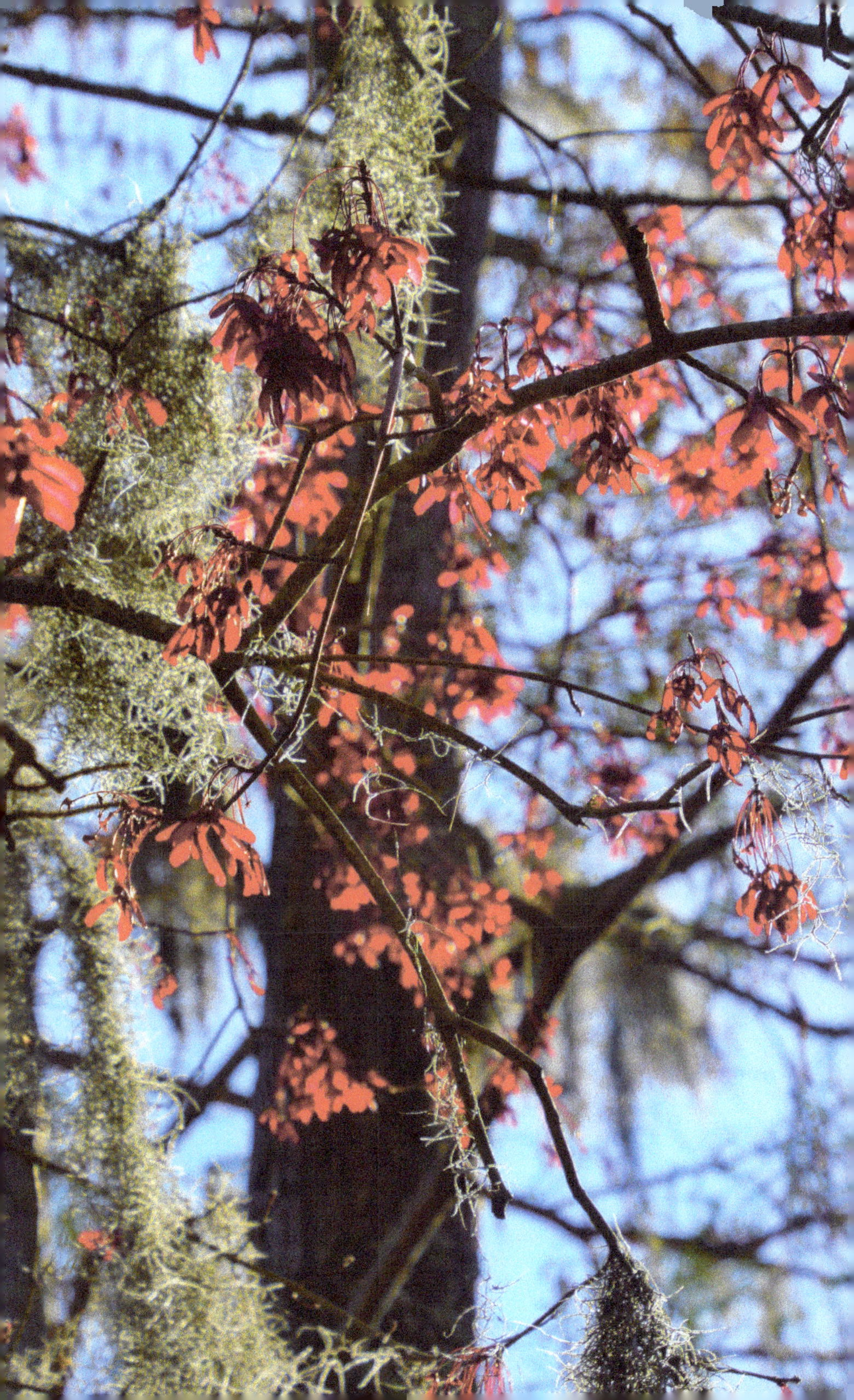

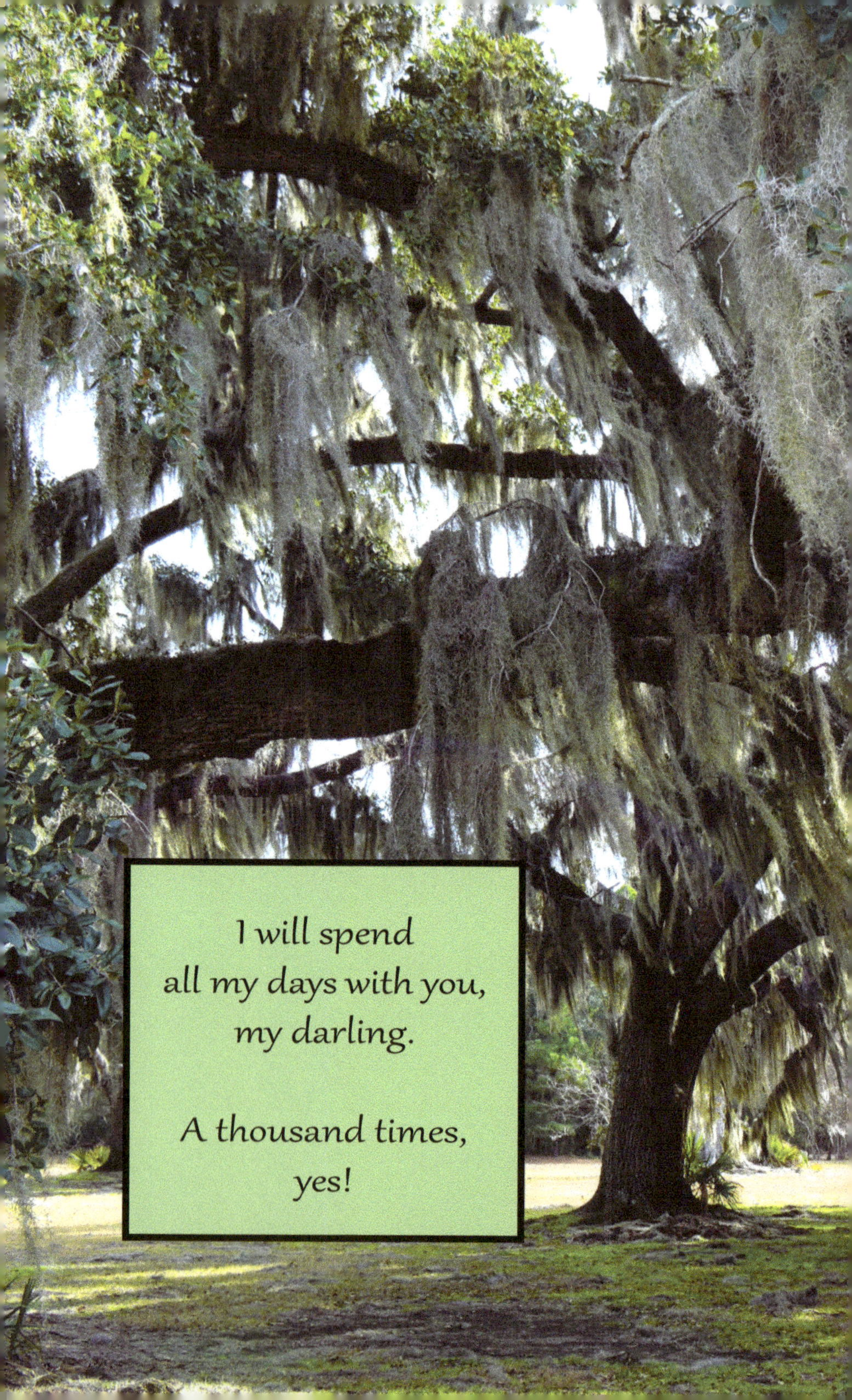

I will spend
all my days with you,
my darling.

A thousand times,
yes!

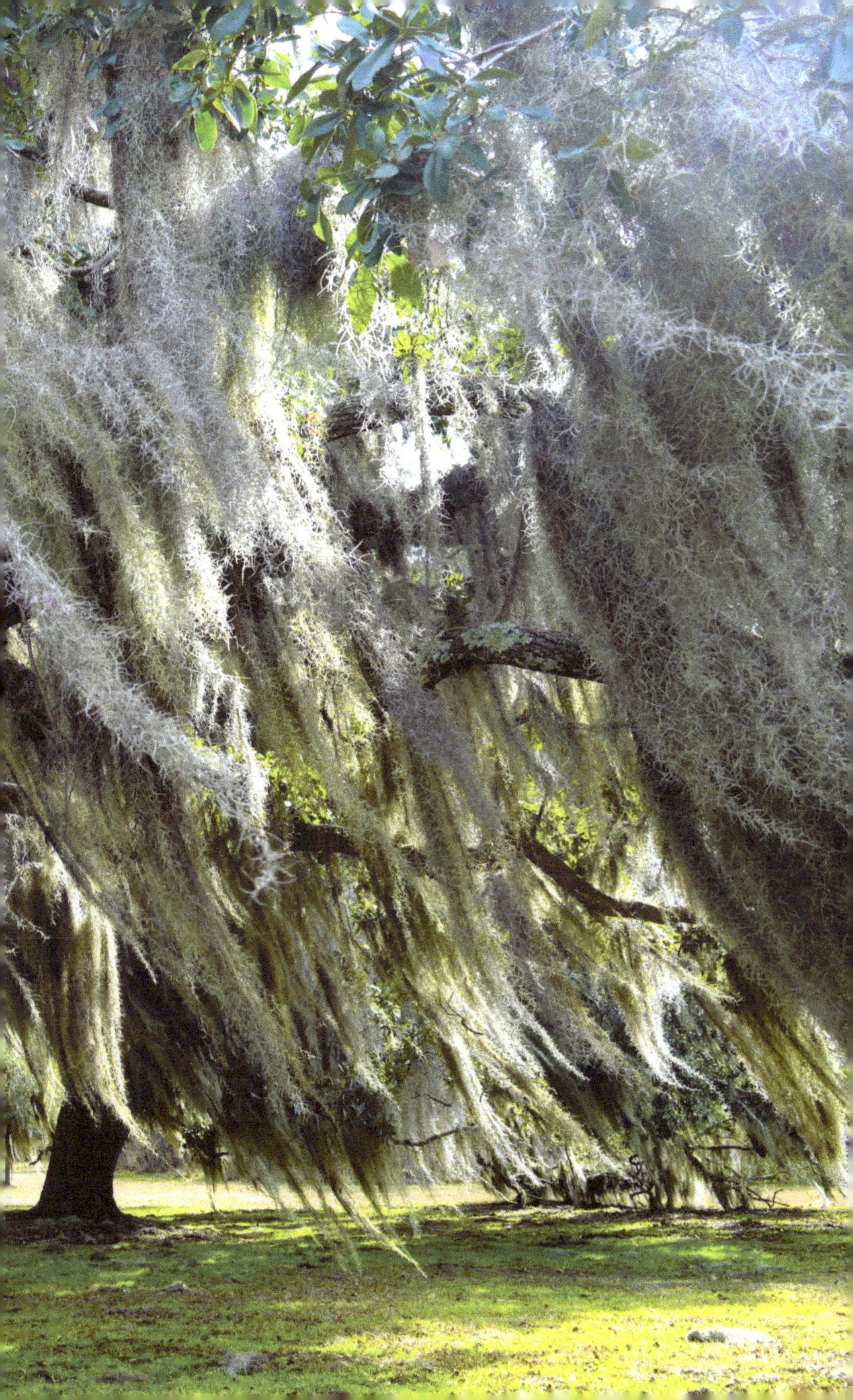

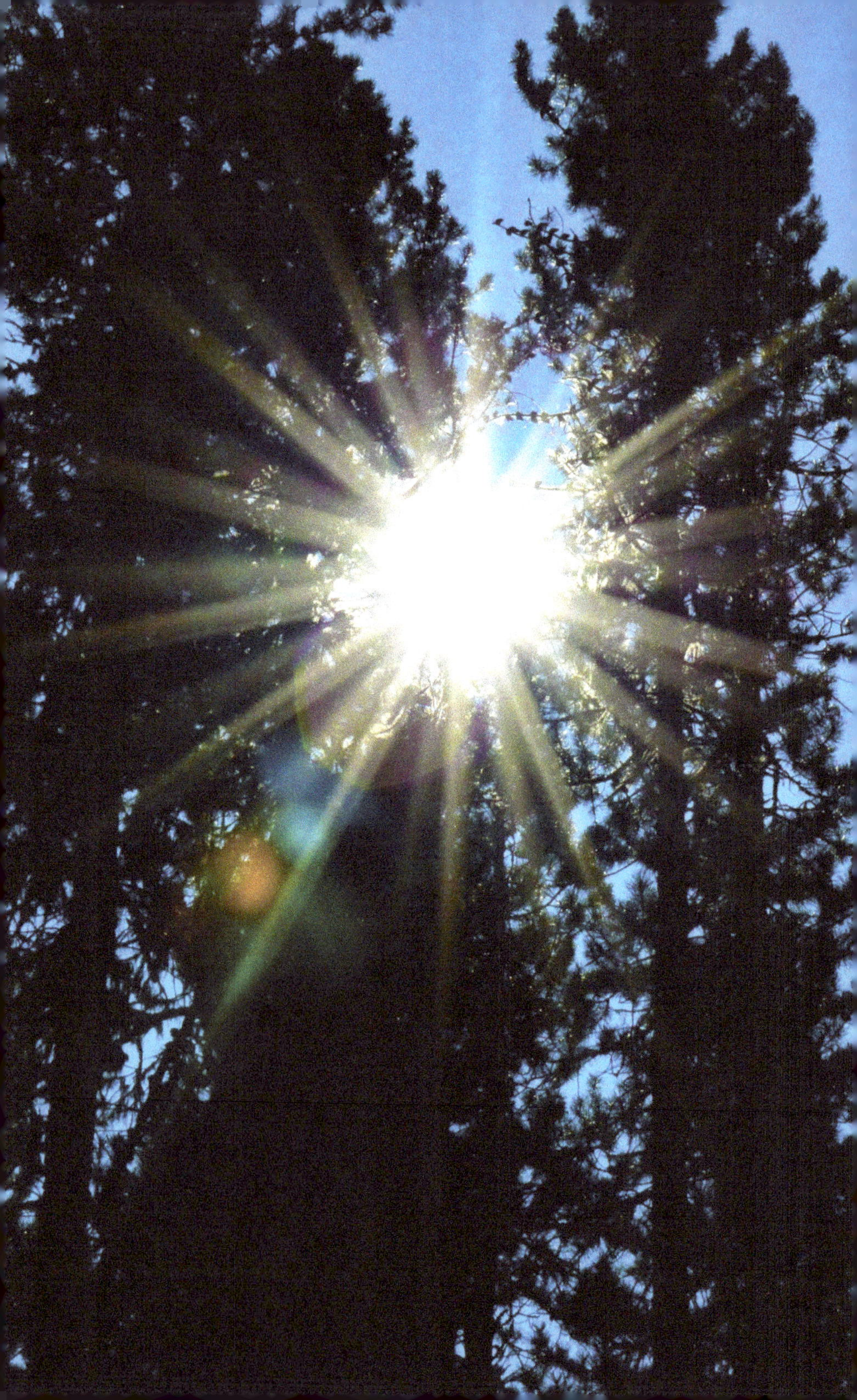

I Didn't Know

I didn't know I could feel this way.
The way the stars shine upon a moonlit lake in the quiet
of the night,
Shimmering, dappling.

The way water eases along the sides of a ketch as it sails
along the deep blue sea,
Licking and lapping.

I didn't know I could feel this way.
The way a fish jumps from safety for its dinner on a cool
summer's night,
Hungering, sacrificing.

The way the warm sun delights the soul on the coldest
of winter's days,
Beckoning and enticing.

I didn't know I could feel this way.
The way fireflies light a path in the darkest of forests,
Captivating, entrancing.

The way the tide flows towards the shore by the command of the moon,
Caressing and dancing.

I didn't know I could feel this way.
The way your fingers electrify my skin with just the slightest touch,
Heart-racing, increasing.

The way your body moves with mine in our most intimate moments,
Enveloping, then releasing.

I didn't know I could feel this way.
Yet here I stand on the sands of our most sacred beach,
Promising to spend the rest of my days with you,
Loving and vowing.

Forevermore.

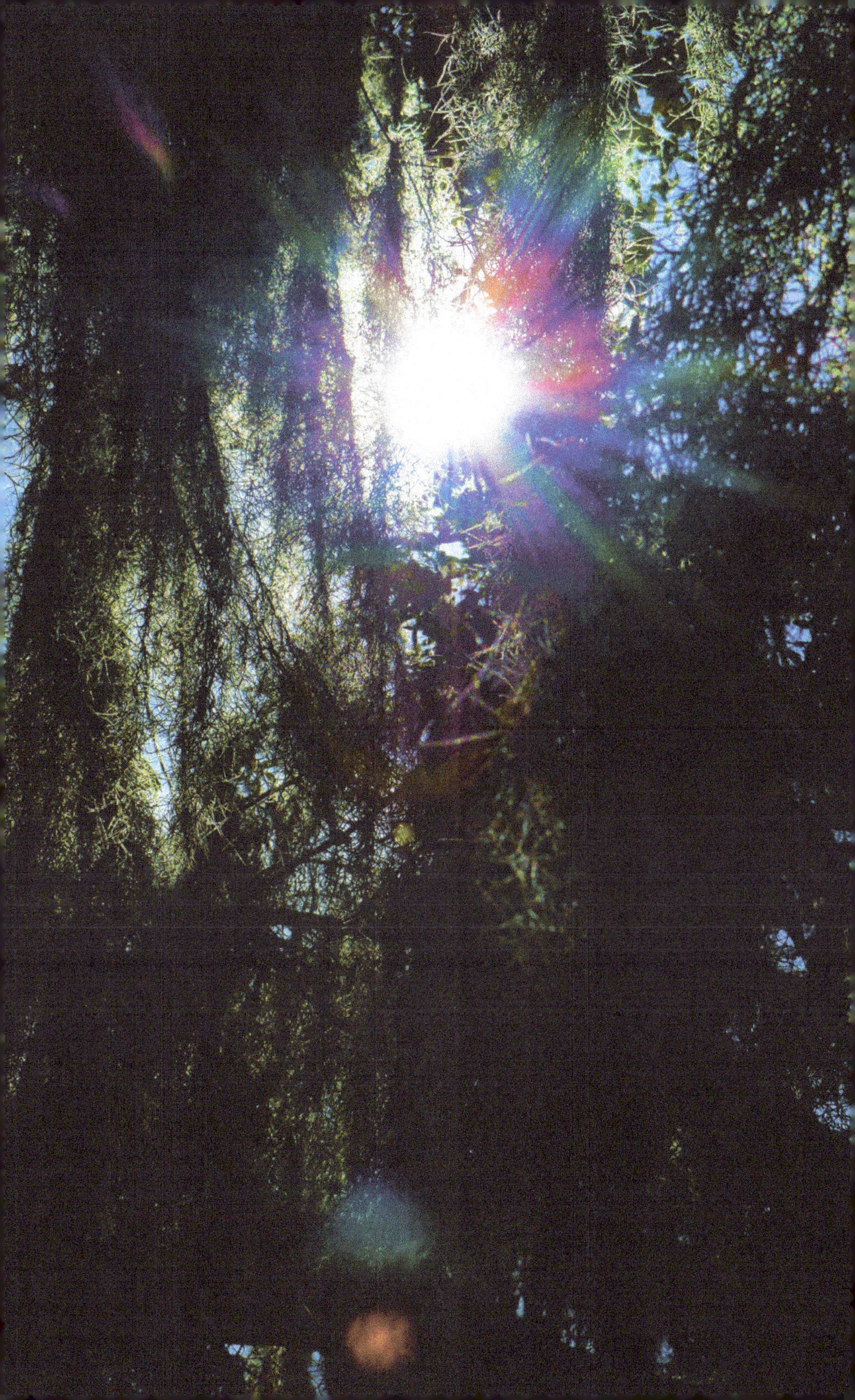

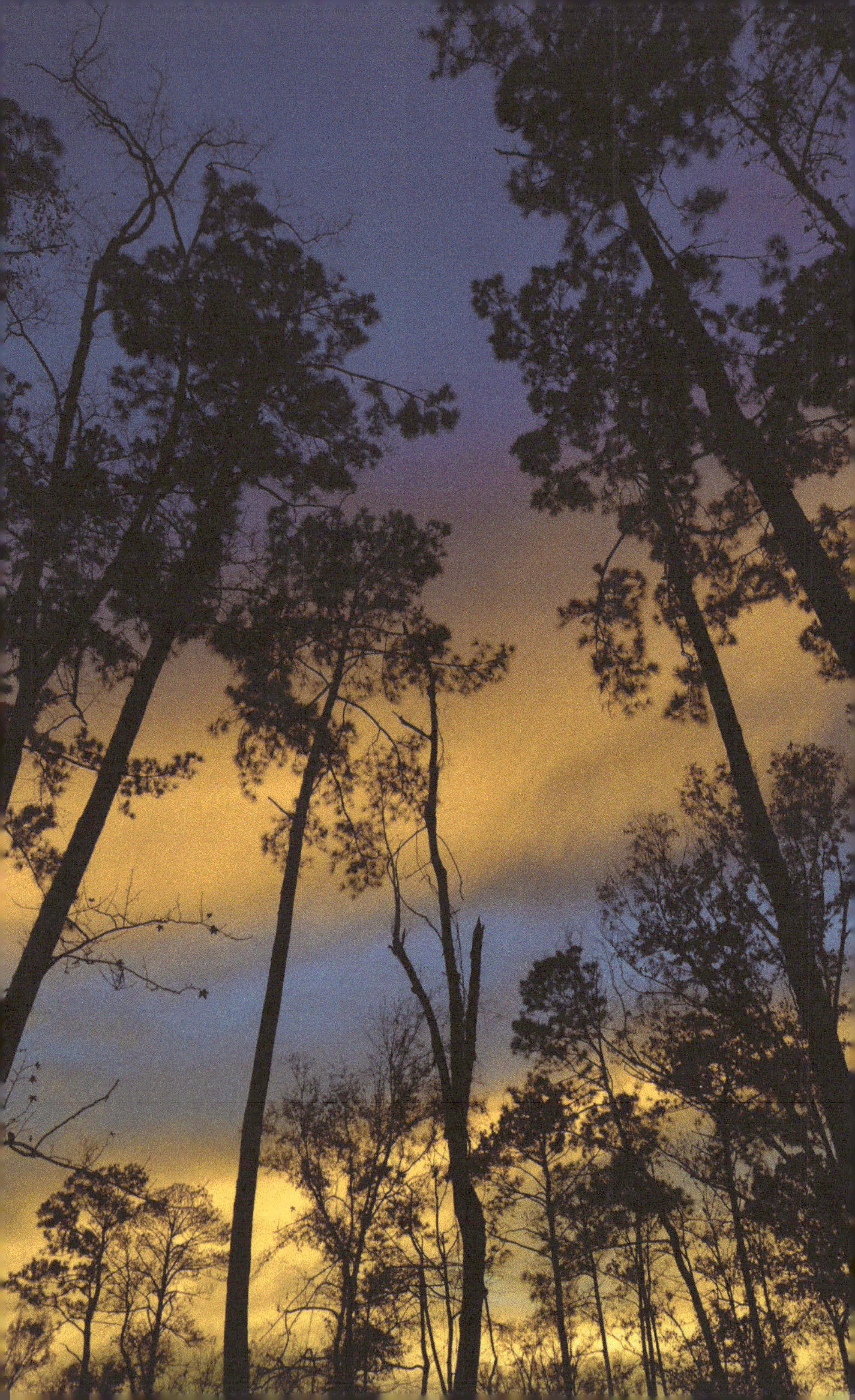

What If?

What if you had never come into my dreams—
Where night lingers amongst the stars that gleam?
Would I know the longing of finding you
With the hope of discovering a love that is true?

What if I had never felt your touch—
The tenderness of you I've come to crave so much?
Would I know what it's like to have my skin shiver
From the ecstasy that melts my body to a quiver?

What if I had never heard your voice
Whispering away my fears into moments of rejoice?
Would I know the tranquility my soul desperately needs
Without ever having heard your words that nourish and
feeds?

What if you had never played me music—
Gracing the keys with every stroke and every lick?
Would I know the poetry that should be wrote
With words mixed with colors abounding from every
note?

What would a life like that be?
What if life was only ever just me?
The thought hurts my heart to its very core—
Never knowing the love of you that is forevermore.

Rather,

What if life continued with the two of us,
With a love in all its beauty that is most glorious?
Would we not set this world ablaze with fire,
Burning and yearning to quench their own desire?

What if we revelled in a life that is you and me,
And let our present carry us to a grand destiny?
Then we could let our *what ifs* propel us forward
To a future set before us that is magnificently assured.

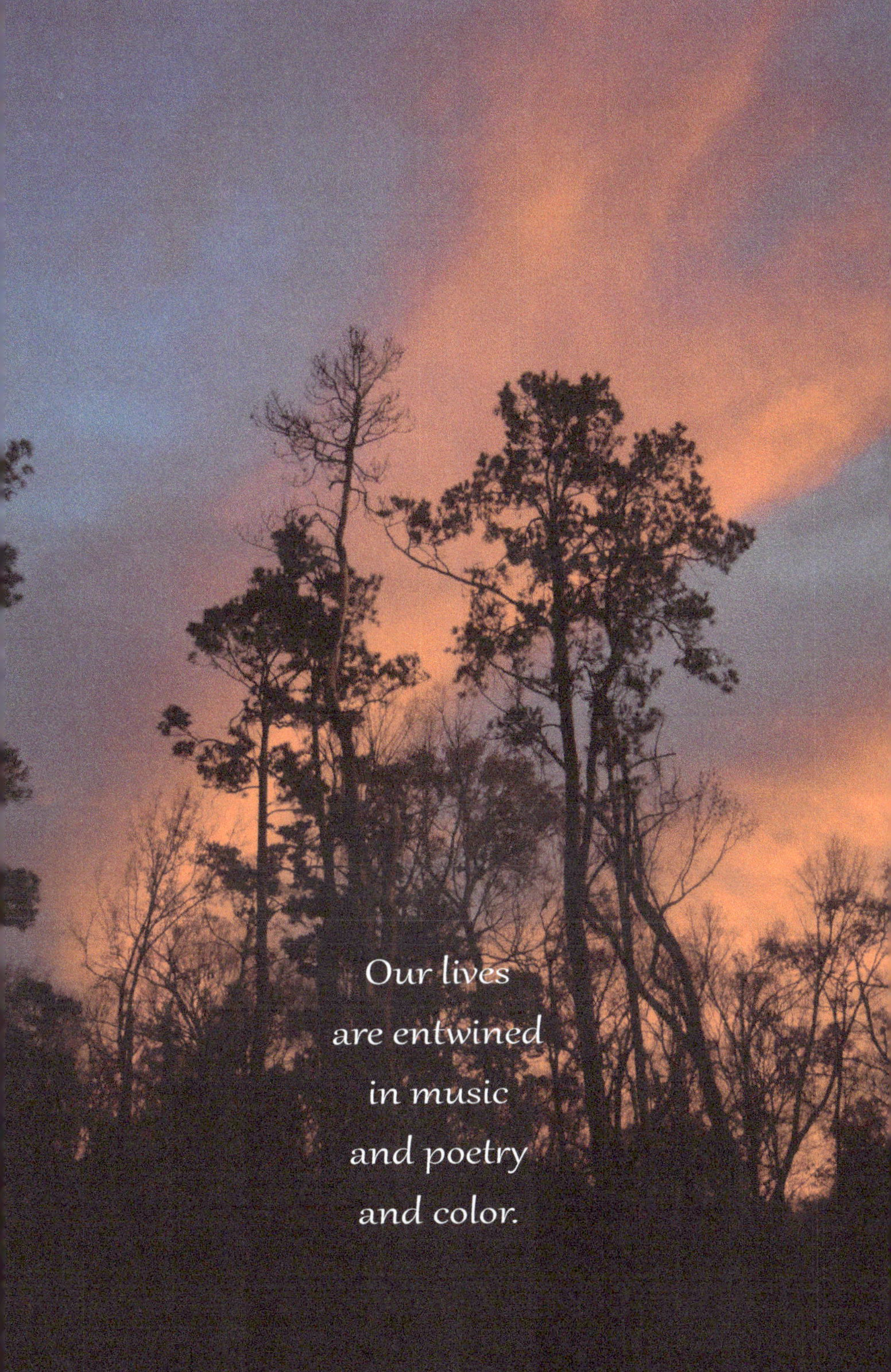
Our lives
are entwined
in music
and poetry
and color.

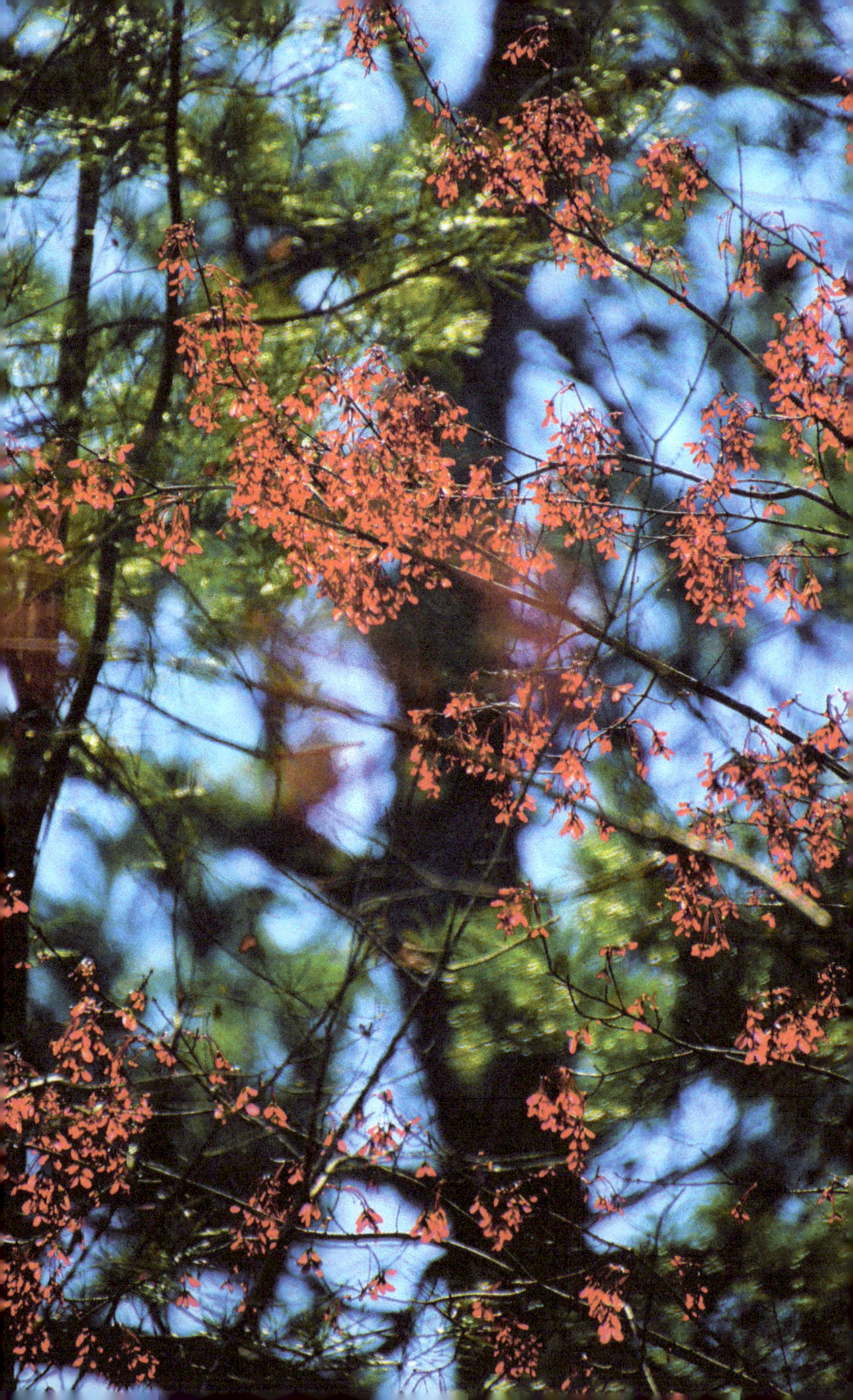

Tease Me

Press me against the wall
And let my hair fall.
Put my arms high up
And watch my eyes light up.

Please me,
Tease me,
Ease me,
And release me.

It started with a peck,
Then a nibble on my neck.
A little bit of cuddling
That became more than snuggling.

Please me,
Tease me,
Ease me,
And release me.

The chemistry of us
Is altogether sensuous.
It's an alchemy of time and space
That transcends us to this place.

Please me,
Tease me,
Ease me,
And release me.

That spot on your shoulder is for me.
How are we bound and yet so free?
Whether we lie, stand, or sit,
There's no doubt about it, baby, we fit.

Please me,
Tease me,
Ease me,
And release me.

Time for room service to keep us fed
With a tray of sandwiches for our bed.
I am so lucky to have found my soulmate—
To love and cherish and celebrate.

But promise you don't just love me for my elbows.

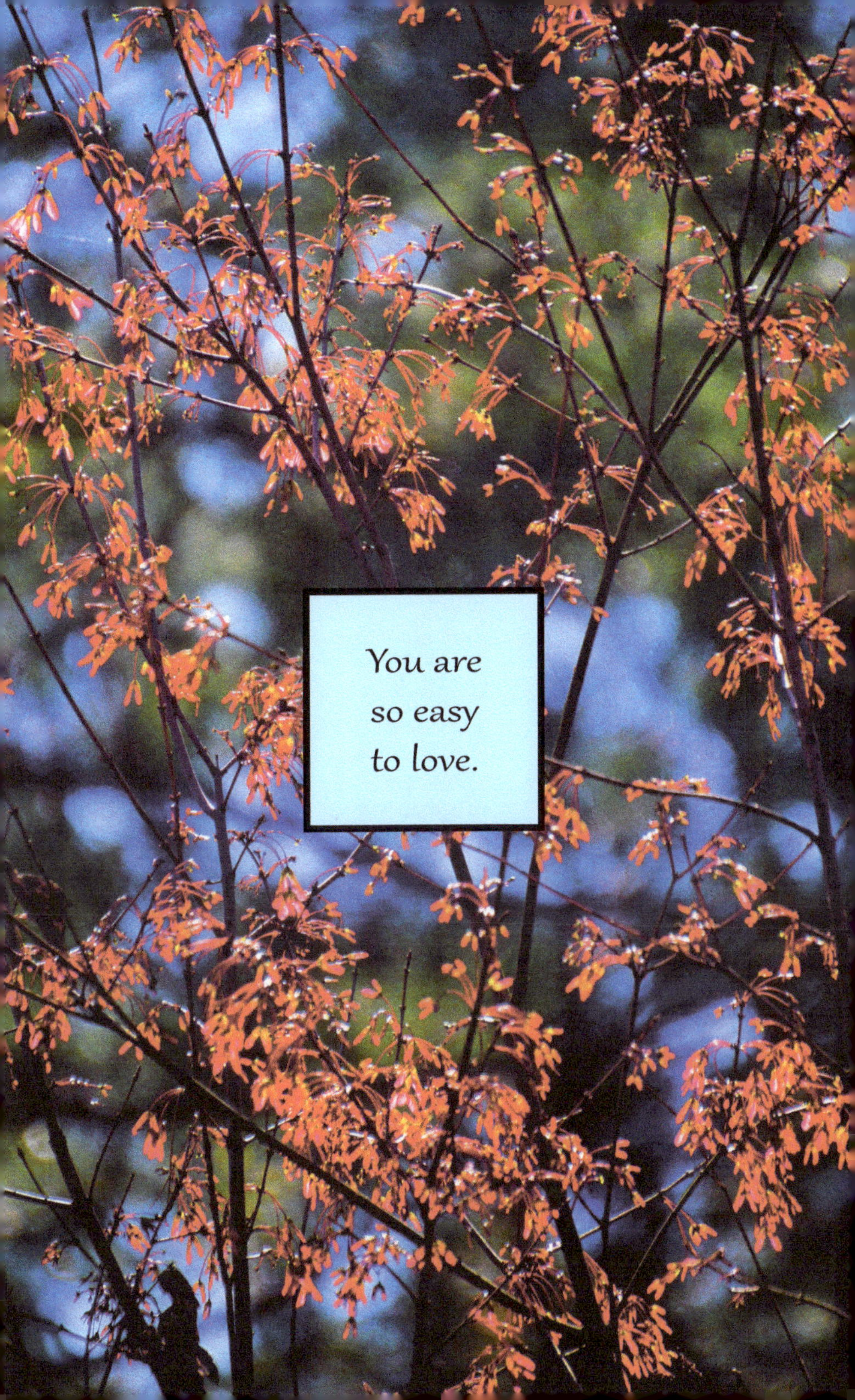
You are
so easy
to love.

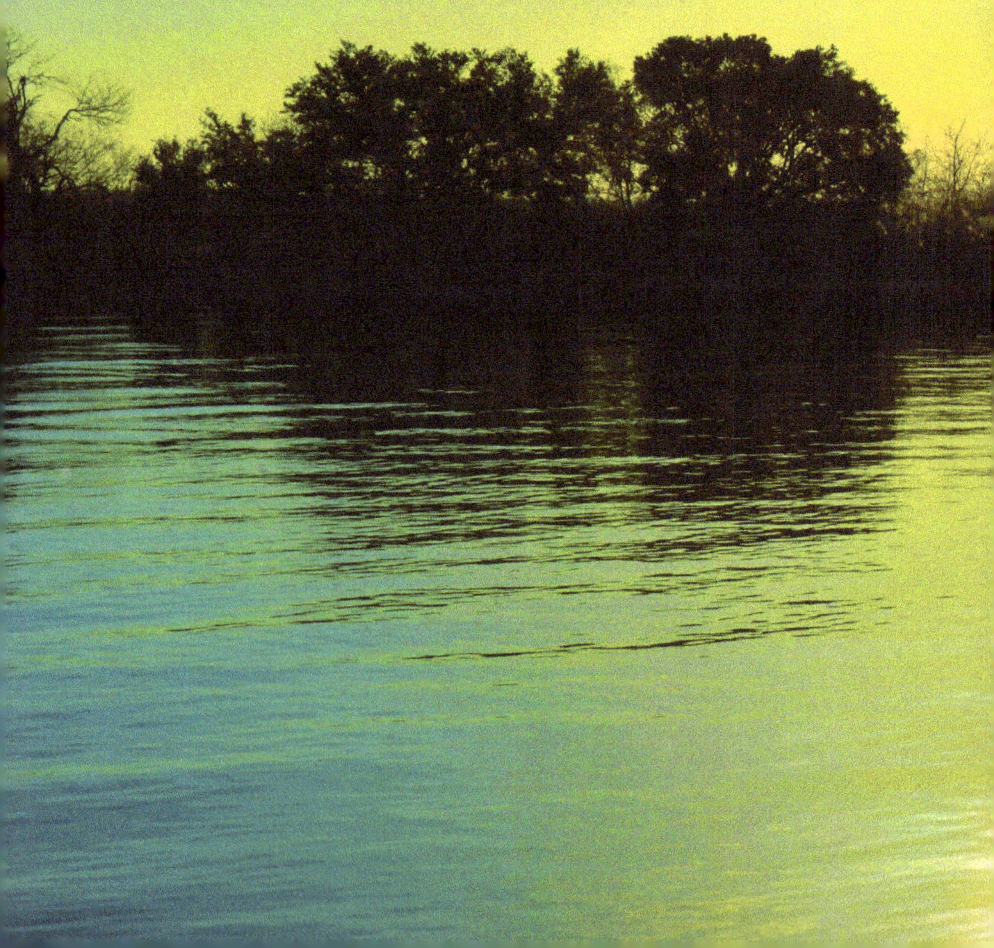
Life is
but a dream
with you
beneath
my eyelids.

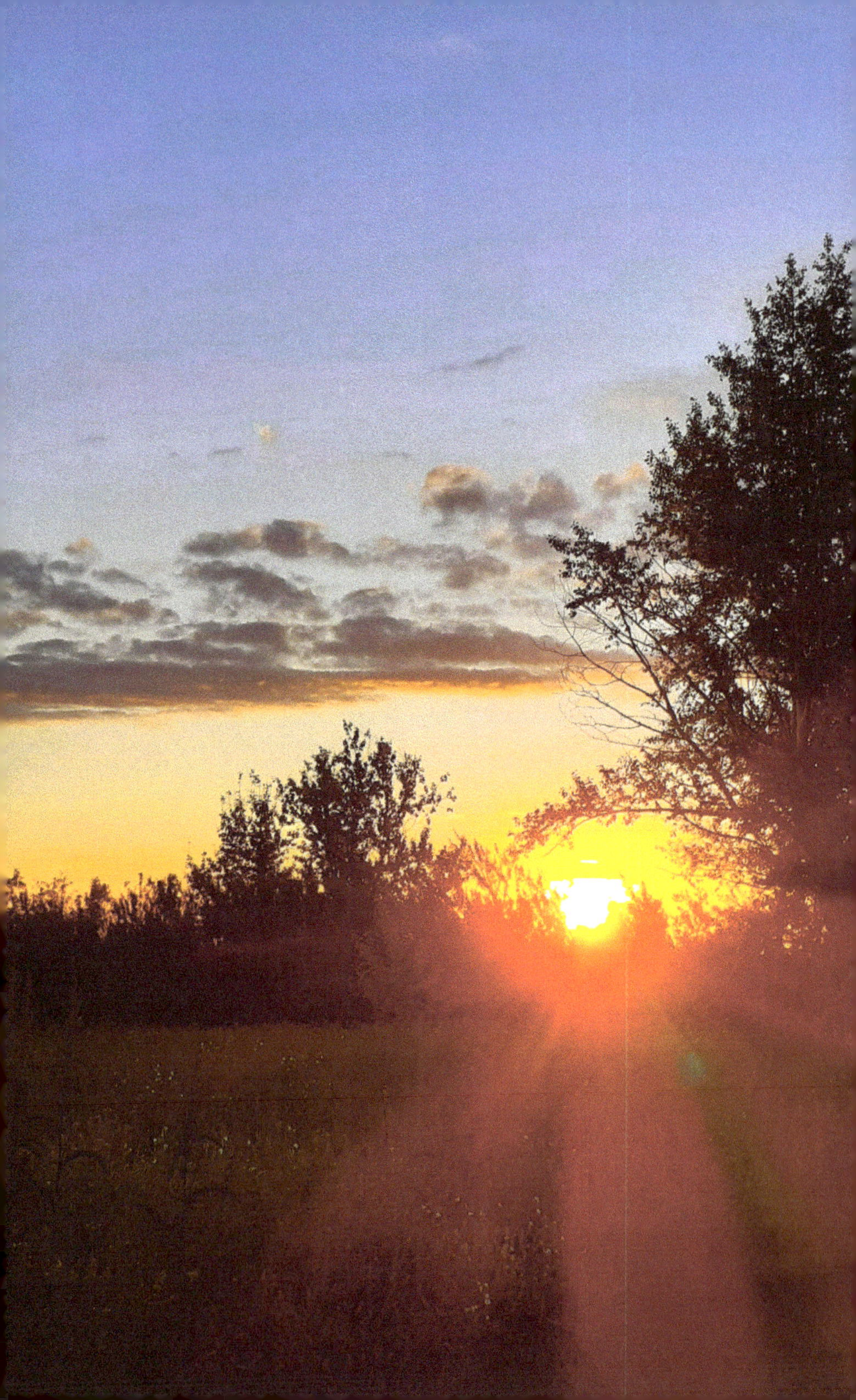

I Hope

I hope I give more than I take,
With love and laughs
And sex that makes you quake.

I hope I inspire you to shine,
With words and deeds
And purpose that is most sublime.

I hope I hold you to great heights,
With honor and respect
And a pride that excites.

I hope I make you smile,
With giggles and jokes
And all things juvenile.

I hope I keep you wanted,
With attention and devotion
And kisses from your little toe to the tip of your head.

I hope I give more than I take,
Because there is not one moment I can bear without
you
Whether I'm asleep or I'm awake.

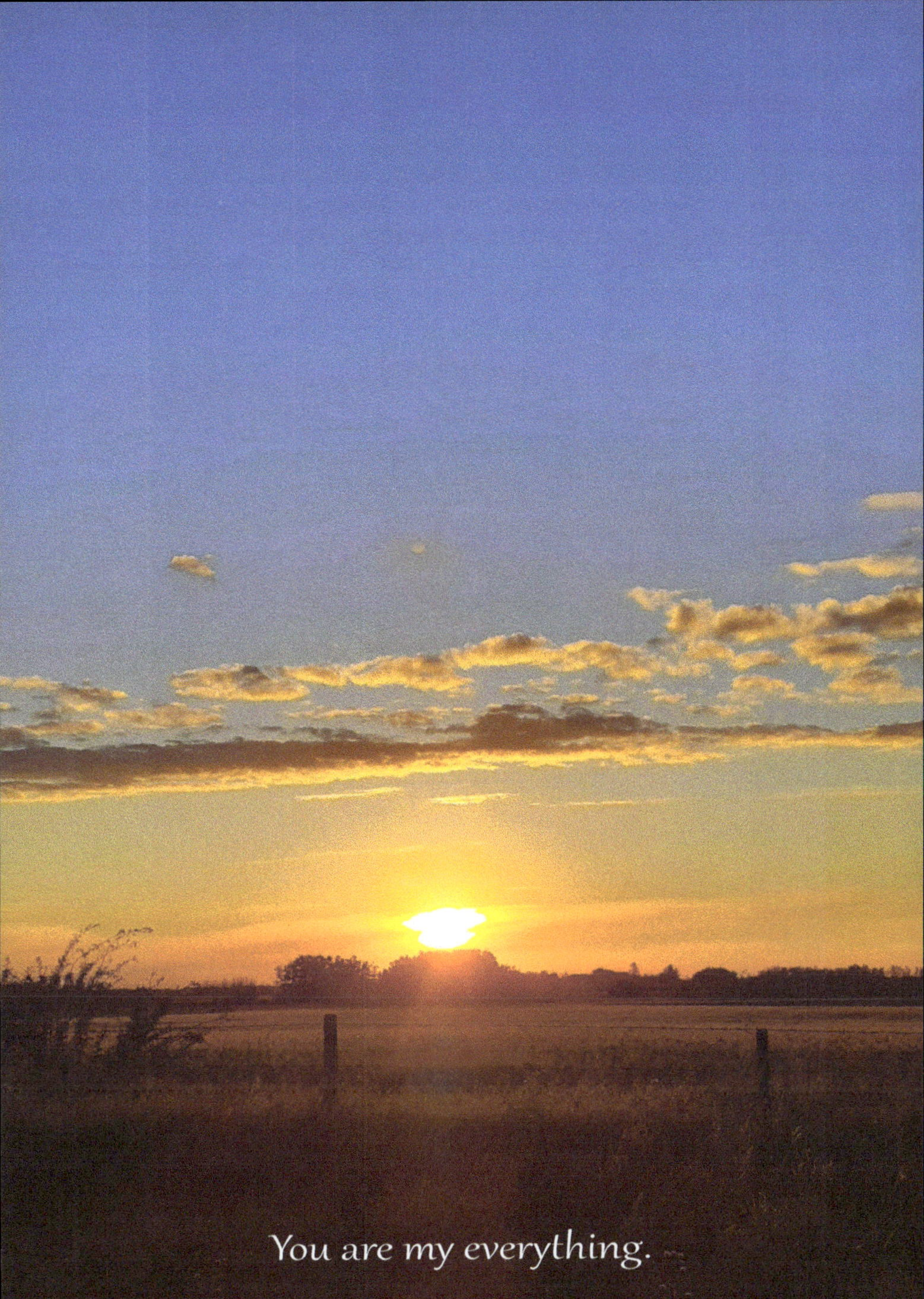
You are my everything.

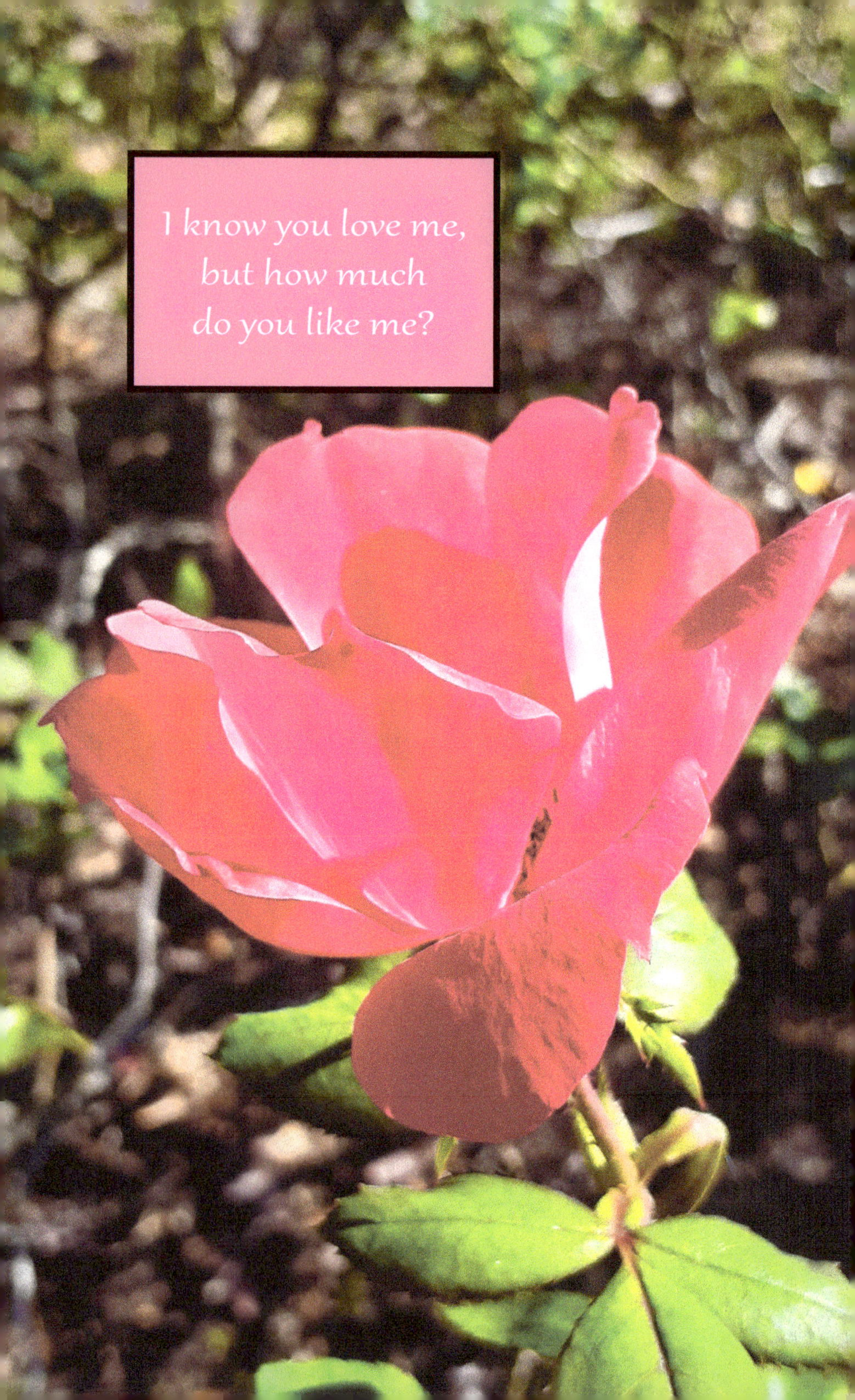
I know you love me,
but how much
do you like me?

I Like You

I like you with the glasses.
I like you without the glasses.
I like you upside down.
I like you right side up.
I like you in front of me.
I like you beside me.
I like you in my sleeping dreams.
I like you in my waking hours.
I like you ridge on ridge.
I like you skin on skin.
I like you soul on skin.
I like you skin on soul.

In every way, on every day,
I'd like you in my life to stay.
Your beauty, my love, turns
Forevermore into a day.

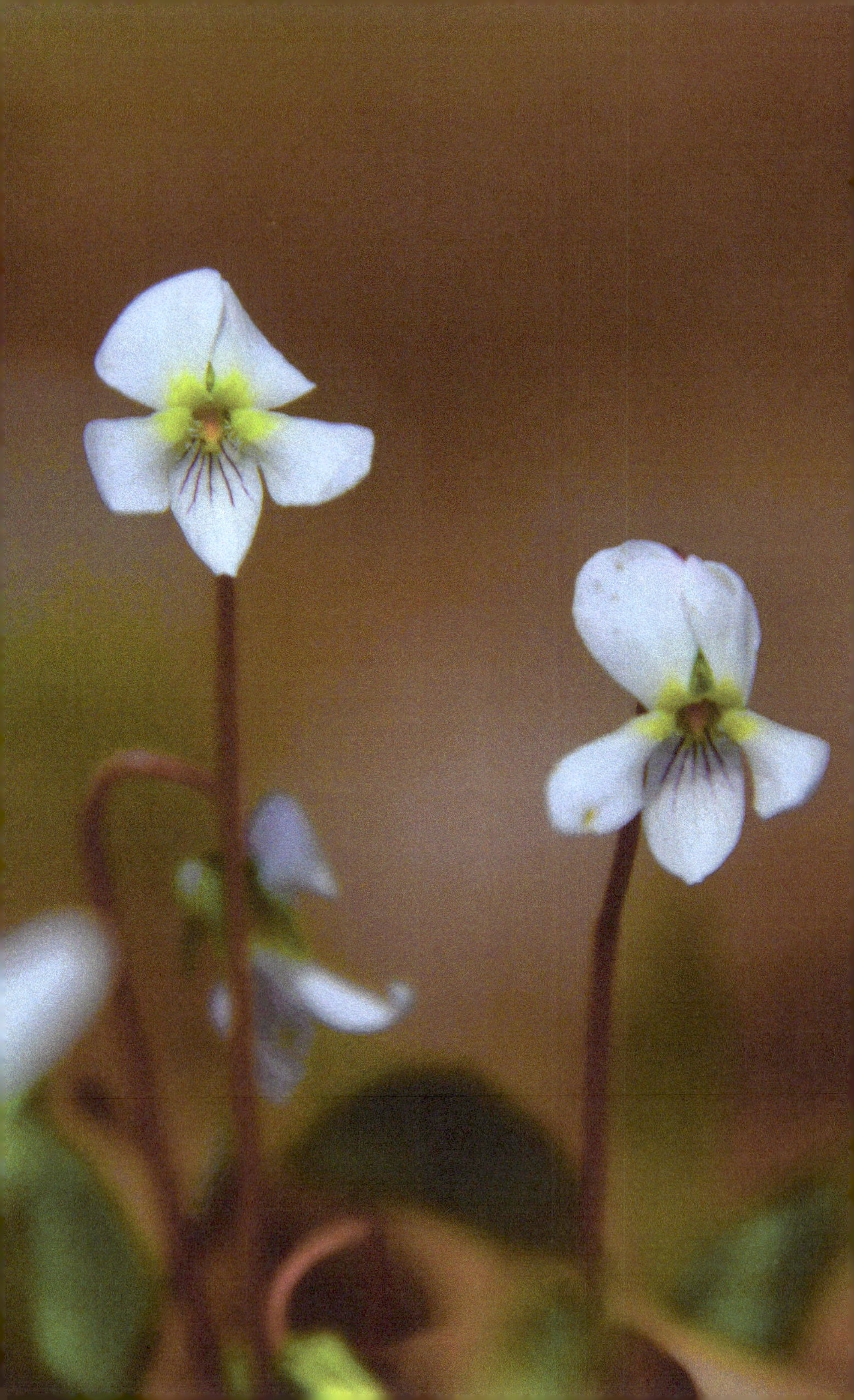

One + One

One plus one equals two?
At one time, yes, when it was me and you.
But no more is it us two that be,
Because one plus one will equal three!

A sweet coo of sound
Will fill our home in leaps and bounds.
For our love has grown
Into a lil person that will soon be known.

A Sassy Lassy with eyes of green
Will be the girl to grace our scene?
Or a thoughtful lad with curly hair
Is the boy ours hearts to ensnare?

Whatever we decide for a name,
Our lives shan't ever be the same
Now that it's no longer you and me.
Because one plus one equals three!

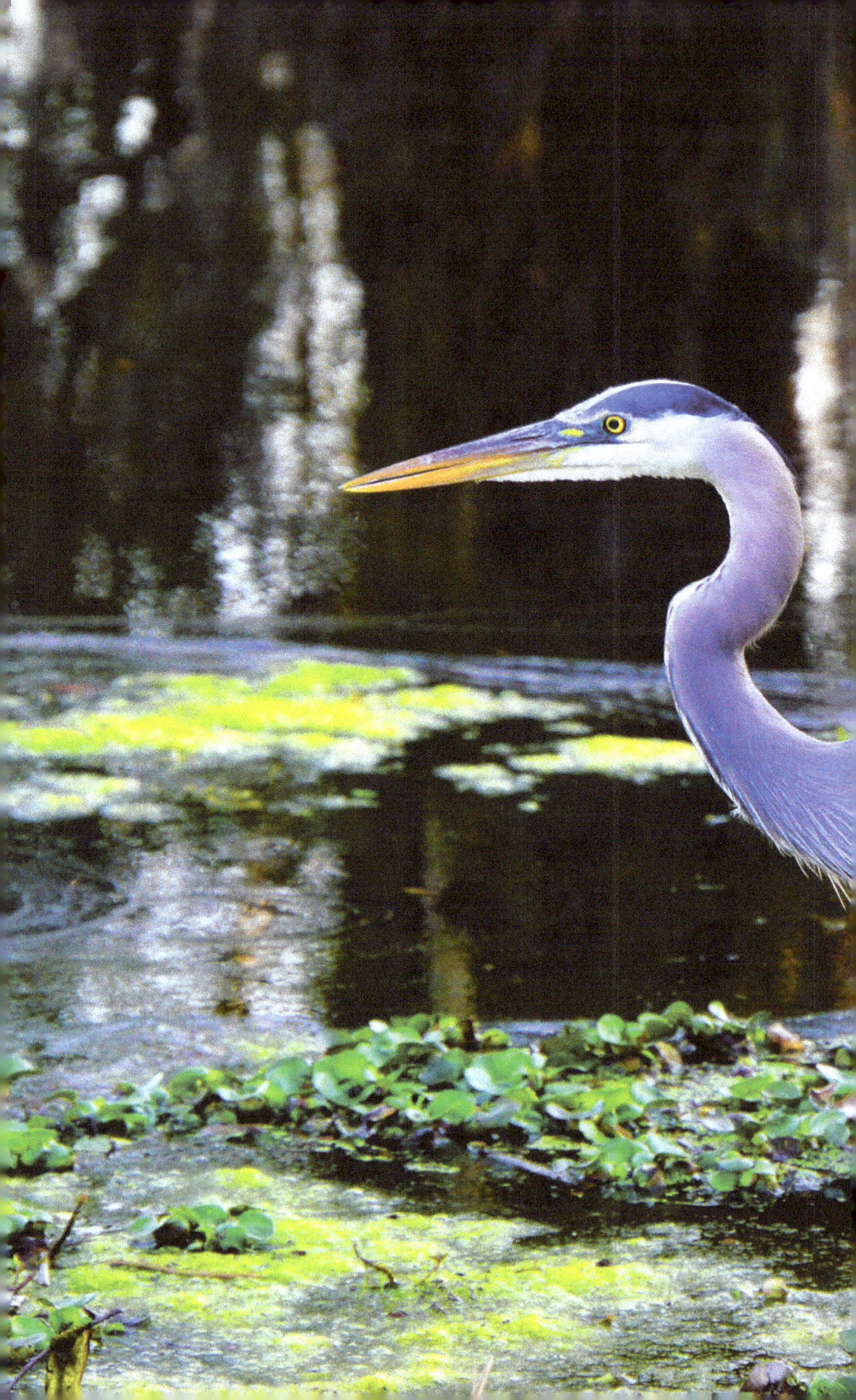

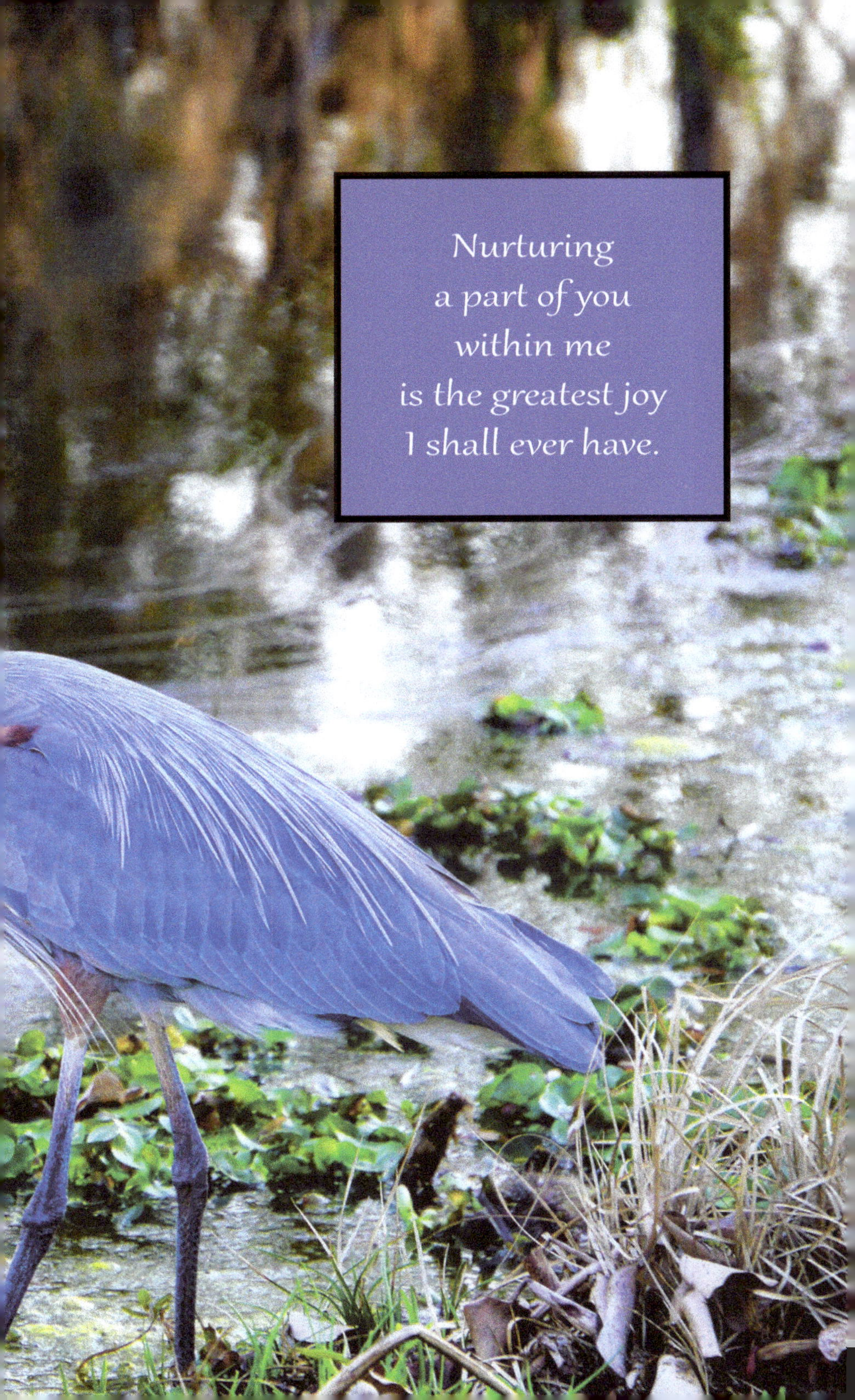
Nurturing
a part of you
within me
is the greatest joy
I shall ever have.

SORROW

&

SOLACE

Scattered fragments
of dreams long lost
become the nightmares
of the dark.

But darkness is cast
for a restoration.

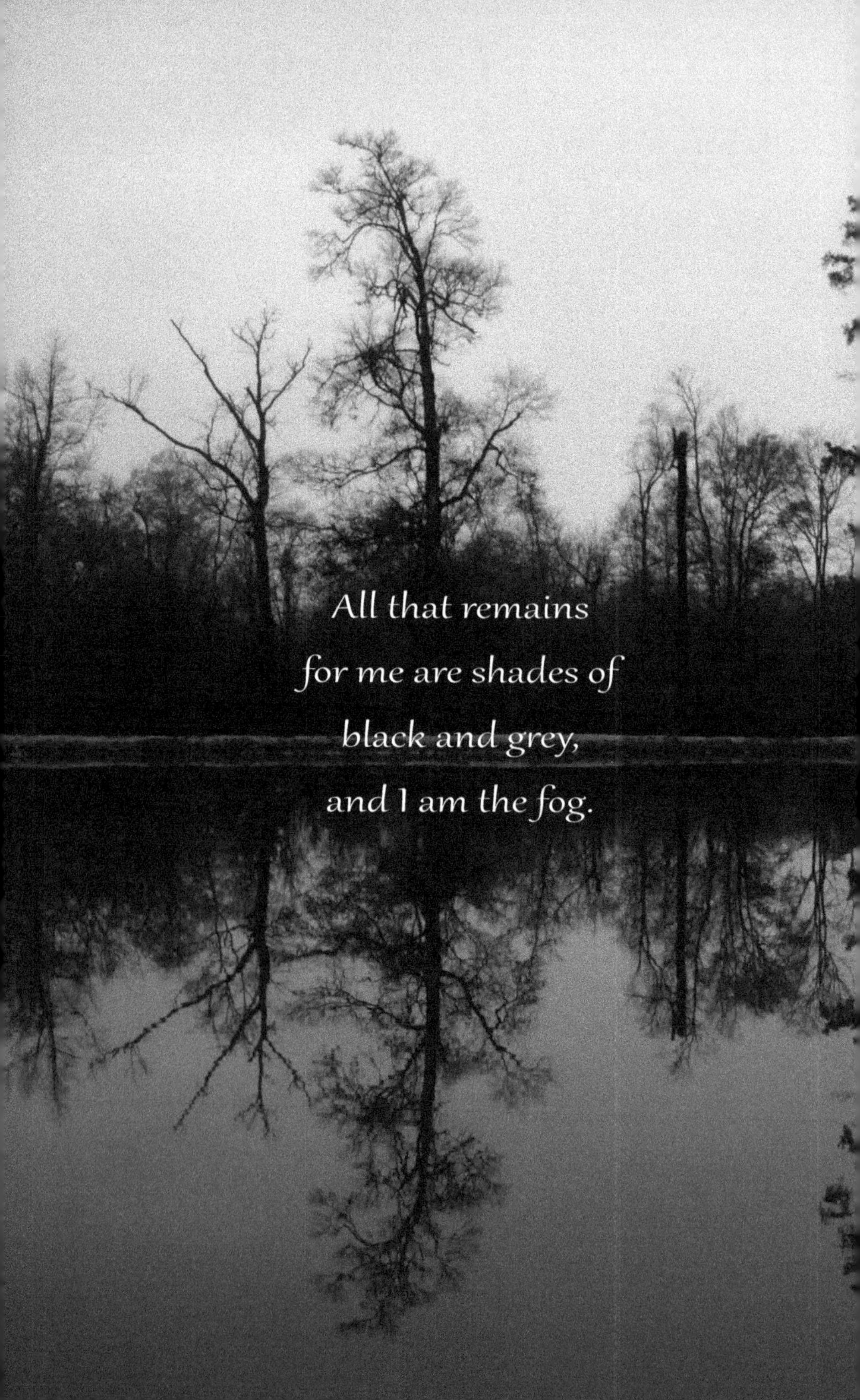
All that remains

for me are shades of

black and grey,

and I am the fog.

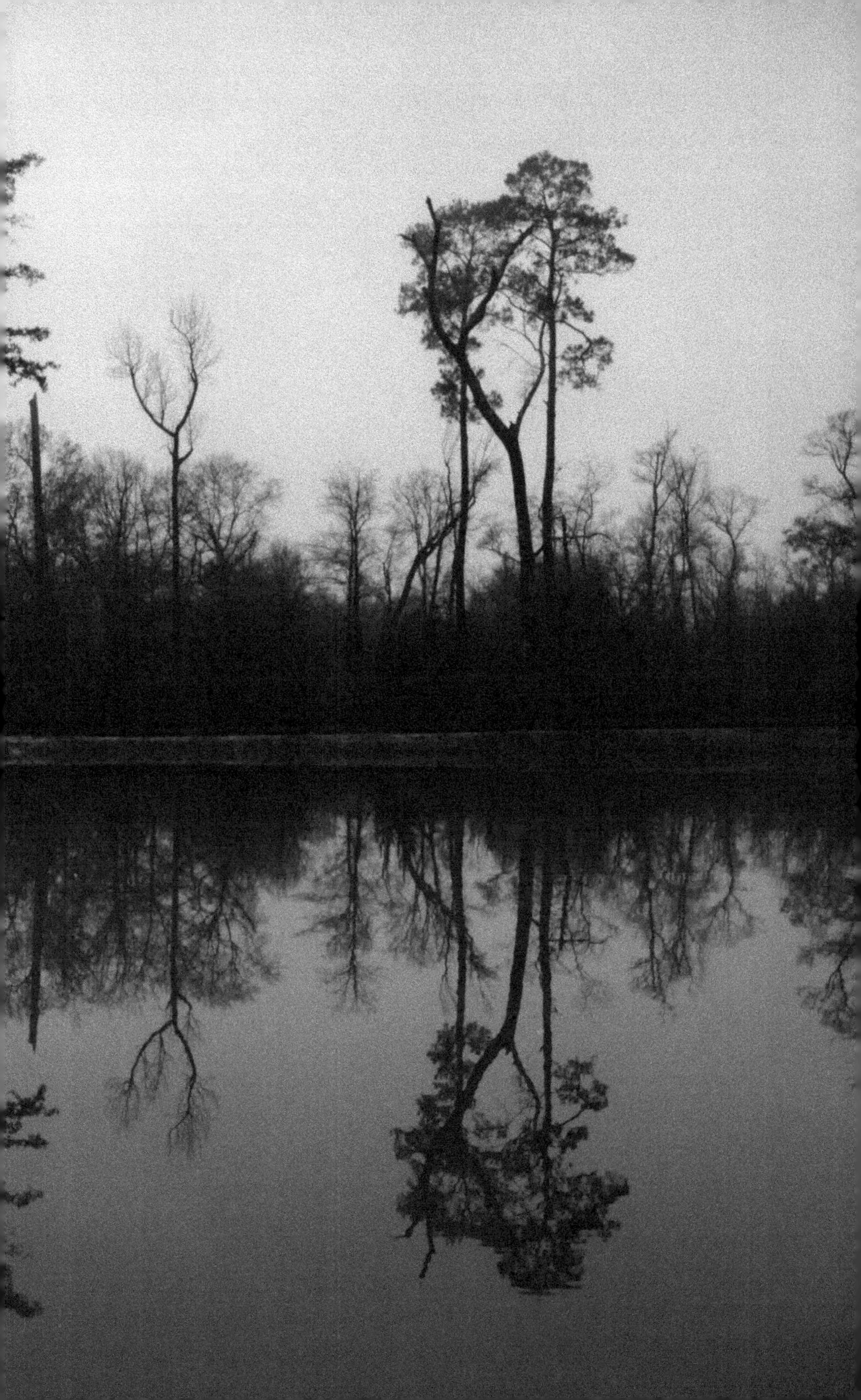

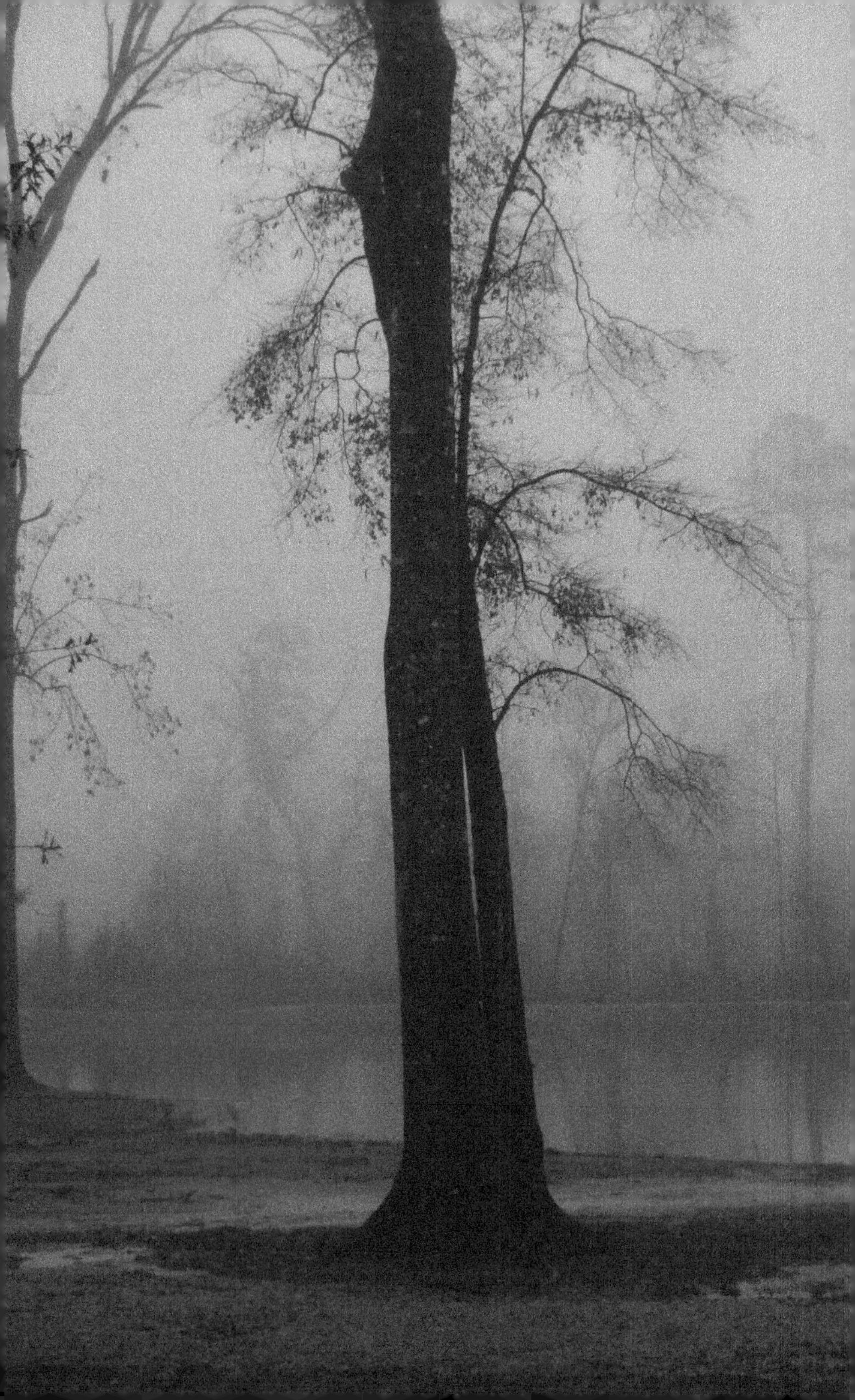

My Heart, My Son

My heart, my son,
You have me quite undone.
The love I feel
Is most surreal,
For your life has just begun.

My heart, my prince,
You have me quite convinced.
You shall rule this earth
From the moment of your birth,
And all the future years since.

My heart, my sweet,
You have made me complete.
I am whole by your presence,
Grateful for your existence,
For your life is but a treat.

My heart, my Timothy,
I long to cuddle thee.

You are the boy of my dreams,
But you will never be seen,
For you were stolen from me.

My heart, my son,
I am quite undone.
The loss I feel
Is most surreal,
For your life had barely begun.

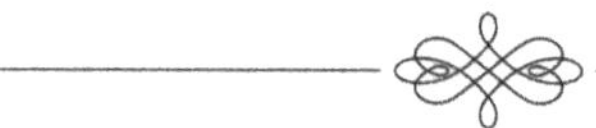

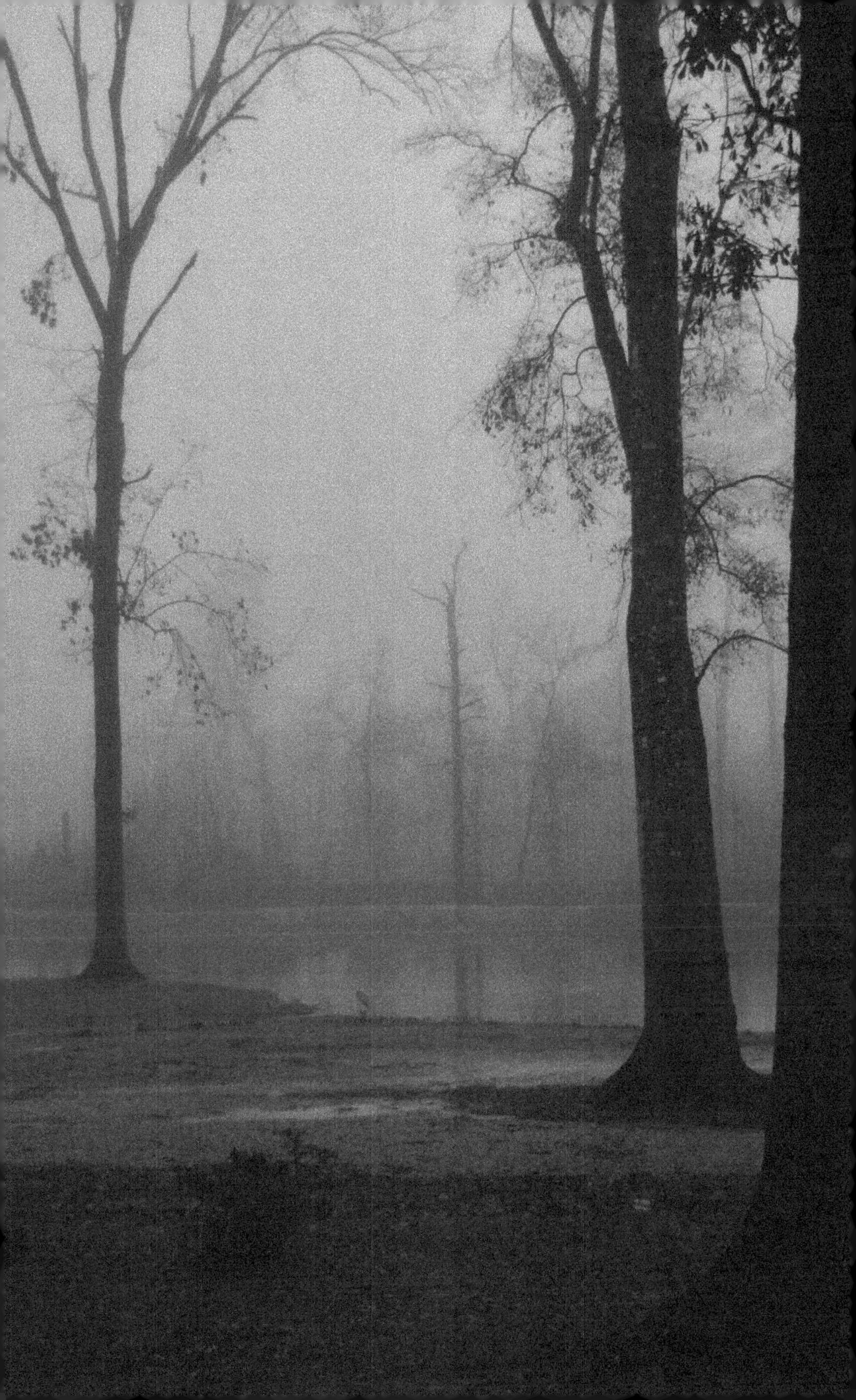

Forsaken

I longed my whole life to be a mother.
There was no other way to be.
It what I was destined to do,
To grow a sweet baby inside of me.

Dear God, I beseech you with this prayer.
I am down on bended knee.
What could I have possibly done?
Why have you forsaken me?

From the moment I was aware,
And felt him kick strong,
I was in love with my boy
Because to me he belonged.

Dear God, I implore you with this prayer.
I am down on bended knee.
For what reason did you take him?
Why have you forsaken me?

He was named Timothy Christian,
And had a room in the color of blue.
But he never got to see it,
And I can't help but blame you.

Dear God, I am begging you with this prayer.
I am down on bended knee.
Please let my son to come back.
Let him come back to me.

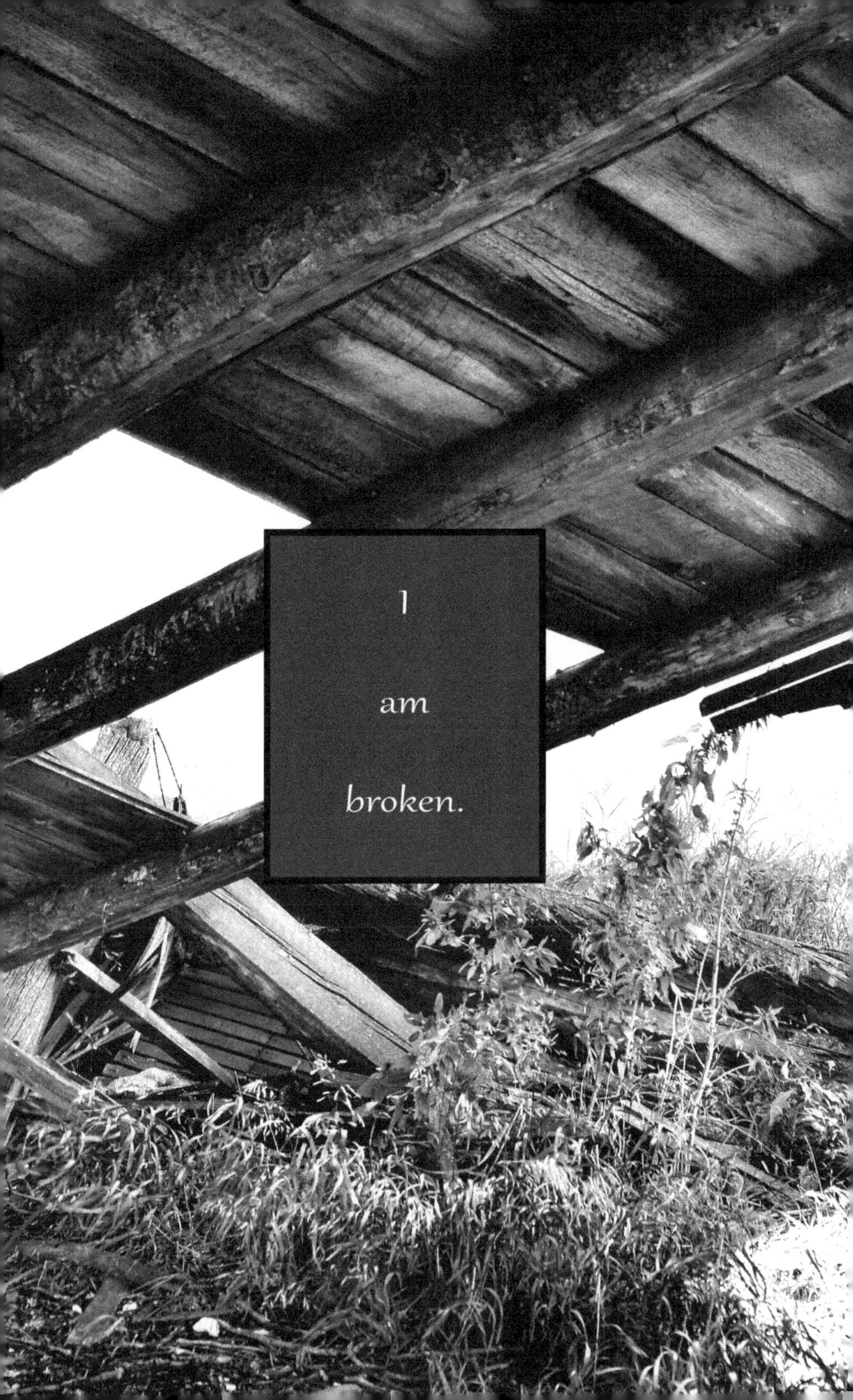
I

am

broken.

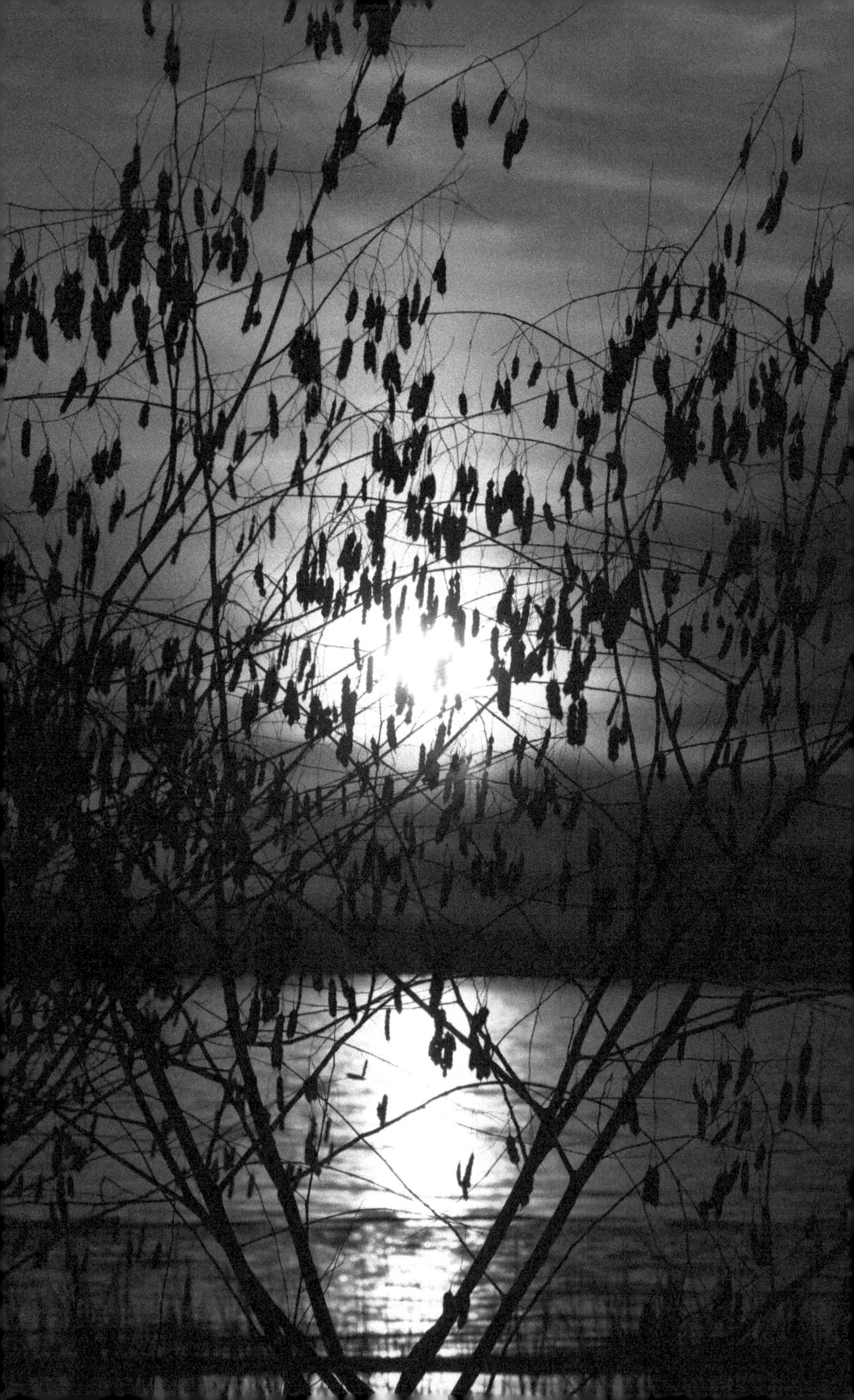

Silence

There's a deafening silence that screams in my head
Of all the words that have been left unsaid.
My mouth opens to articulate,
But my throat is in constant suffocate.

I cannot breathe from this cacophony,
And am overwhelmed by the enormity
Of this harrowing sound of silence
That tears through me with a vengeance.

I long for a different kind of cry—
One that can be soothed by a lullaby.
But only the clanging cymbal rings
With a creepy stillness that pierces and stings.

I'm out of tears and am out of words.
Nothing to self-soothe or reassure
This emptiness I feel within me
From the tragic loss of my sweet baby.

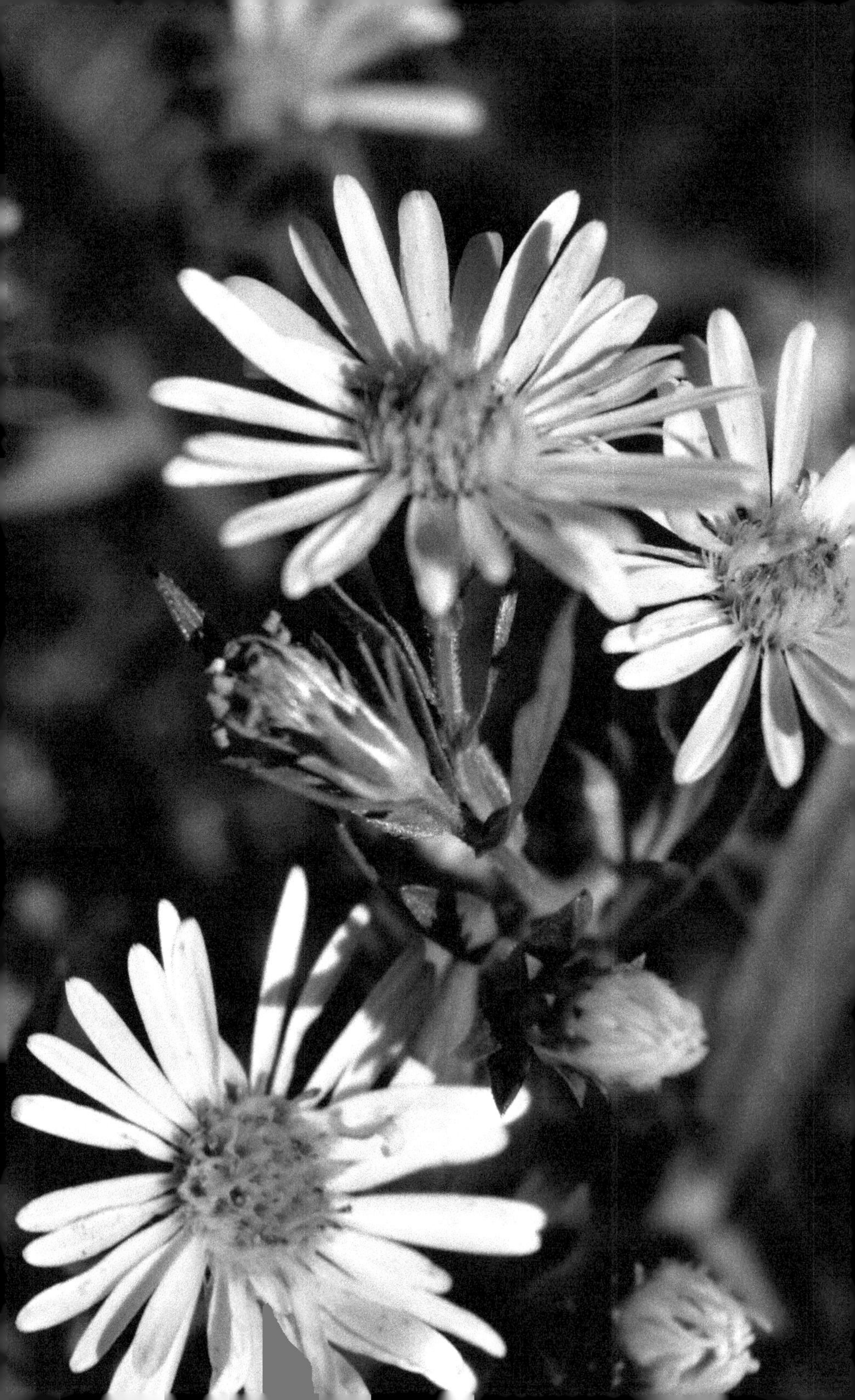

Oh, My Little Girl

My daughter is on my mind.
She is sweet, gentle, and kind.
She has curls in her hair,
And plays devil may care.

Oh, my little girl,
I long to see you twirl.
Beautiful child of mine,
Your eyes sparkle and shine.

She hops and skips with her run
As she greets the morning sun.
She wears a flowered dress,
And is filled with happiness.

Oh, my little girl,
I long to see you twirl.
To hold you in my arms
And keep you from all that harms.

She is my Hope, my Grace,
With goodness about her face.
She loves and hugs with much might,
And brings nothing but delight.

Oh, my little girl,
I long to see you twirl.
I will find you one day, my dear,
And always keep you near.

Although she is away,
My love will never sway.
Of my heart she has the key,
And one day, she will know me.

Oh, my little girl,
I long to see you twirl.
I love you, my sweet girl,
Every smile, every curl.

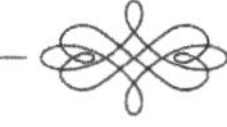

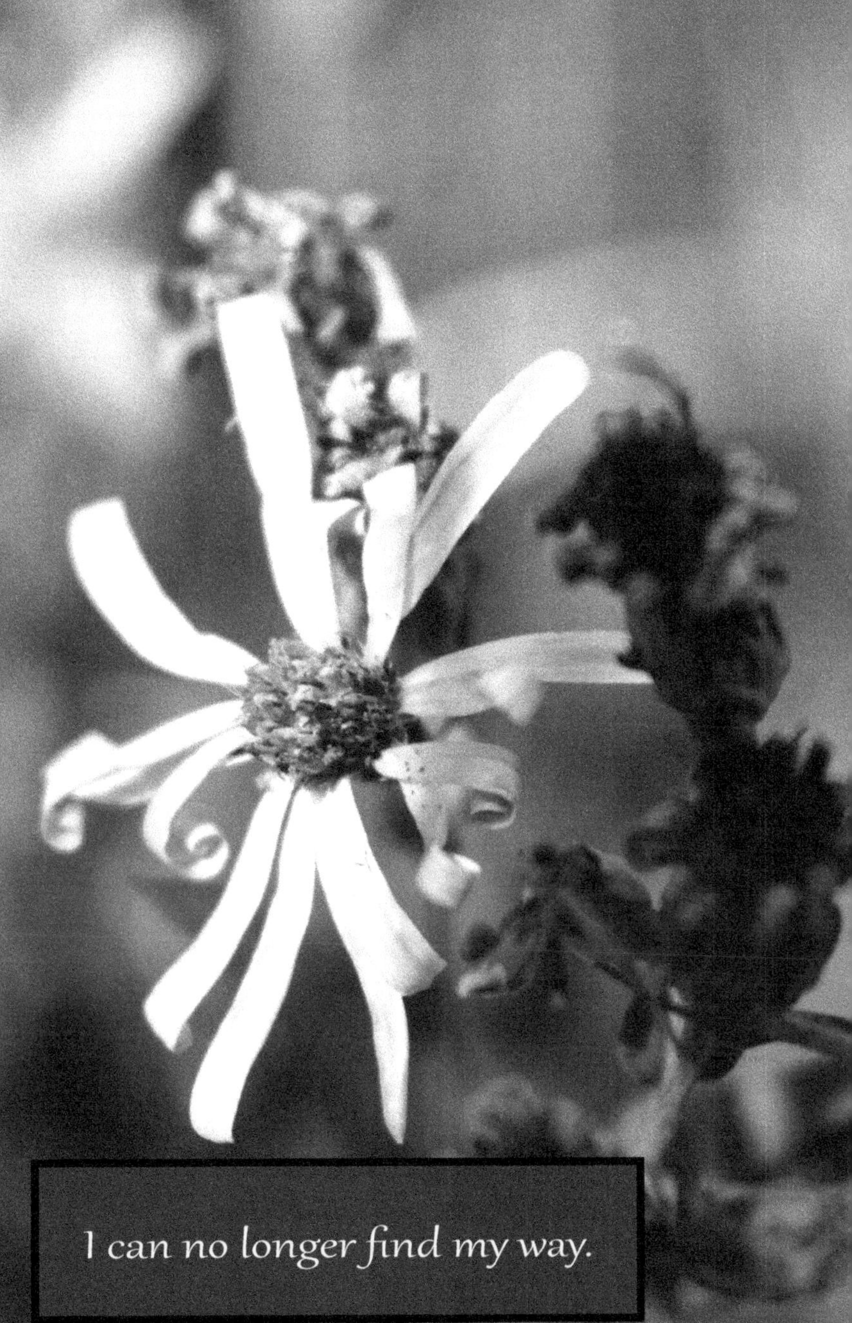
I can no longer find my way.

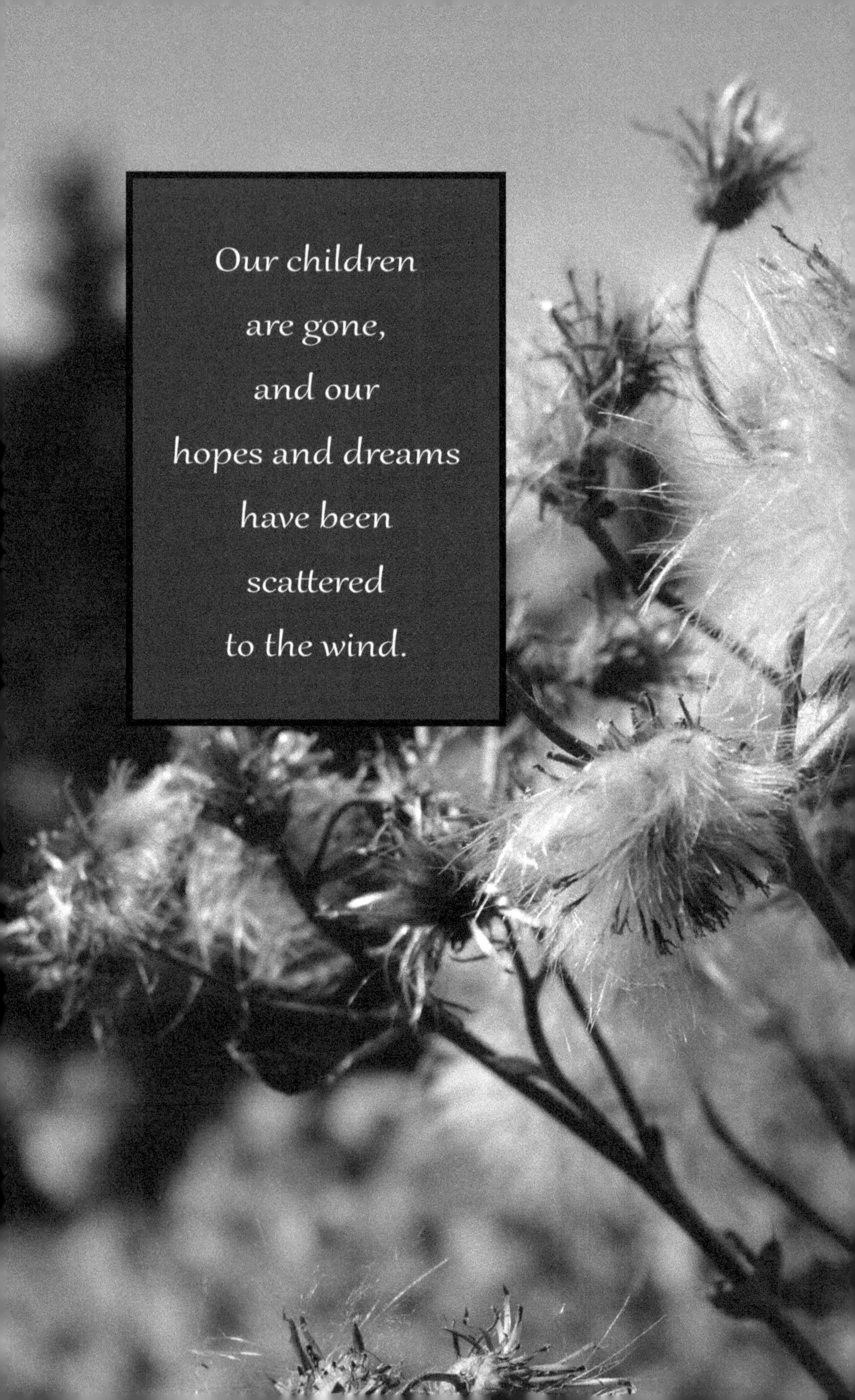
Our children
are gone,
and our
hopes and dreams
have been
scattered
to the wind.

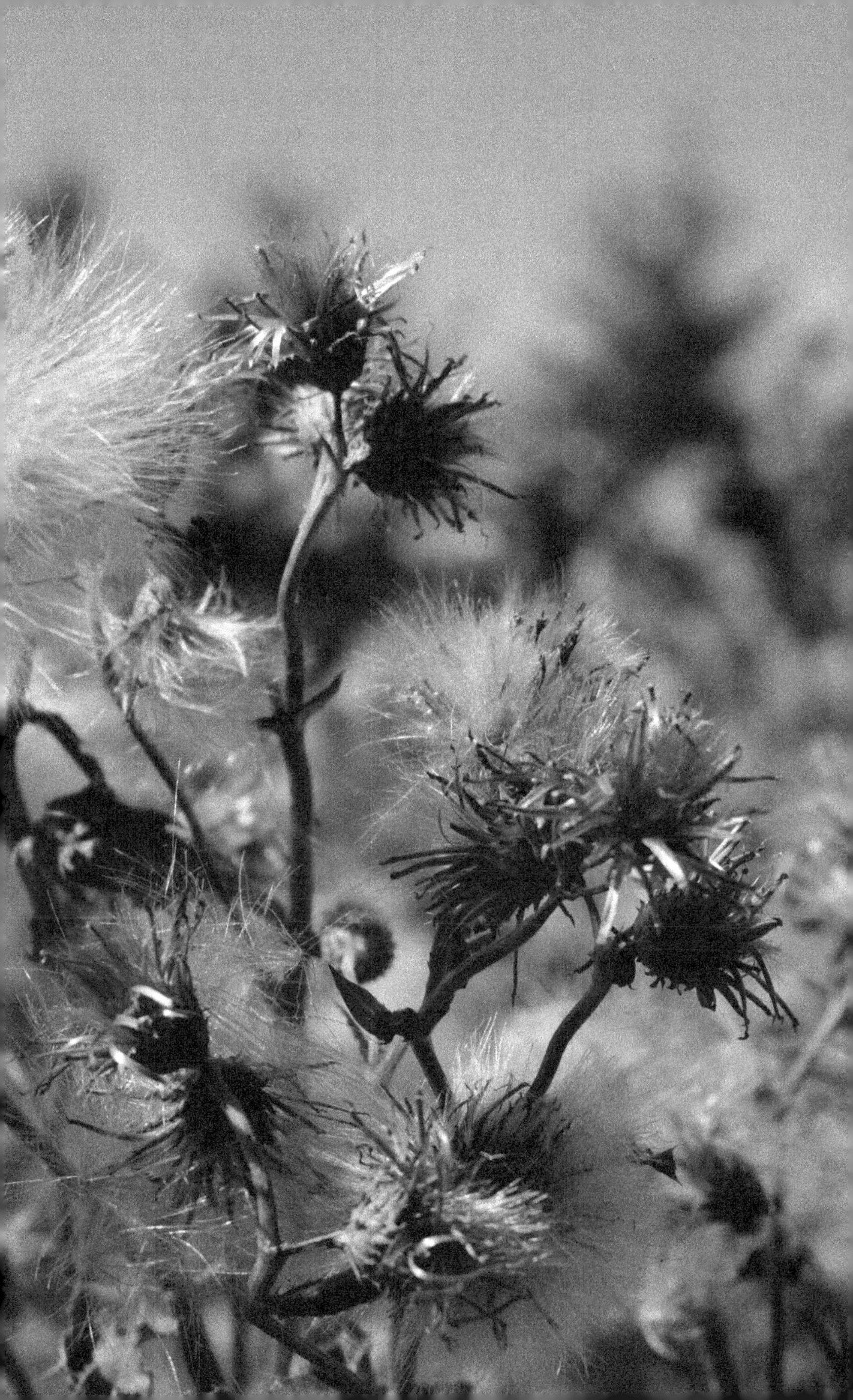

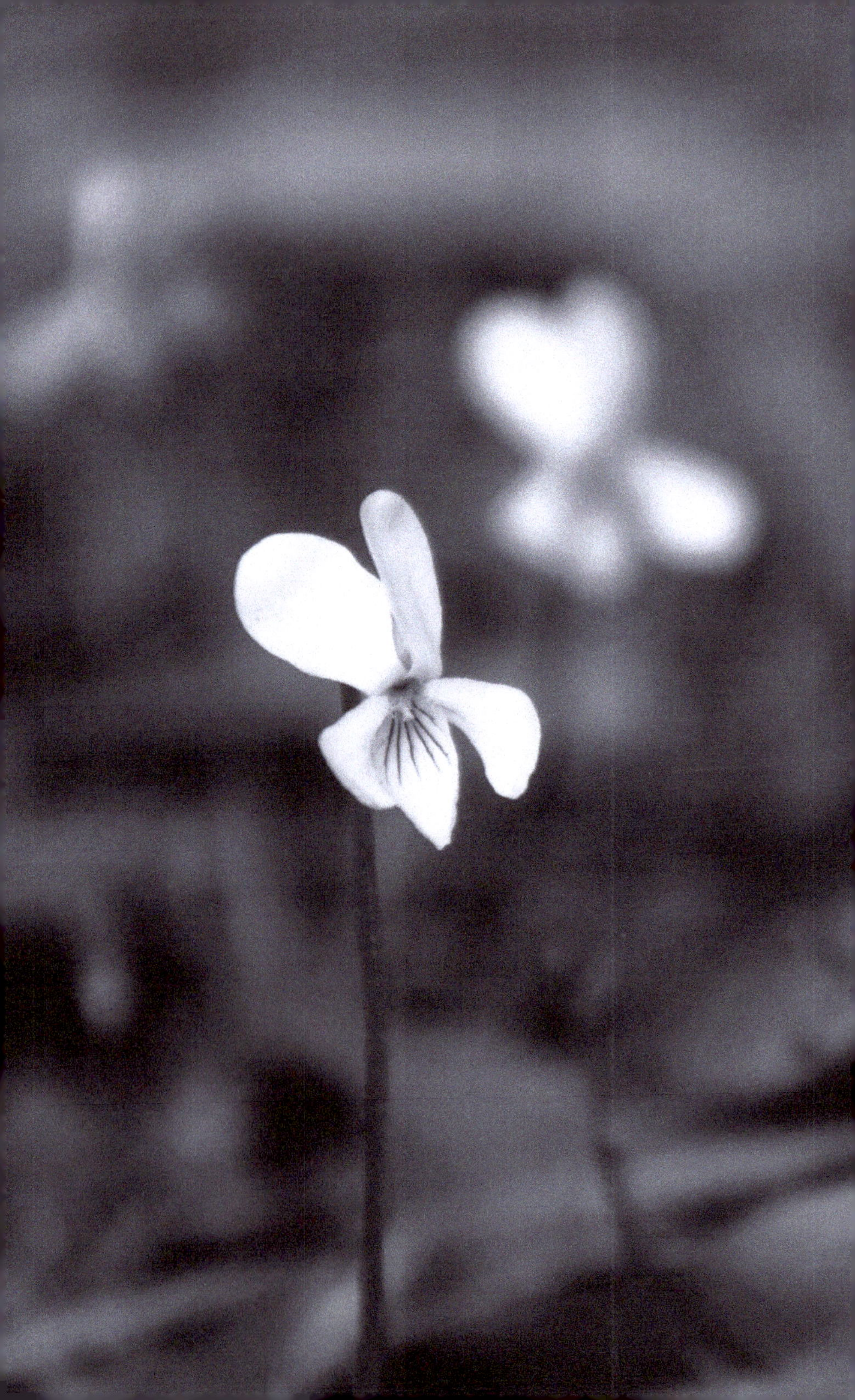

My Little Echo

I tried to write these lines
A hundred times in vain.
Just bleed, they say,
Make sure it rhymes,
Include a brief refrain.

But words, like lives,
They don't resolve.
The nouns and verbs
Don't fit at all.

I'll have to break a rule or two
To make it plain for me and you.

I'm sorry I was not there . . .

To rock you in your crib,
To hear your first big word,
To read you stories
Of grand adventures,

To guide you
On this pilgrimage
We call life.

I'm sorry I was not there . . .

To teach you what
I've had to learn—
That roads are made
By walking them,
That life is best lived
Inside out.
And down is always
The best way up.

I'm sorry I was not there . . .

To watch you take
Your first brave step.
First steps are always the hardest.
But I'm learning.

I'm sorry I was not there . . .

To pray with you,
To play with you,
To dance and run
And stay with you,
To somehow find a way for you.

For us.

I tried so hard
To make us rhyme,
To make my life
And yours
Align.

It would've been divine—

If I was yours,
And you were mine.

My chest cannot contain
This fire
That burns unquenched
When I retire.
Each night,
Its flames grow higher,
Stealing my desire.

The hottest flame, they say,
Is blue.
And with each passing day
Anew,
I feel the melancholy hue
That comes from
Never knowing you.

The mirror knows this to be true.

It sees my blueprint
Stamped on you.

It sees my purgatory, too.

This hell in me
Within this shell of me,
This aching heart
In love with thee,

I am
A thousand miles
from sanity.

This mind of mine,
A vanity
Of unremembered
Memories . . .

And you don't even know my name.
(It's your name, too—we are the same).

There is a word in Japanese
That drives me daily to my knees:
"Sonzai-Kan" – it's used to mean
That feeling when you are aware,
Without a sound or stare,
The presence of another there
With you
Within a room.

I feel you, darling,
When you wake.
My heart, you know,
Is yours to take.

And all the loss,
And all the strife,
Was worth it when you spawned to life.

You're worth it, baby girl.

And broken words
Can sometimes heal
The deepest wounds
We feel.

But all the oceans
Can't contain
The tears I've shed,
The fears I've tamed
In search of you.

But one great Fear
I fear the most—
A lie that took me as its host:
That I am nothing
But a ghost

To you.

But someday soon,
And by God's will,
I'll get the chance
To know you still.

And though *His* grace,
My smile you'll trace,

Someday at last
When we embrace,
My life with yours
Shall interlace.

And what was blue
Shall be made new,
The flame will meld
Us through and through.
This ghost, then fleshed,
Will be to you
The parent of your dreams
Come true.

My past, my present,
Future too,
With all my heart
Belong to you.

I'll see you soon,
My little echo.

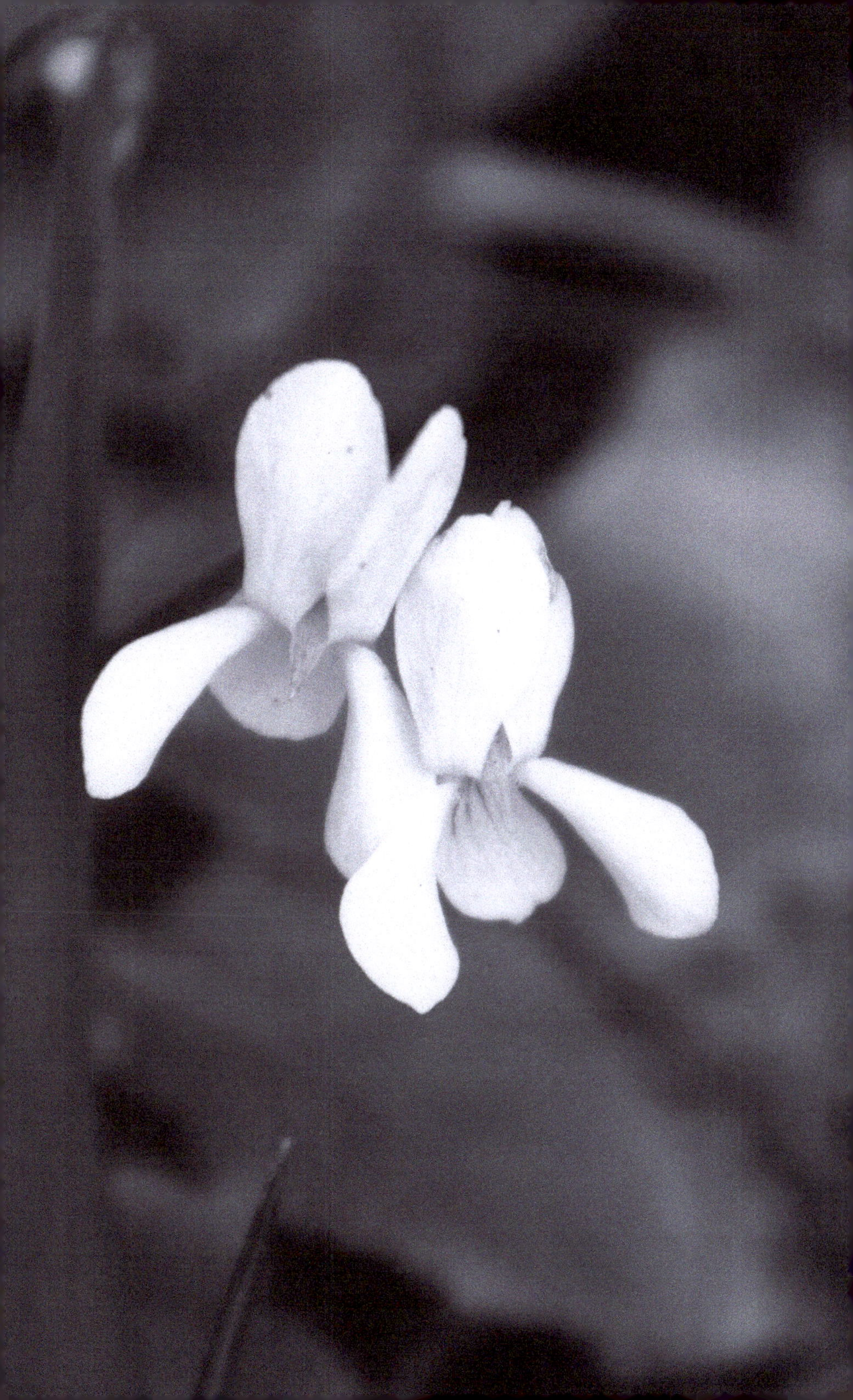

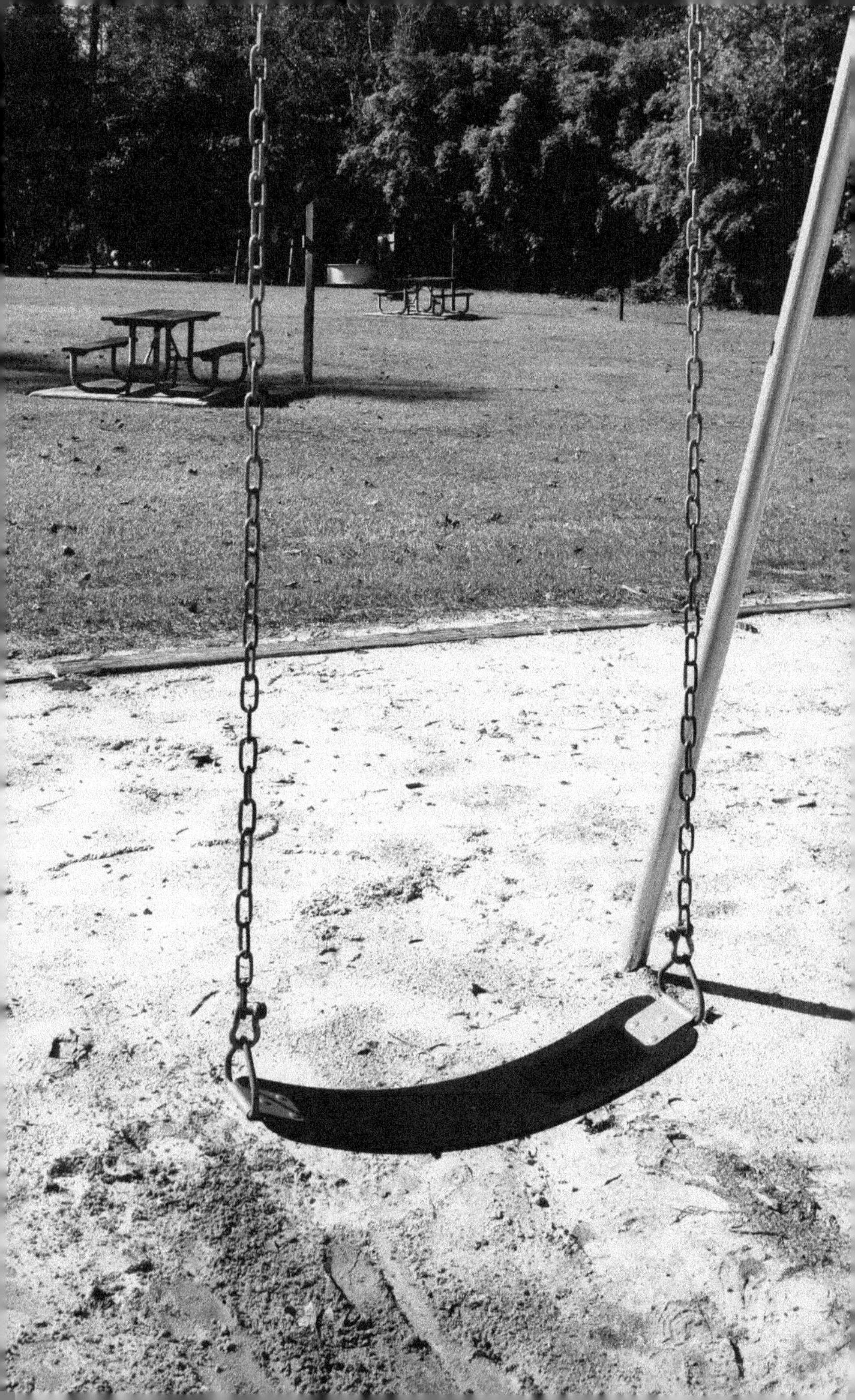

The Life We Could've Had

I imagined our life with littles running about,
With shrieks of joy, a holler, and a shout—
The kind children make in the moments of fun
As they play together in the days of the sun.

On rainy days they'd whisper a story,
Something scary and definitely gory.
Then in the night they'd crawl into our bed,
Knowing we'd protect them from the things earlier said.

They'd grow together and be forever friends,
And take care of us until the bitter end.
In my mind I see it all as clear as day.
It's the only place I can see them at play.

I'm haunted by those faint echoes.
Another life? God only knows.
Sometimes I smile by the life we could've had,
But today I only feel misery and sad.

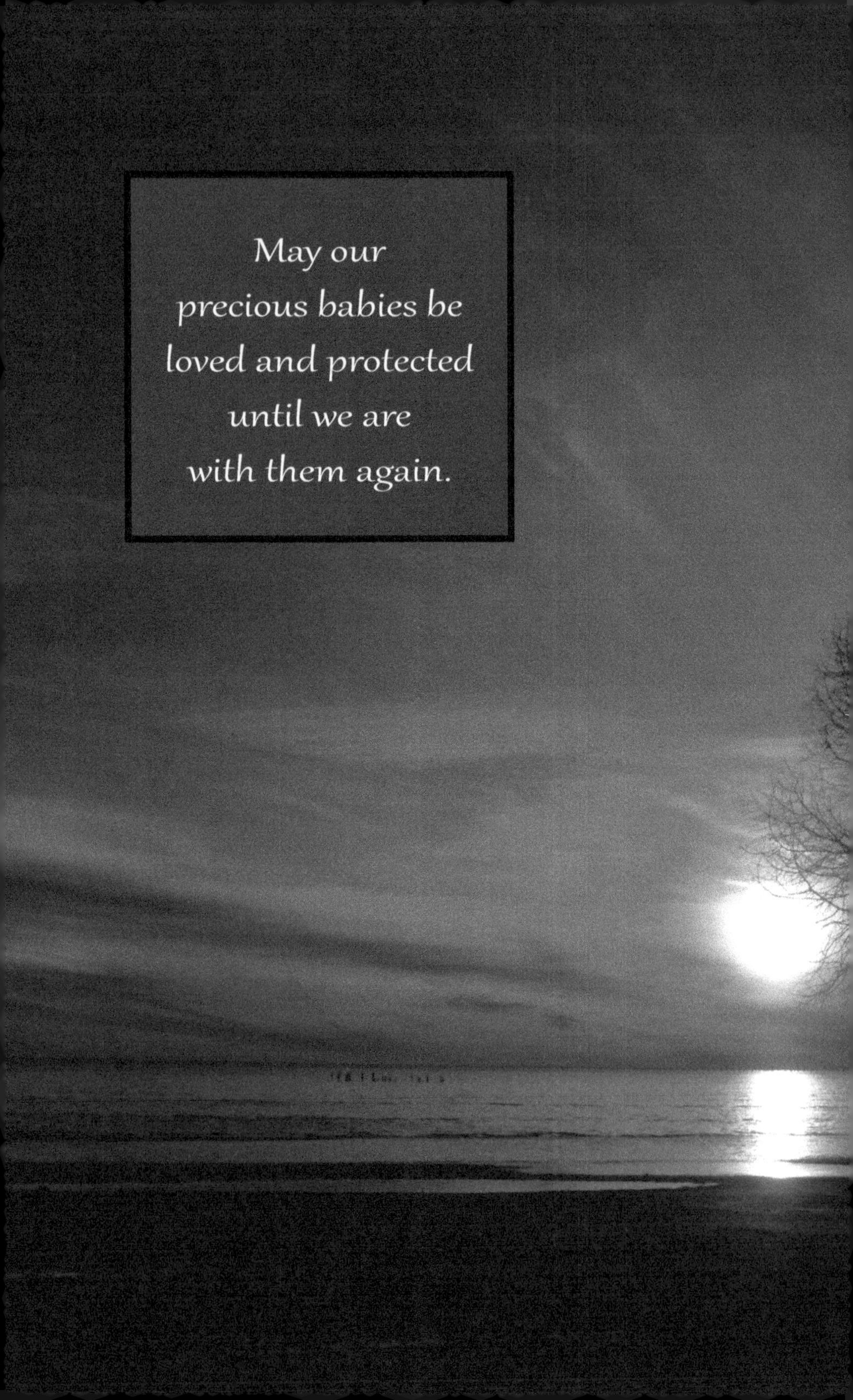

May our
precious babies be
loved and protected
until we are
with them again.

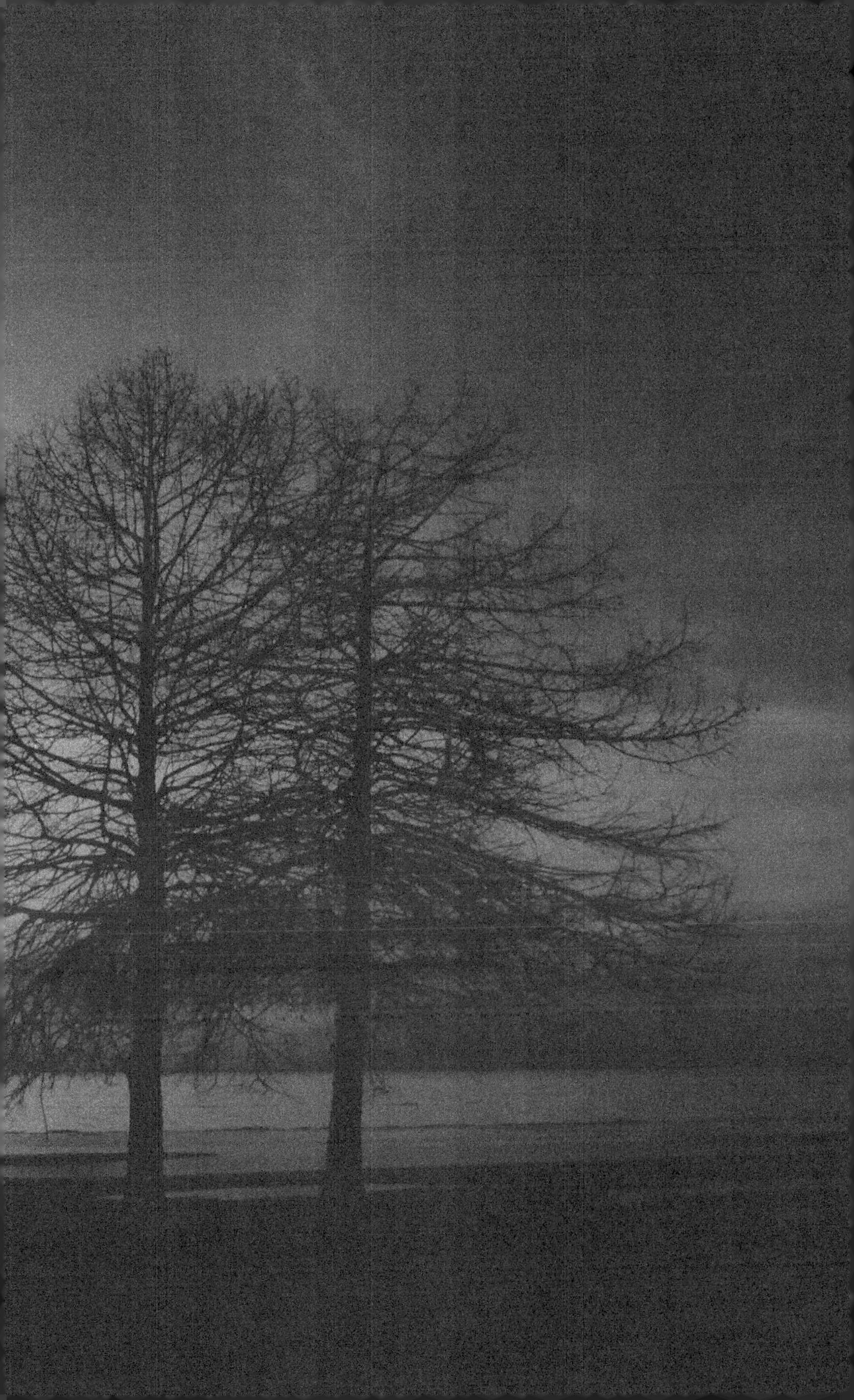

In Darkness I Will Hope

I told my story the other day,
And said I was over it.
I was completely believable,
But inside I was total shit.

No one really cares,
Nor do they want to know
This feeling deep inside
That screams to be shown.

I'm applauded by my strength,
With how I've moved on.
But the only thing I've done
Is live my life as a con.

It's not acceptable to grieve
For any length of time,
'Cause people can't handle anything
That isn't perfectly sublime.

In silence I shall weep,
And in darkness I will hope
That one day peace falls upon me,
And I finally learn to cope.

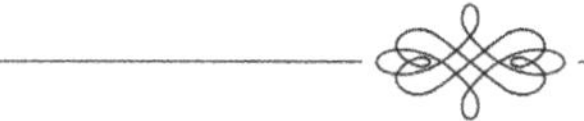

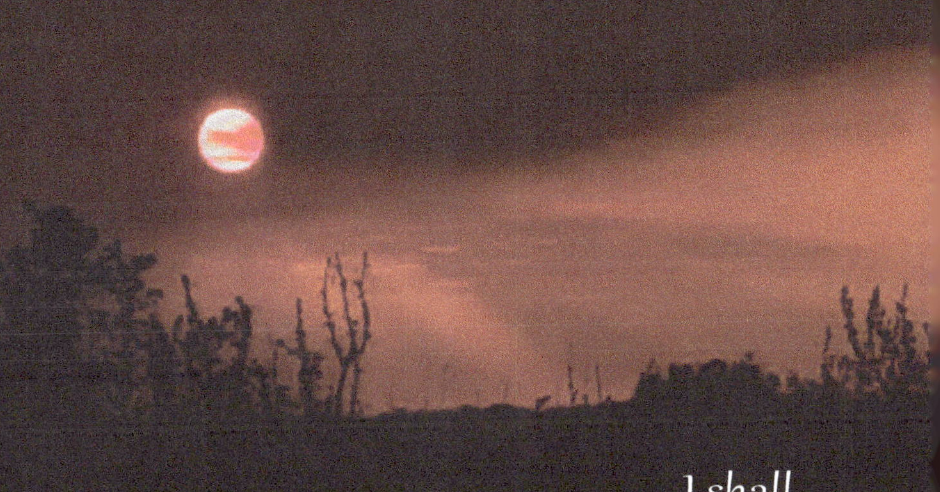
I shall
be brave
for the
both of us.

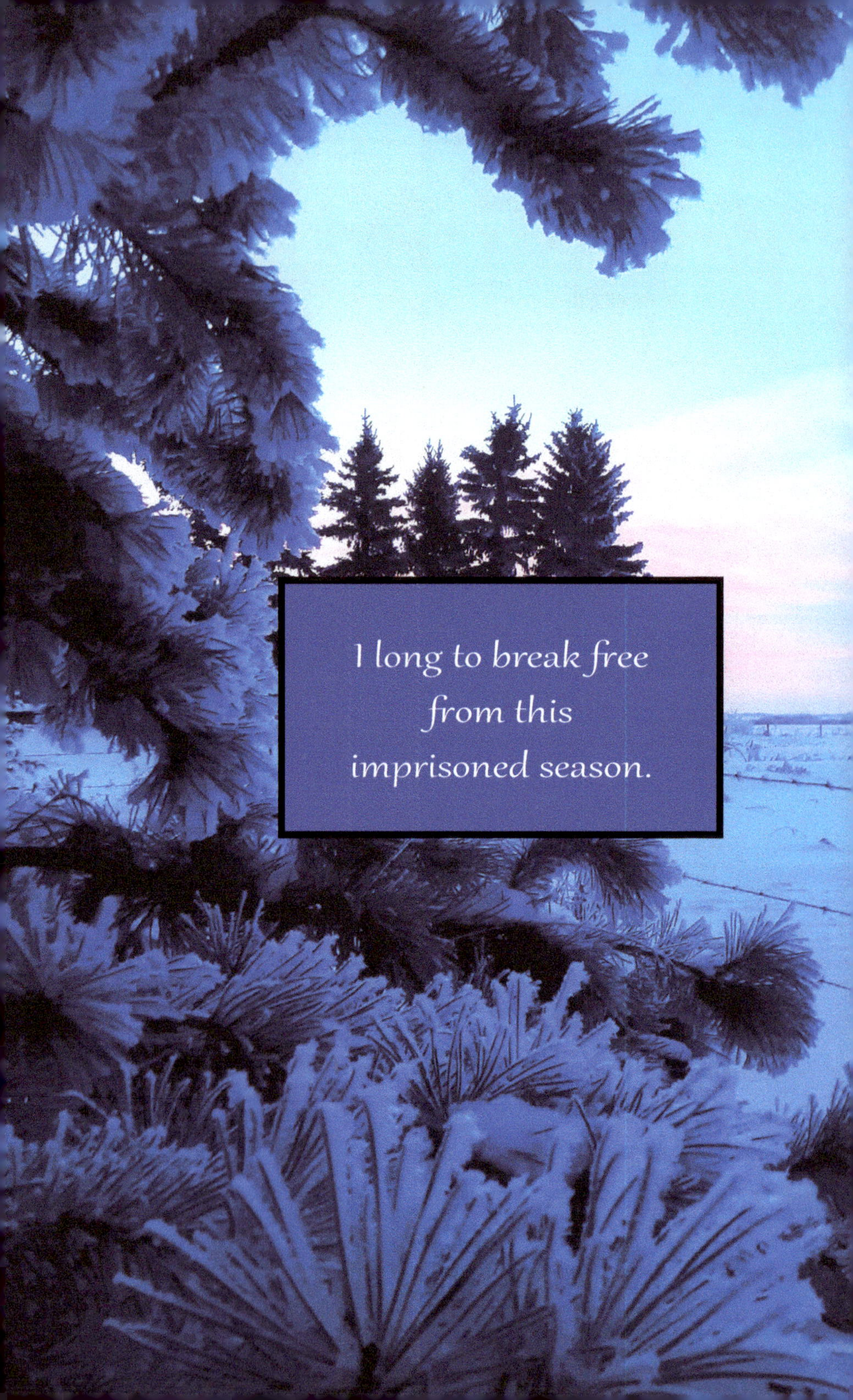
I long to break free
from this
imprisoned season.

Grief

There's no right or wrong with the stages of grief.
I can do everything by the book and still get no relief.
Sometimes I have all the feels, and other times just one.
It's never in any particular order, and I'm never truly
done.

I can't ever "get over it" like a horse jumping a fence,
Because these emotions I have are far too intense.
I must embrace this grief and work through all the pain,
With the hope I will somehow find a way to keep sane.

Will I ever be able to find a true kind of healing?
Does my sweet love understand? Does he feel what I'm
feeling?
I'm trying with all my might to get through all of this,
'Cause I long for the time when our lives were filled
utter bliss.

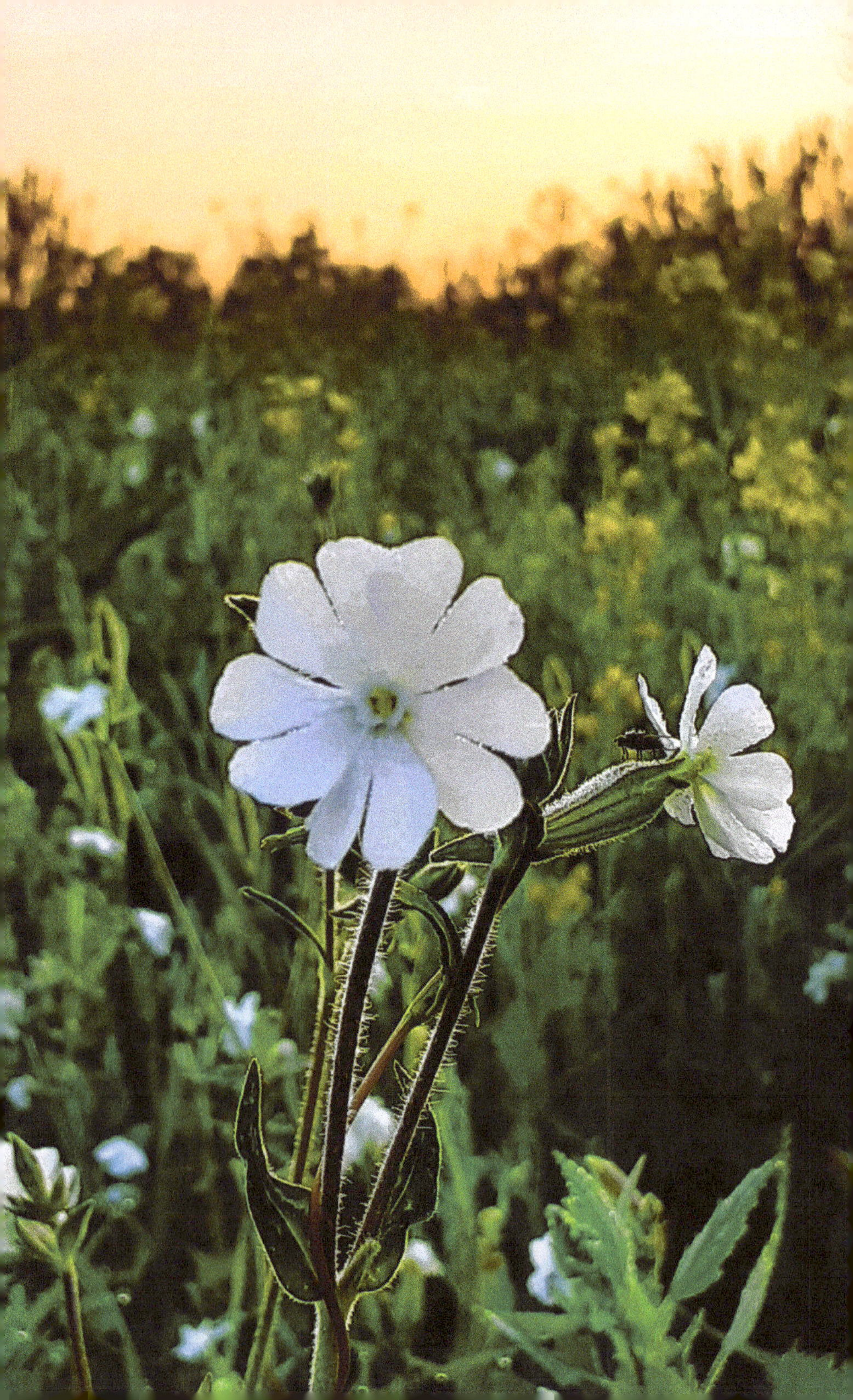

Finding My Way

It's been a long road of pain and sorrow.
It's been a long time since the yesterday of tomorrow.
I've been searching for the other half of the glass,
Often hoping for the greener side of the grass.

I know the change that's needed is really up to me,
But this place I'm in is a strange place to be.
My thoughts and emotions have become all a blur,
Keeping me from a healing that's supposed to occur.

I will give myself just a little more time,
For it is quite the mountain I have yet to climb
Through my grief and sorrow and sadness and dismay.
But by the grace of God, I promise to find my way.

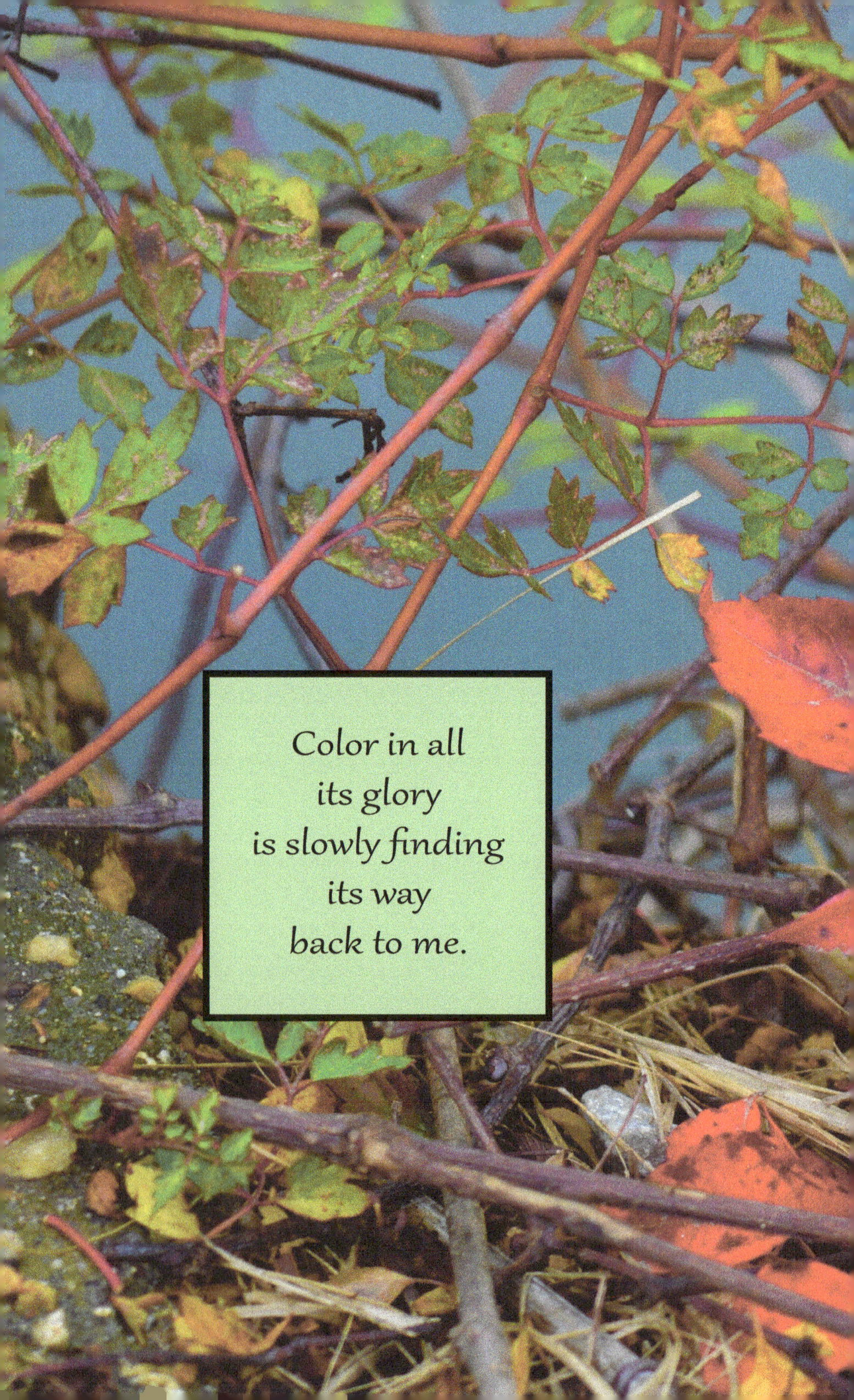

Color in all
its glory
is slowly finding
its way
back to me.

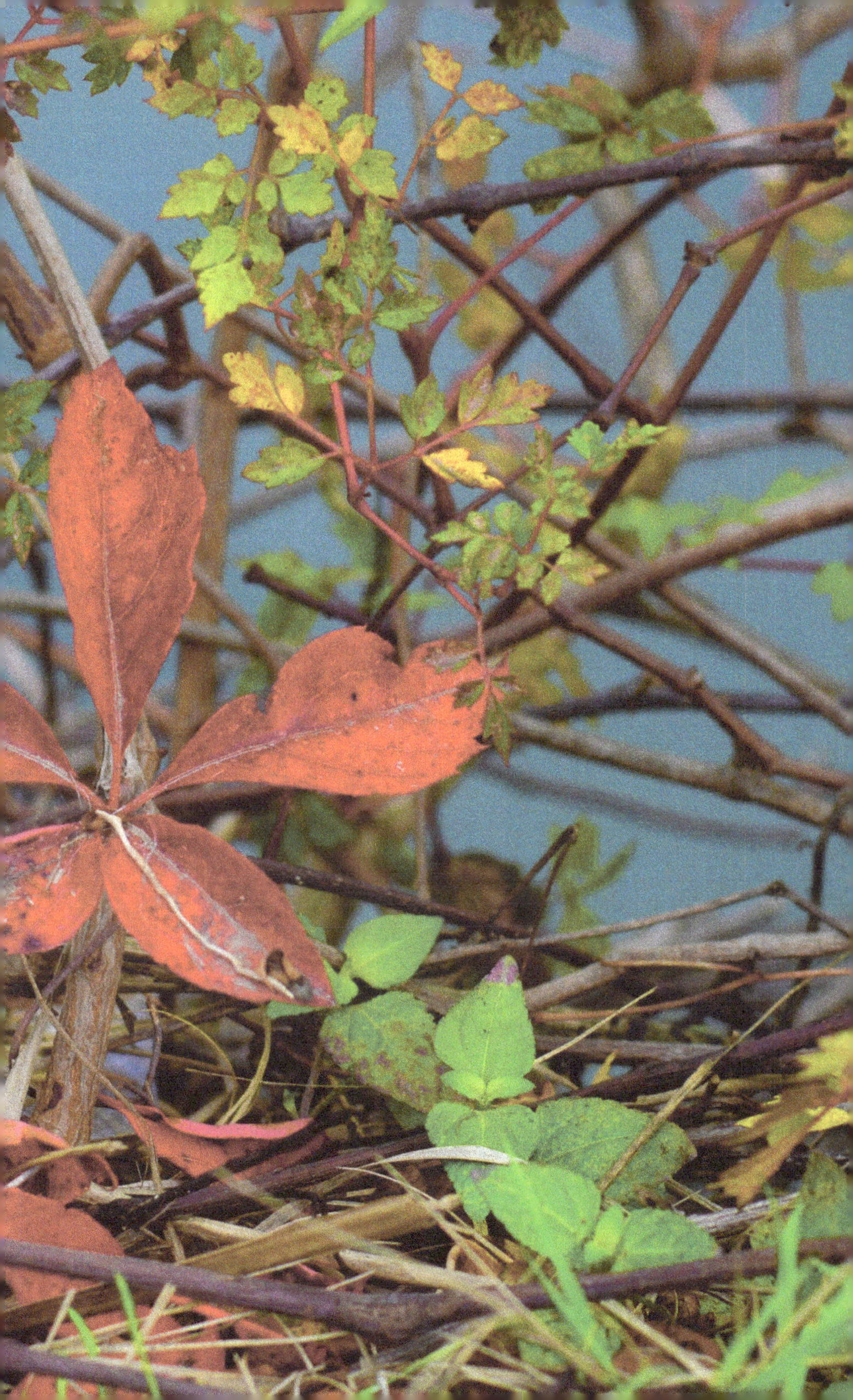

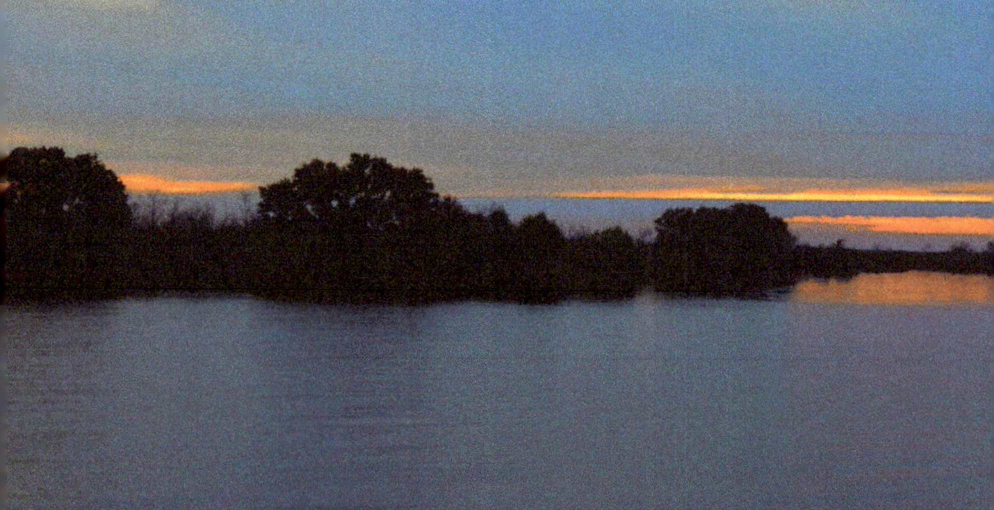

I have tried
with all my heart
to take away
this trauma,
but the best I can do
is hold your hand.

I Smiled Today

I smiled today
When your fingers overlapped mine.
I smiled today
And for first time, I felt fine.

I laughed today
When you made your eyes wiggle.
I laughed today,
A lot more than a giggle.

I loved today
When you held me tight.
I loved today
When I found my inner light.

I healed today
When you showed me that rainbow.
I healed today
When I finally let it all go.

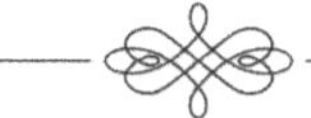

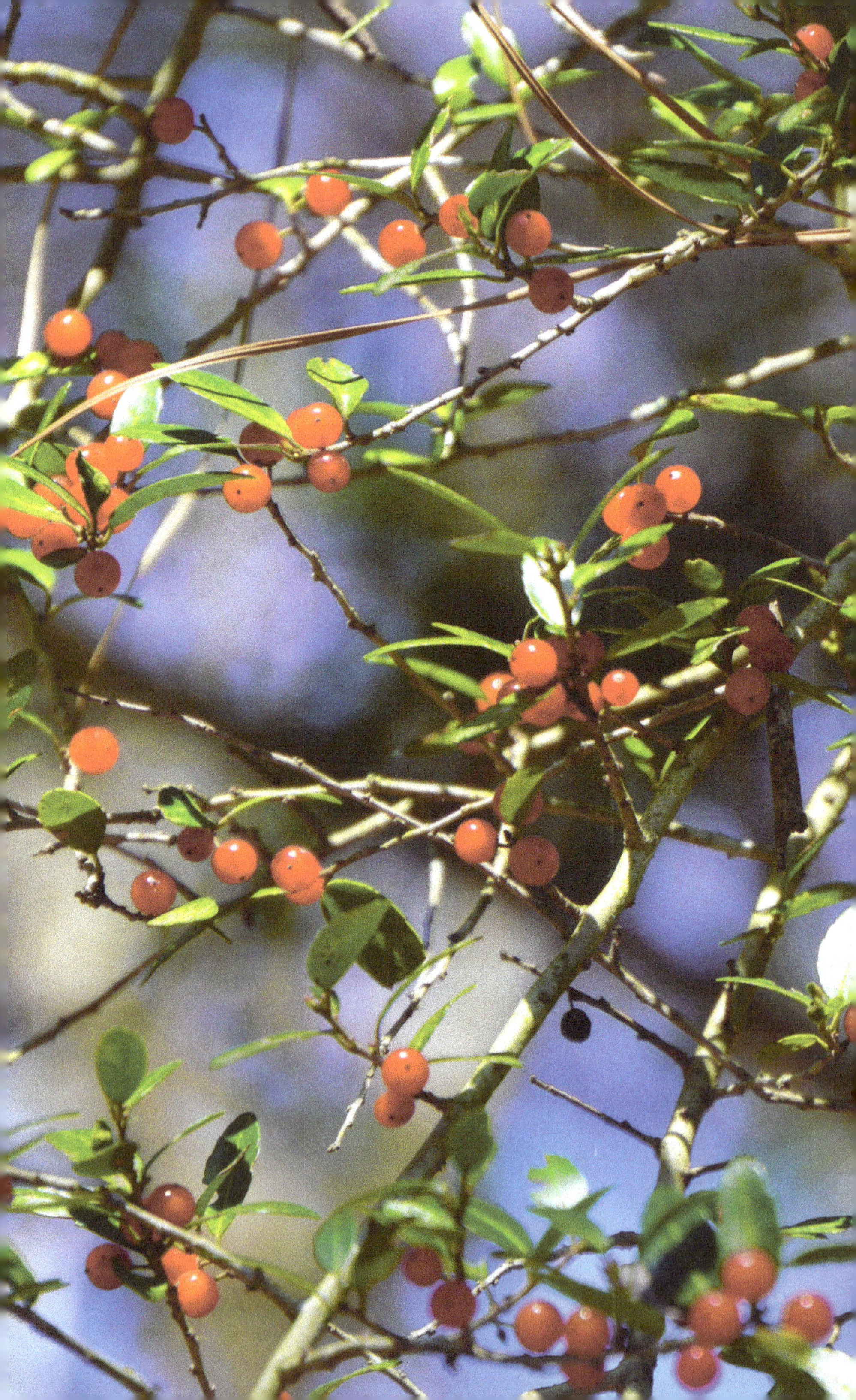

Dots on a Thing

A projected light forms a sky above,
With neon stars gracing the dark.
Nebulas swirling in royal blue,
Calling for magic to light its spark.

Freed from the chains of reason,
I am flying through this night—
Exploring, creating, imagining
On and on until dawn's first light.

A whole universe is mysteriously revealed,
And a soulful healing it does bring.
For me, it means utter bliss,
But to others, it's just dots on a thing.

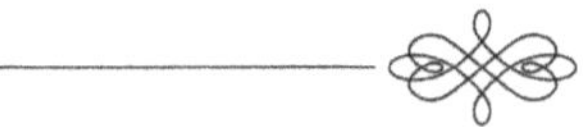

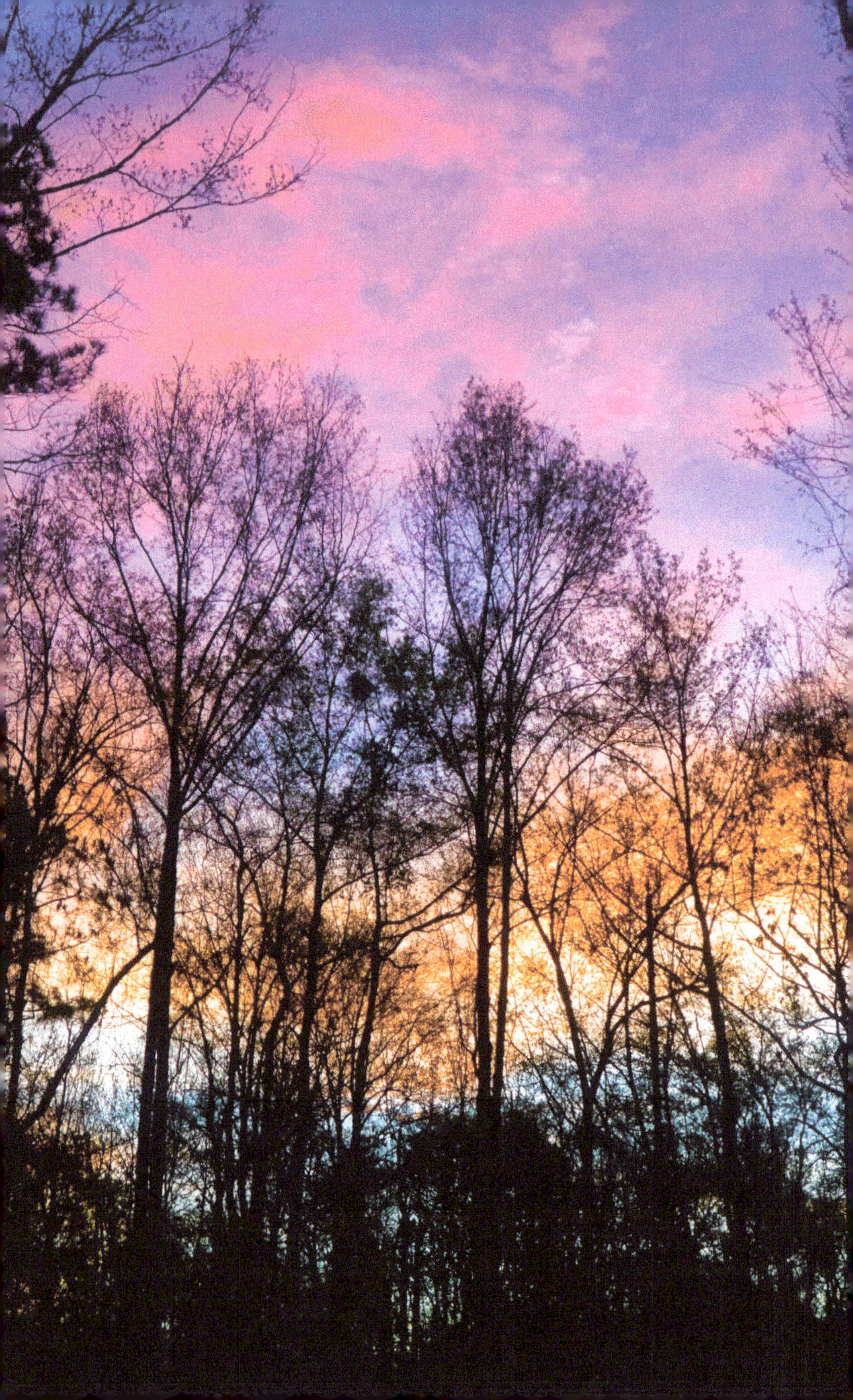

Champagne Delight

A sorbet of colors painted above,
And on the street, a mourning dove.
The sound of its coo brings a smile
As it struts around with great style.

The day is waking with a bustling sound,
Noises heard are all around.
Too busy to notice the sky,
How sad! They don't even try.

The fiery sun lifts the shroud,
Sugaring the expanse of a dawning cloud.
With raspberries and champagne delight,
It bids adieu to the gloomy dark night.

A circus of creatures comes alive,
Drinking the color that makes them thrive.
So much to be had from nature's cup!
And all I had to do was just look up.

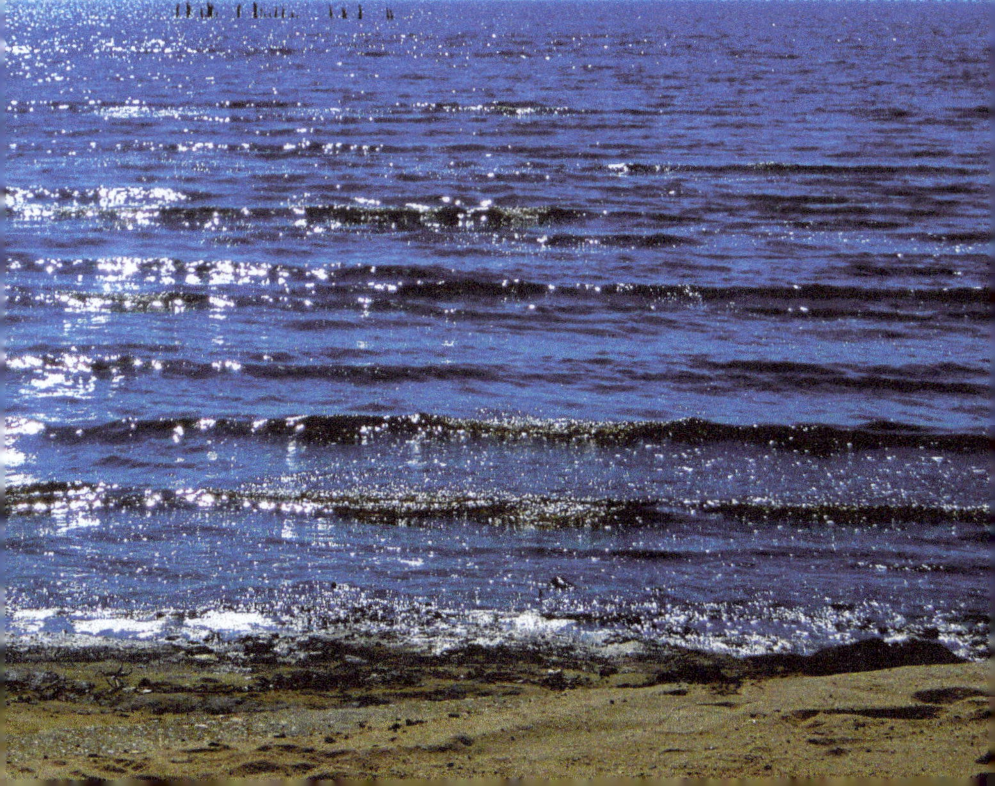
I shall play music for you again.

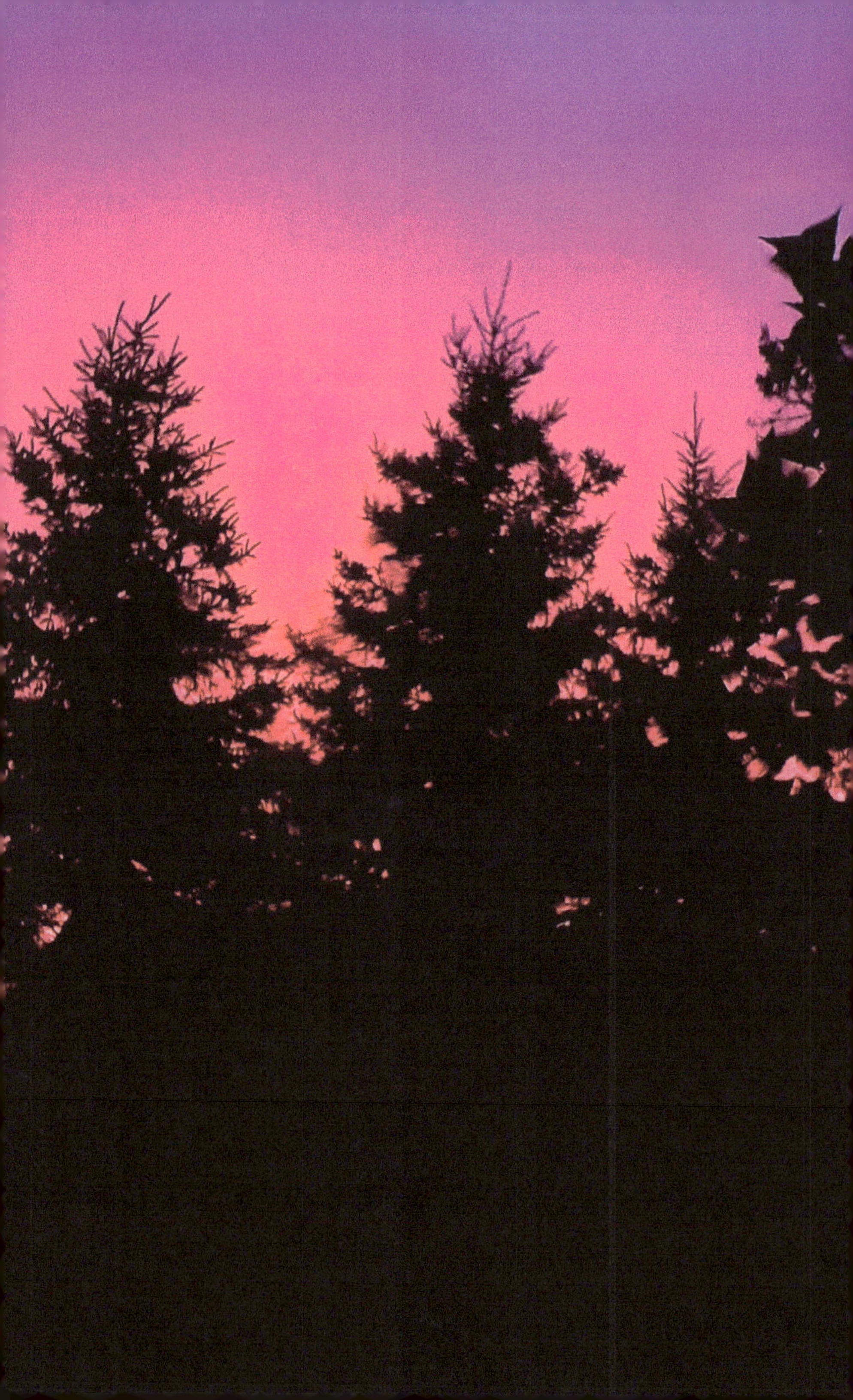

Jewels of the Night

There exist jewels so precious.
They are kept far from reach,
And only come out
When all have gone to sleep.

They mingle with the stars,
And dance about the sea,
Dappling over mermaids,
Creating their own artistry.

They linger within the woods,
Twinkling like the firefly.
And with their voices they sing
Unto all creation to glorify.

They are angels from beyond—
Jewels of the night.
And although we can't see them,
They protect us with their light.

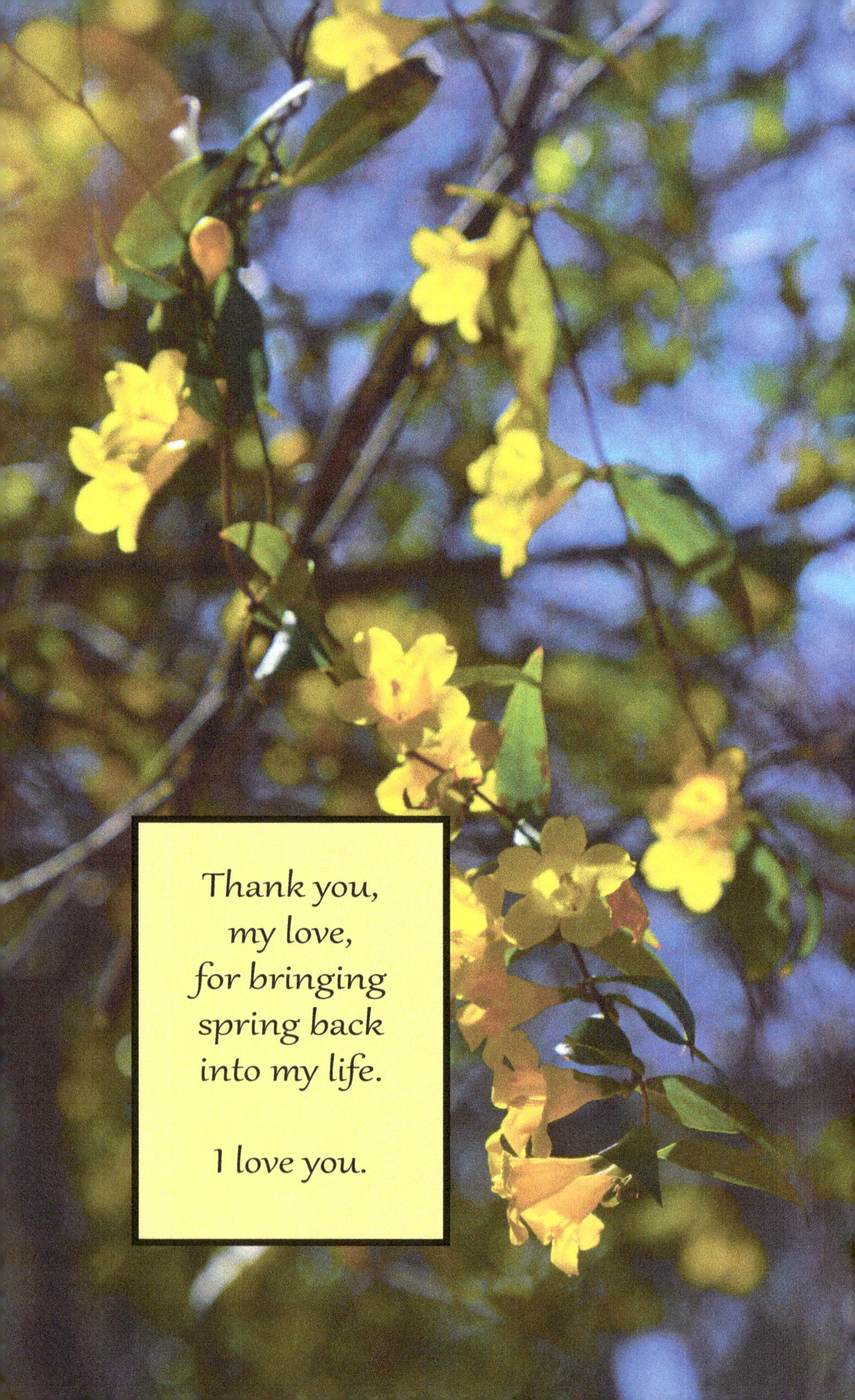

Thank you,
my love,
for bringing
spring back
into my life.

I love you.

The Simple Things

It's the simple things that bring joy,
Like the kiss of a girl and a boy.
Or watching a butterfly flit
Until it finds a scented flower to sit.

I've been walking along this path,
Soaking in the sun as though it were a bath.
All the while listening
To the chitter of squirrels visiting.

Nature has everything I need
To move forward and succeed,
From the bumble of the bees
To the rustle of the trees.

The fragrance of a wooded pine
Is but pure divine,
And the sight of a blue jay
Reminds me that all is okay.

There are lessons all around
If only I give ear to the sound,
And allow the meanings to penetrate
For my heart to resonate.

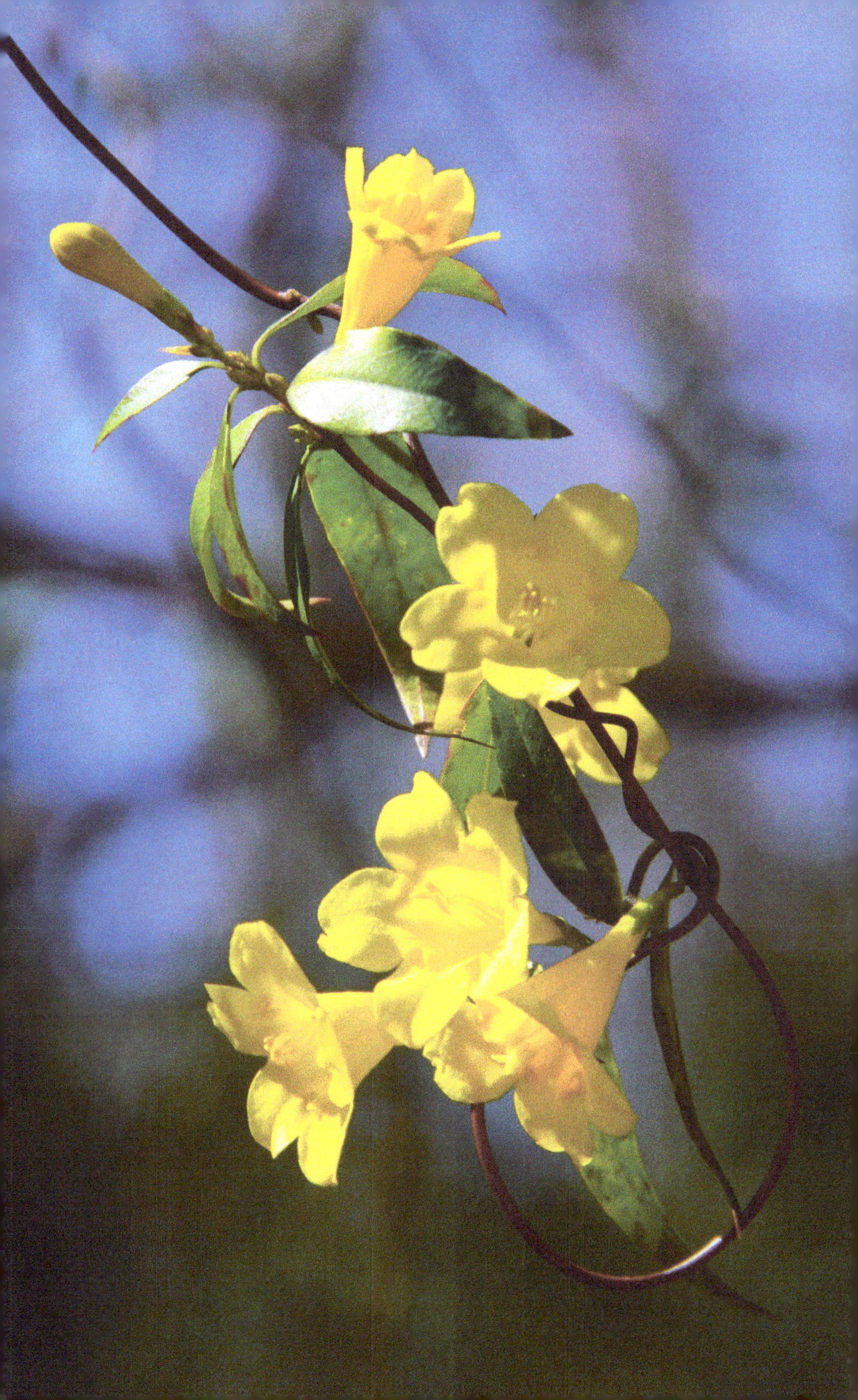

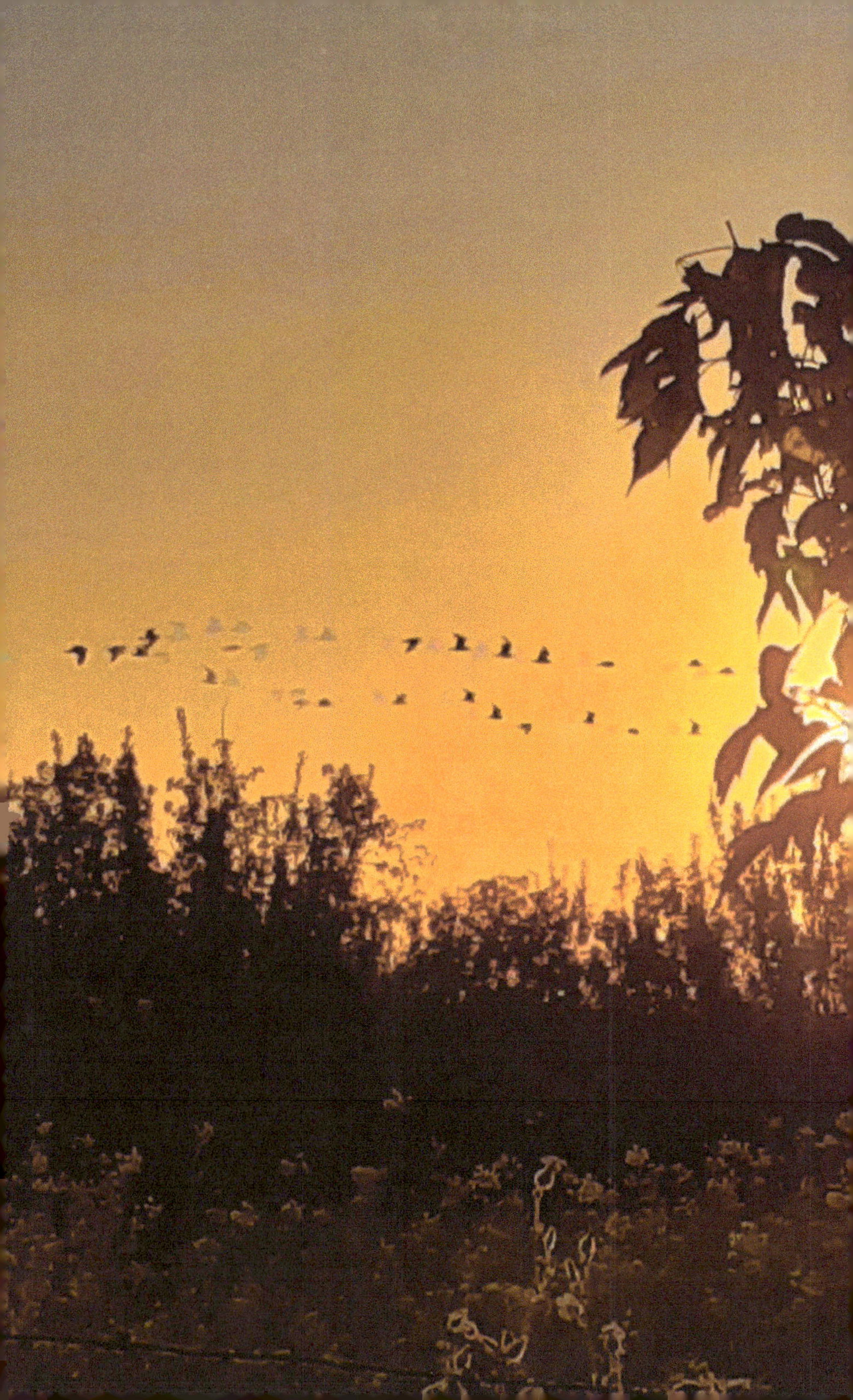

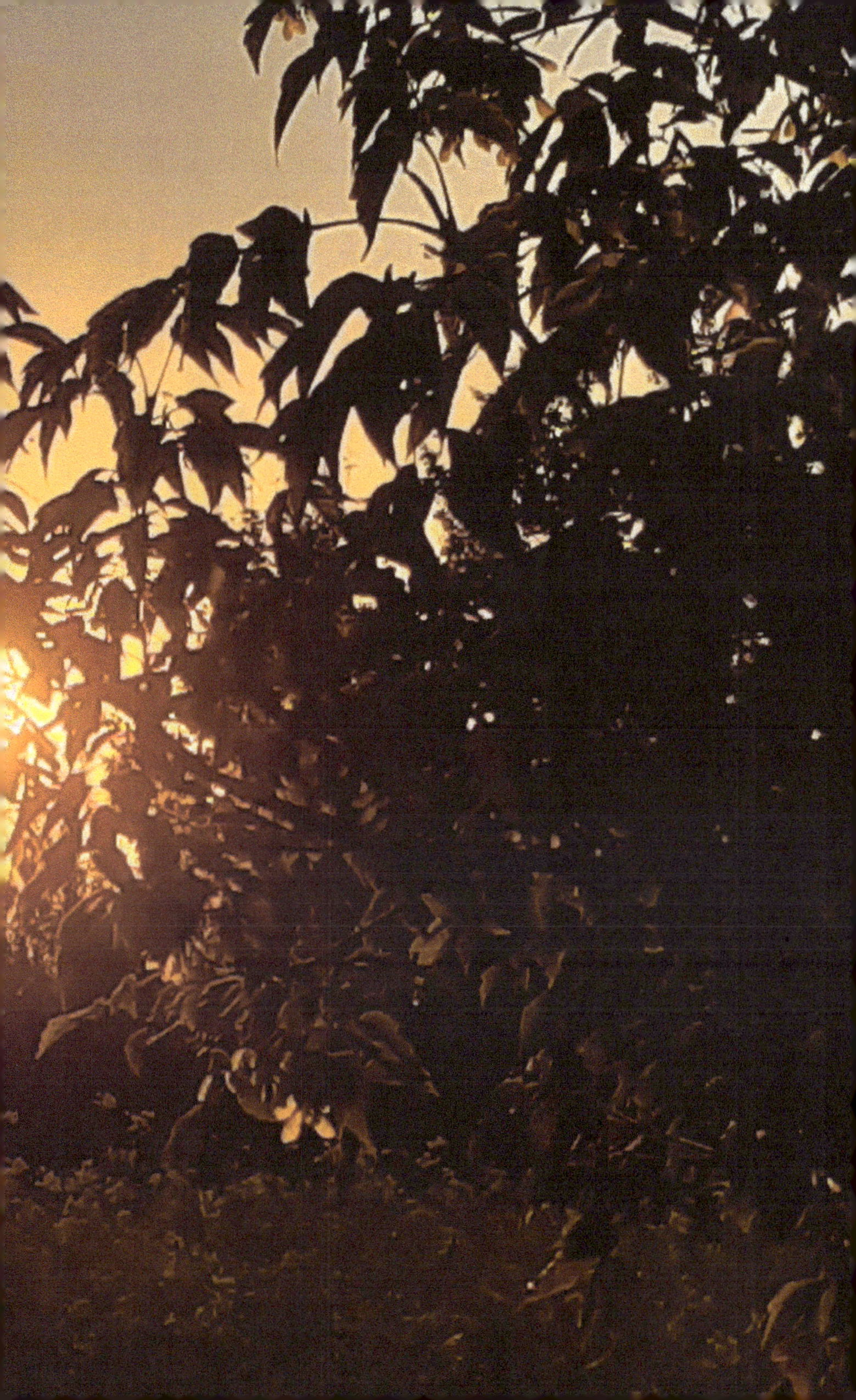

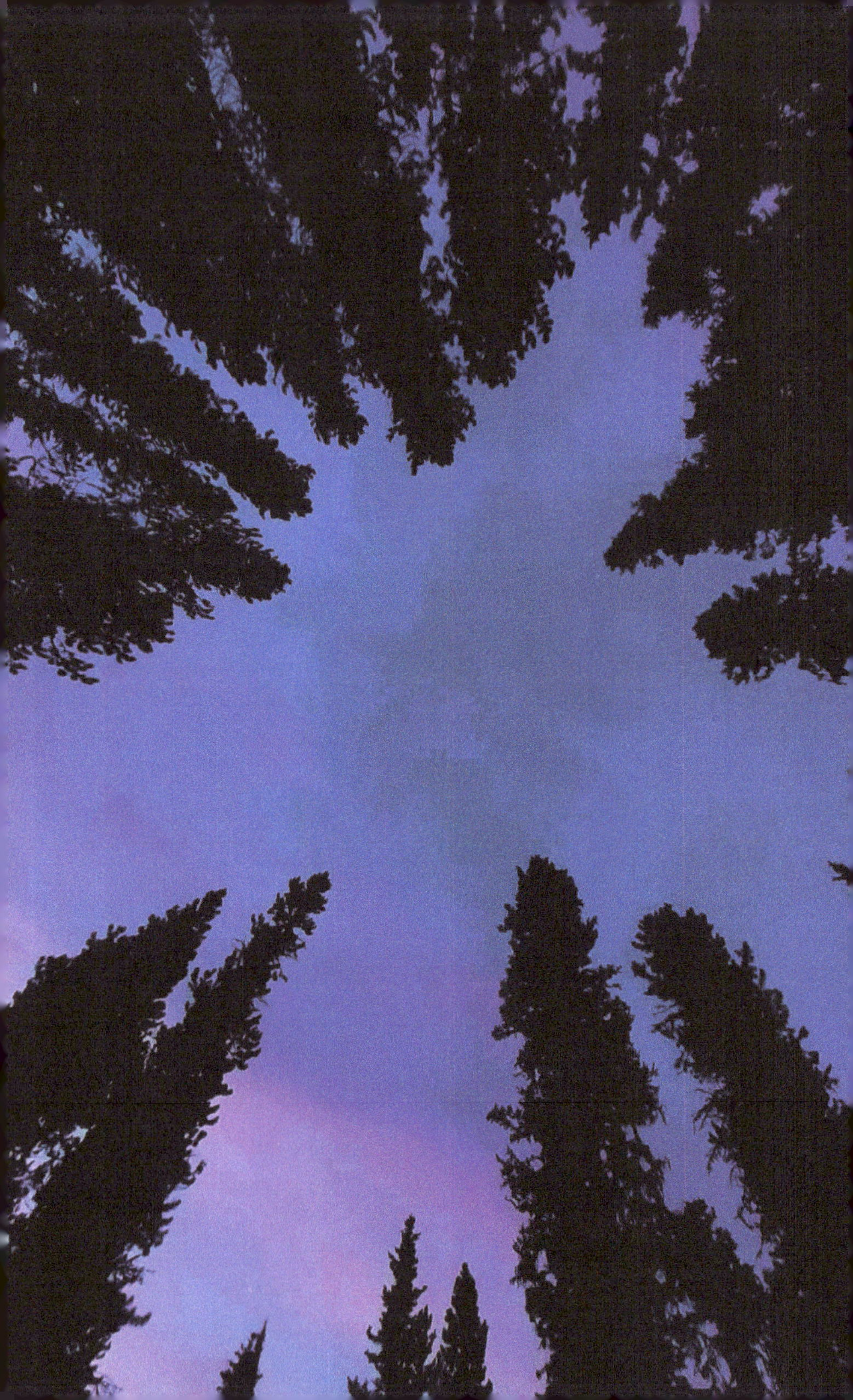

Let It Be Me

I heard the news today,
Words that will haunt forever in my mind,
So much to my dismay.
How can I go forward? What will I find?

A life without him,
When he is the best of us.
This can't possibly be true!
It is ludicrous!

Dear God, "Let it be me.
I willingly take his place.
Please, hear my plea!
And his life, do not erase."

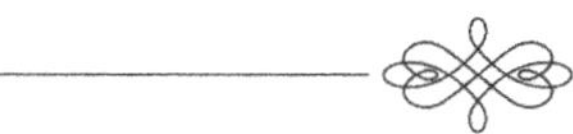

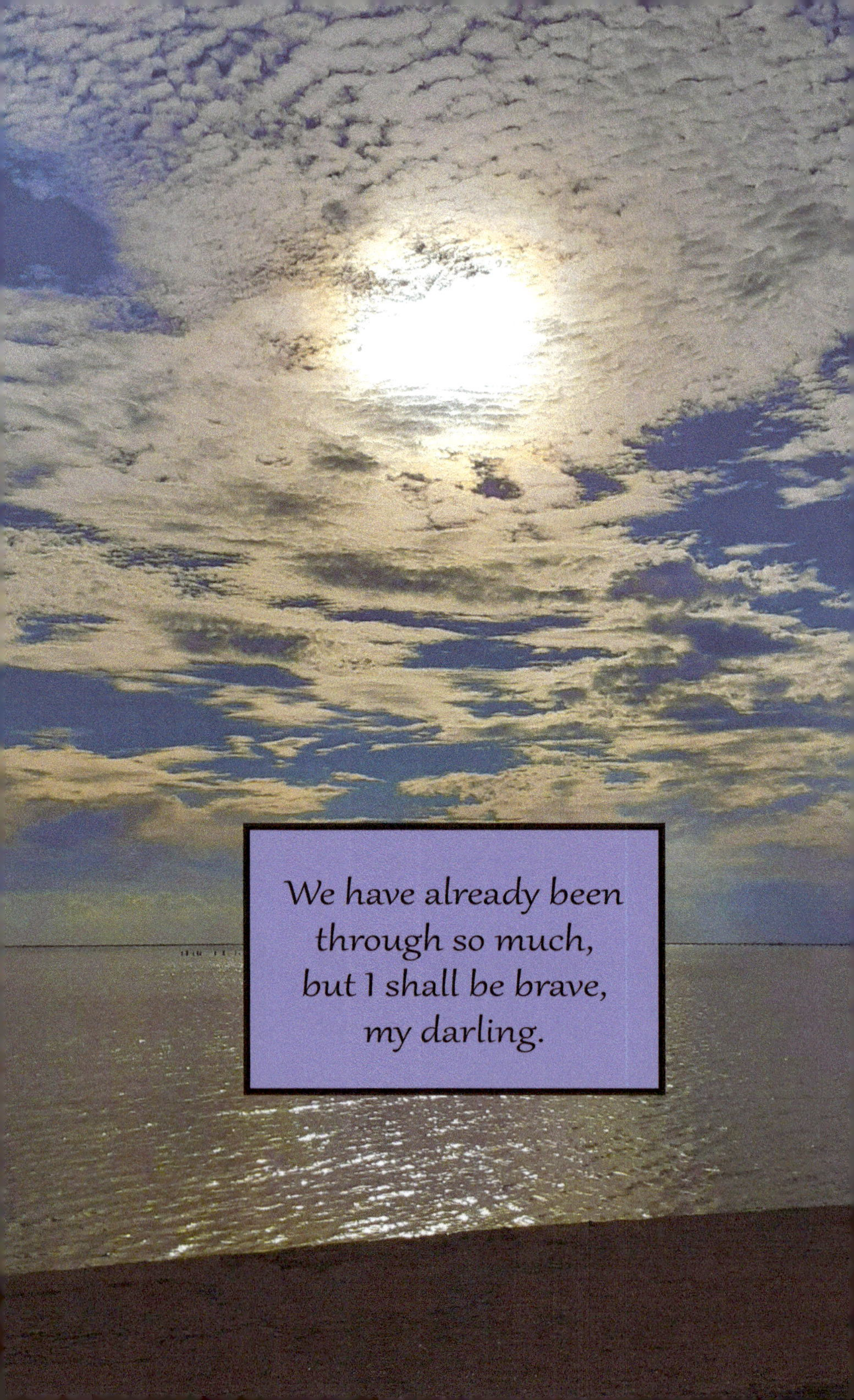
We have already been
through so much,
but I shall be brave,
my darling.

More Time

I wish I had more time
To make it all sublime.
I want to trust my gut,
Except for the word "but".

Life keeps getting in the way,
Each and every day.
And I can't keep going,
For this pain is showing.

I'm so sorry for it all,
And wish I could make it stall.
But I'm tired, my dear,
And soon you will die, I fear.

So my sweet love,
My emotions I will shove
To give you some peace
Until the time that you cease.

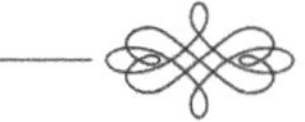

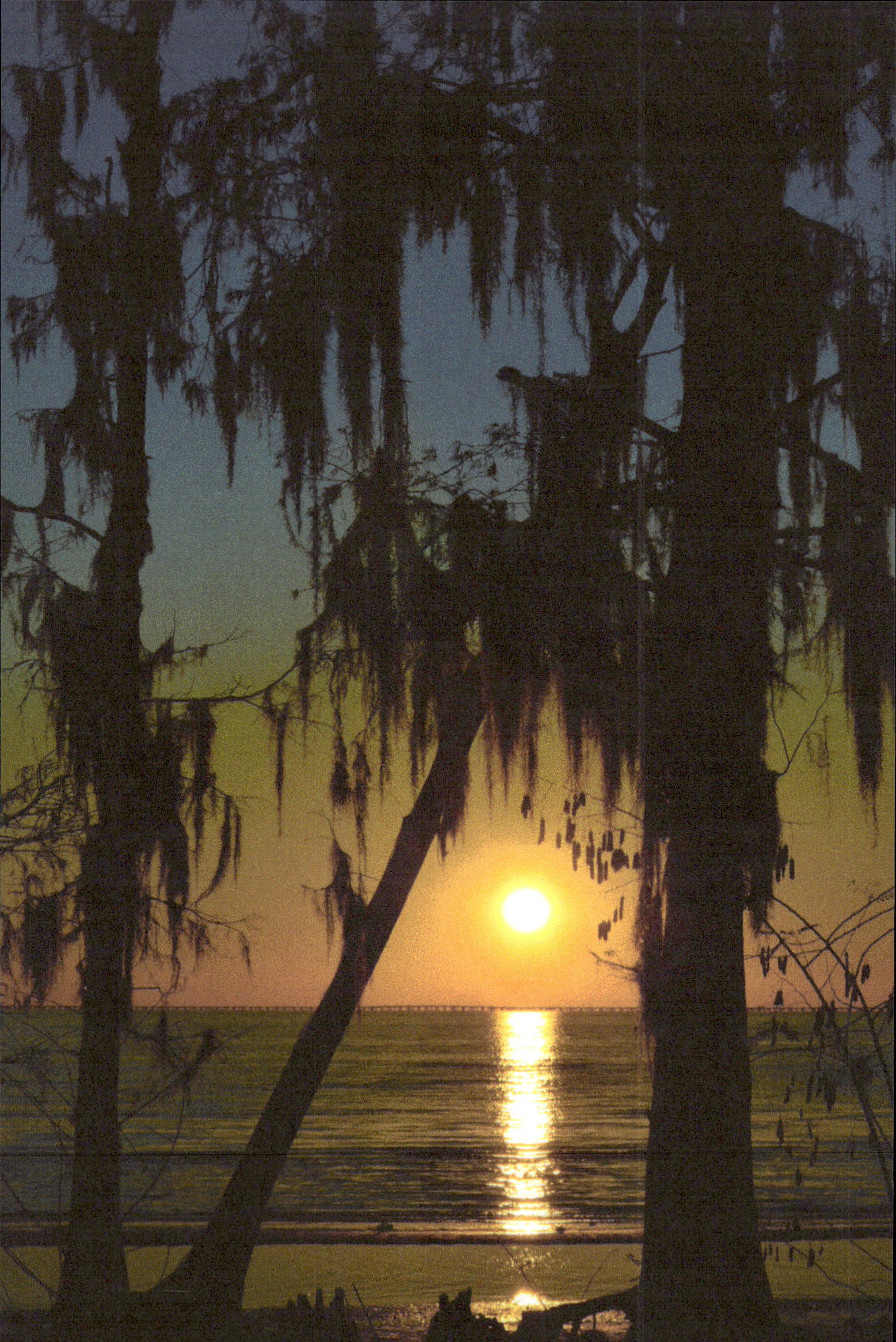

The Lull

There is true joy in the lull after ecstasy—
A quiet, gentle bliss of complete harmony.
In that moment when your eyes meet mine,
It is foreverness and a stillness of time.

We giggle and laugh and play,
And wish we could stay in bed all day!
But sometimes we hold on and cry
For fear we soon have to say our goodbye.

You know my light and my dark shadow.
Still, your love streams to an overflow
Like the rippling tide cleanses the shore,
With the quiet moon shining on all the more.

The lull has a strength beyond all power.
It is the binding of two delicate flowers
Softly blowing in a field's breeze,
Yet will grow again after the winter freeze.

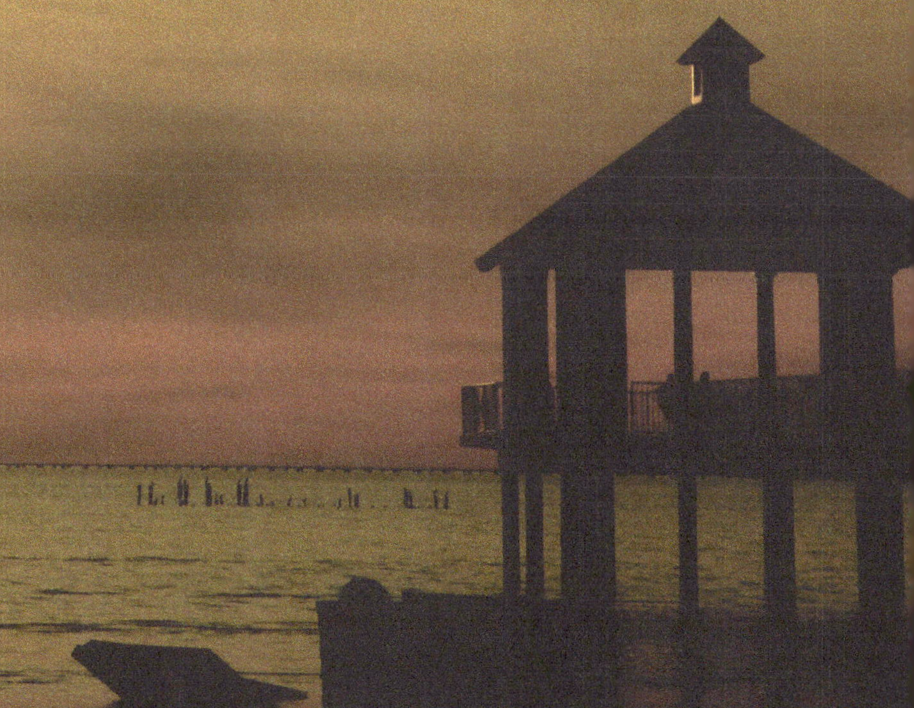

I was meant to help you.

And I was meant to heal you.

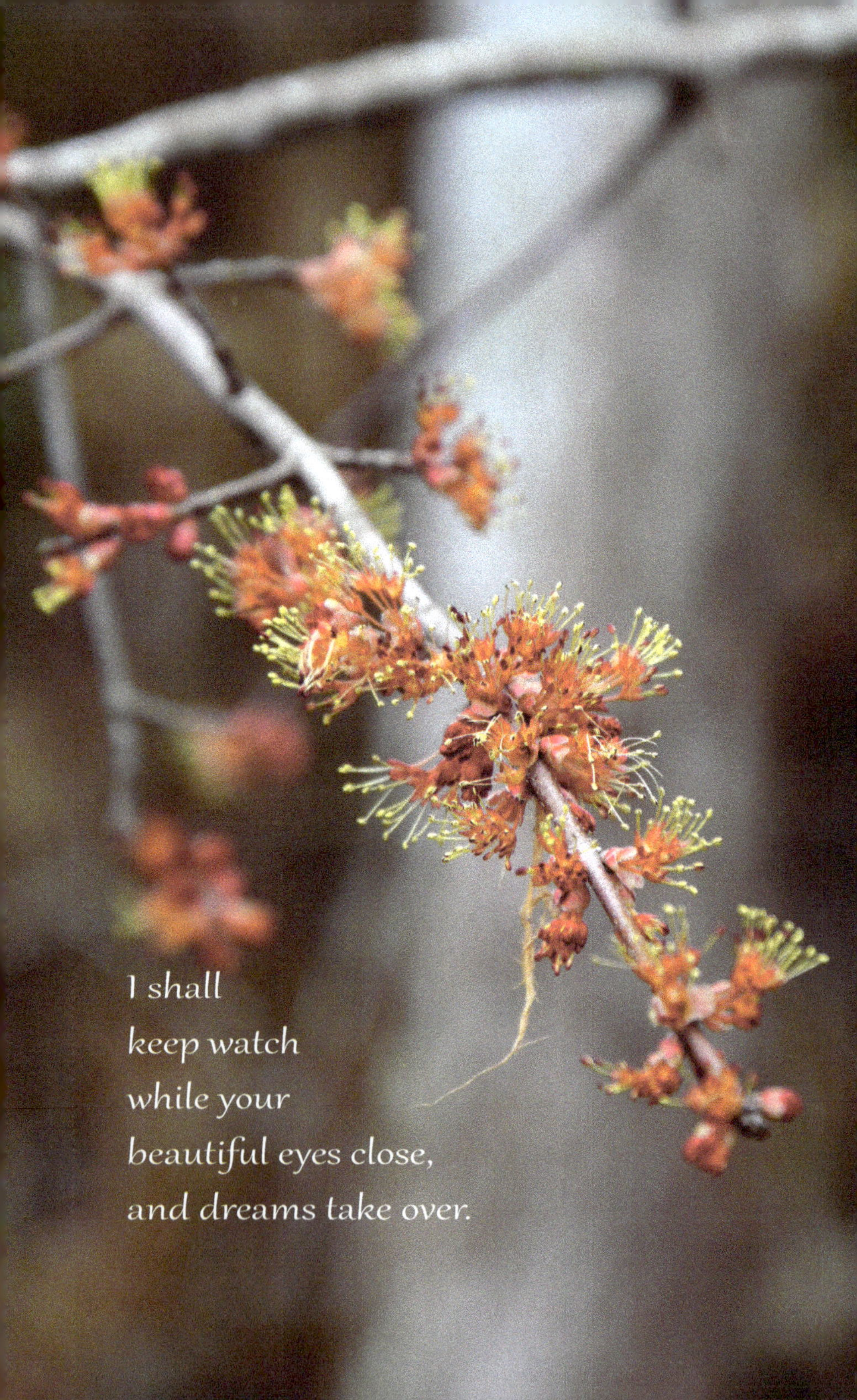

I shall
keep watch
while your
beautiful eyes close,
and dreams take over.

Breath

With a faint light shining upon your face,
The movement of your mouth shows barely a trace
Of the effortless breath propelled by your beating heart,
Holding me entranced, wishing to never to be apart.

Lying by your side, watching you drift
From dream to beautiful dream is but a wondrous gift.
And to be with you before you open your eyes
Is for me life's greatest and superlative prize.

For I'm in love with you—body, mind, and soul—
And this close proximity makes me want to lose control.
But I will be content just to be in your presence,
'Cause your effortless breath gives meaning to my exis-
tence.

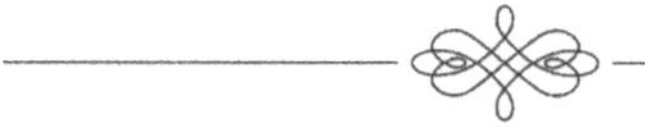

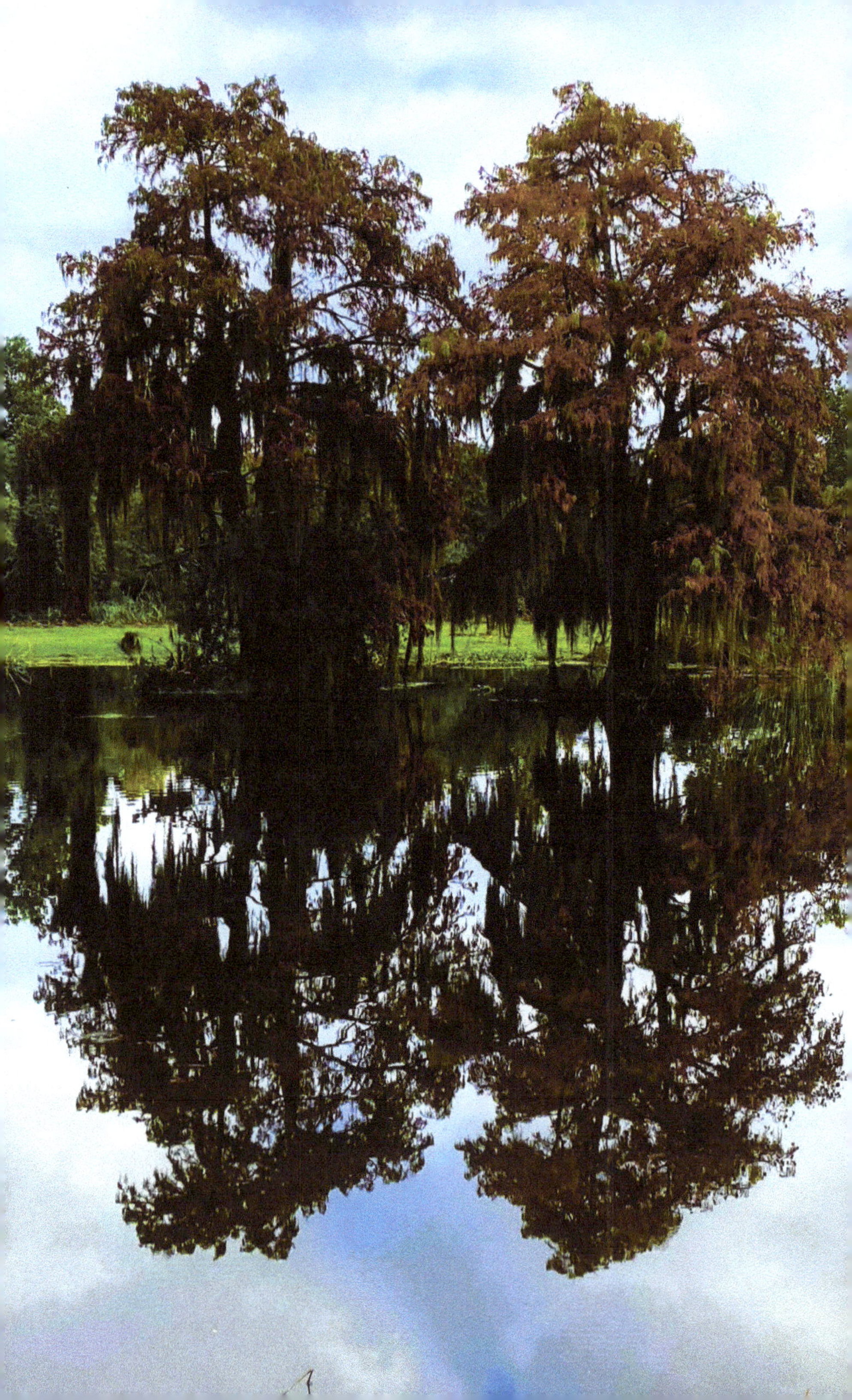

While You're Here

While you're here, I wanna say
Things from my heart, if I may.
Words are not easy for me to express,
But there are some things I need to stress.

While you're here, you need to know:
I've loved you more than I could show.
It came when you were unaware,
Surrounding you like the breathing air.

While you're here, please remember:
Summers of fun when it's cold in December.
In this season of your life,
Feel my warmth to heal your strife.

While you're here, hold my hand.
When things don't go quite as planned,
I'll be here to keep you steady,
And anticipate things before you're ready.

While you're here, feast your eyes
Upon the legacy that did arise.
Those you've helped are all around.
Your kindness shown is truly profound.

While you're here, I wanna say,
You've been the best part of my day.
From the beginning until time's end,
You've been forever, my best friend.

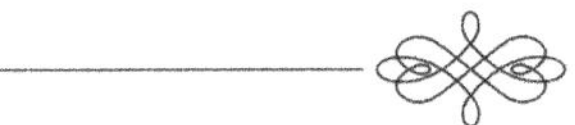

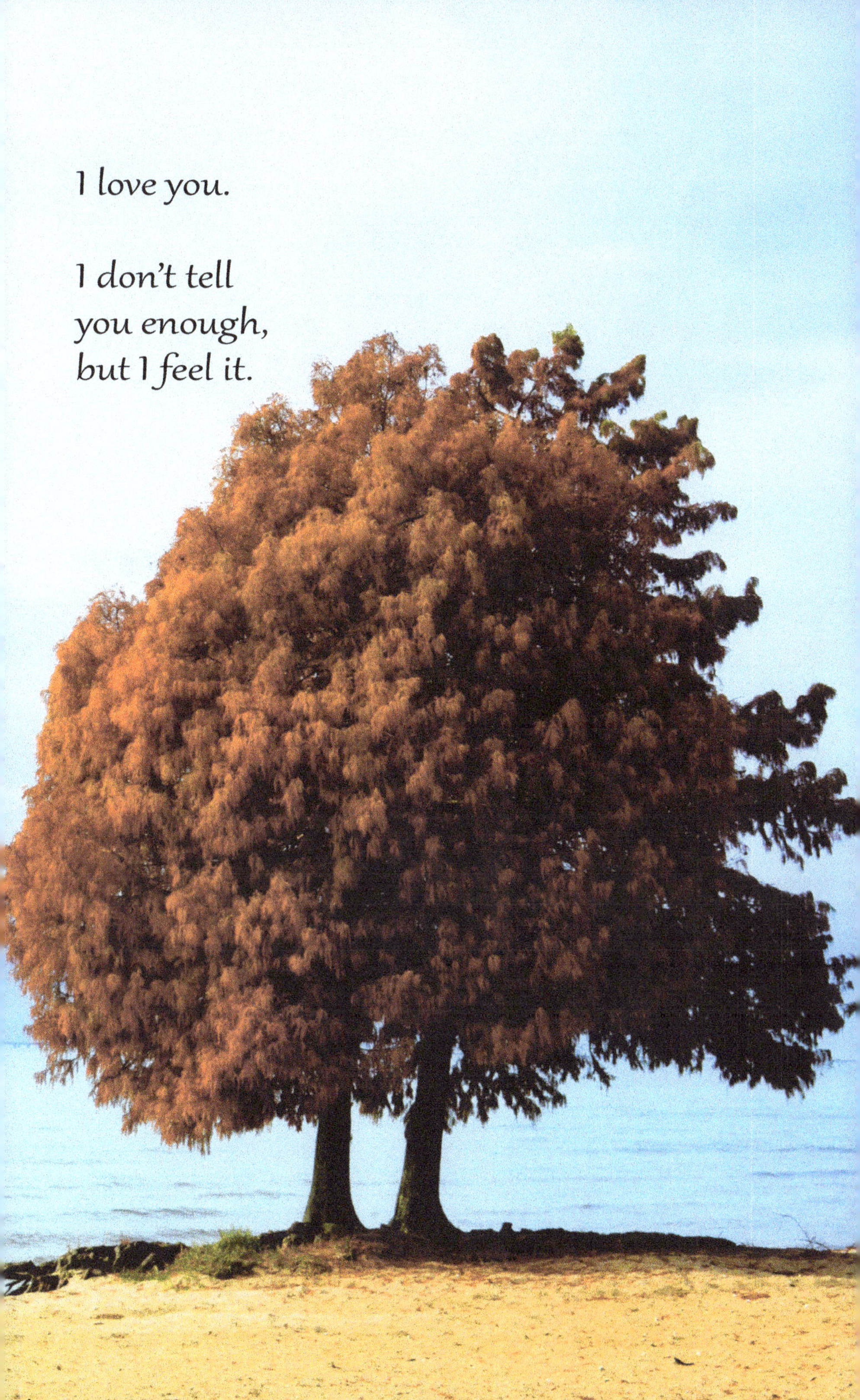
I love you.

I don't tell
you enough,
but I feel it.

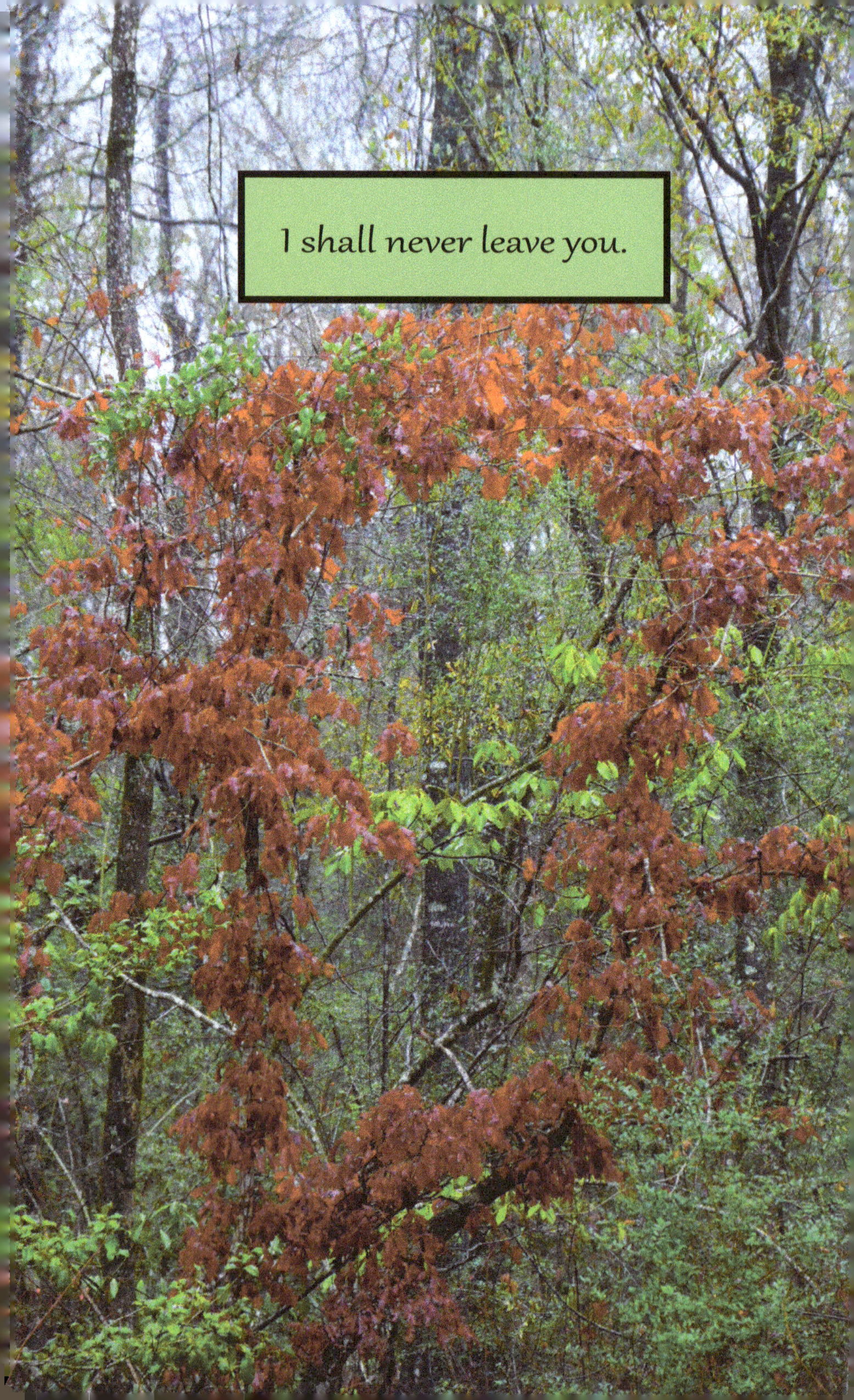
I shall never leave you.

Ever Waiting

Please come now.
Hear my voice.
Walk my path.
Seek me out.
Find me soon.
I need you.
I am here.
I won't leave.
I love you.
Take me hand.
Stay with me.
Feel my heart.
Kiss me now.
I am yours.
You are mine.
We are one,
By our love.

Always.

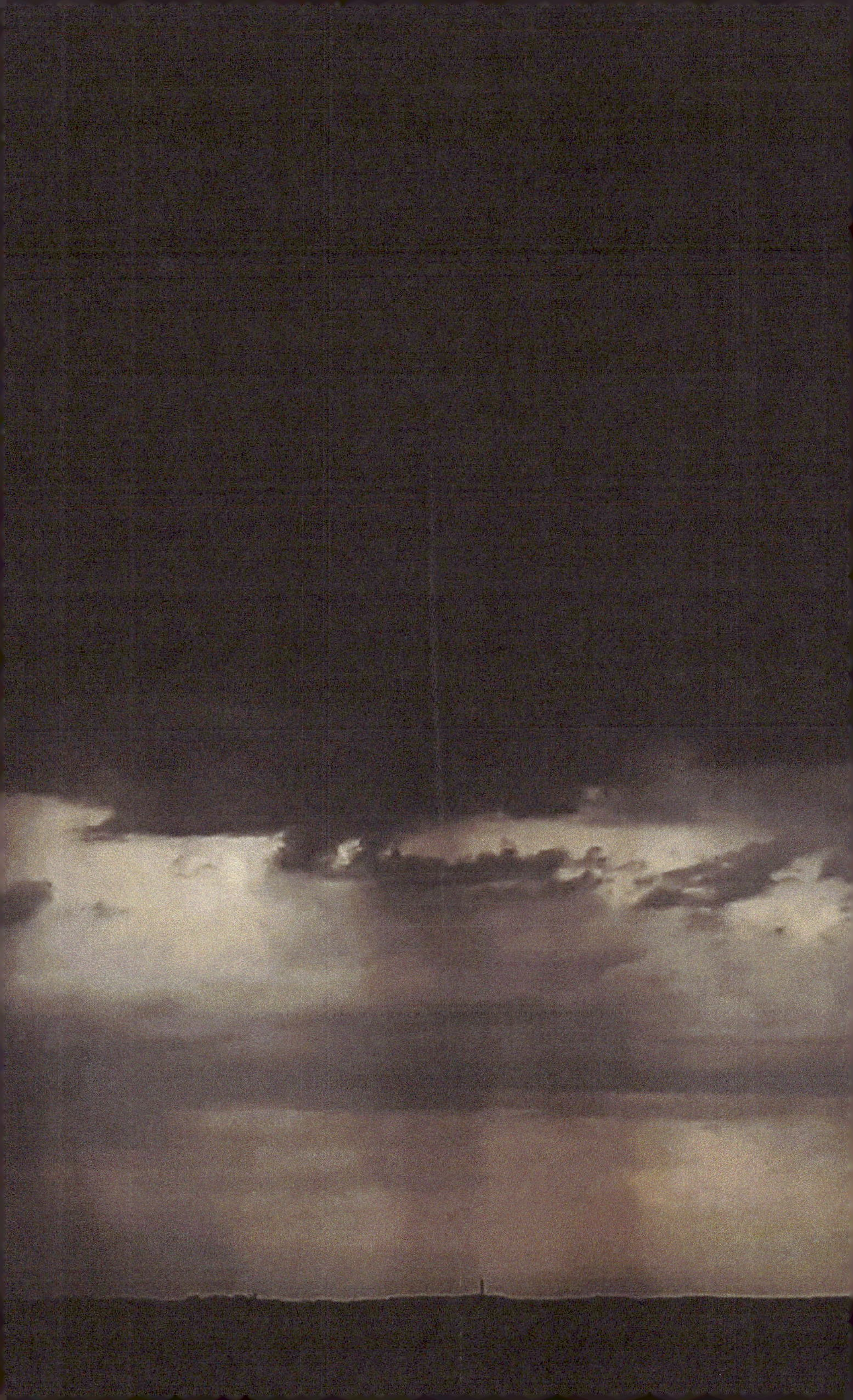

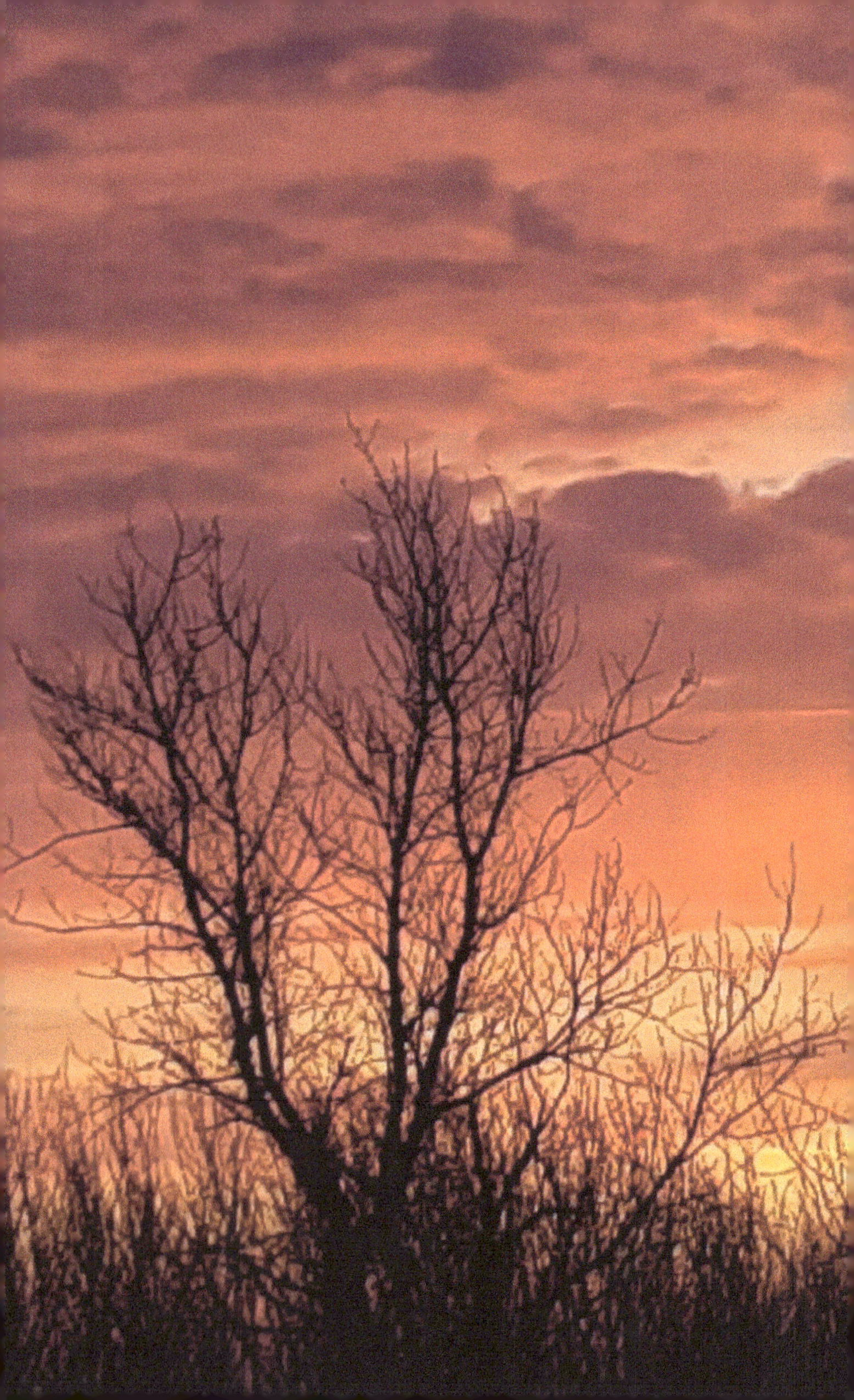

Endlessly

Barefoot, I ran.
Sweet clover intoxicating,
Dew splashing.

With eyes focused
On the prize ahead—
You.

I did not falter
To the right or to the left,
Scaling every stone.

Your outreached arms
Pulled me close,
Your beating breast against mine.

Our love abounded
And resounded.
Beauty reigned.

Time stood still.
The sun in all its glory
Shined.

Then darkness fell
With no moon in sight
To light even the smallest of paths.

You were taken.

Now thorns close in,
Gnashing at my skin.
Tears of blood drip.

Naked and alone,
I stand weeping
With nowhere to go.

The clock is ticking,
And I stay still.
Endlessly.

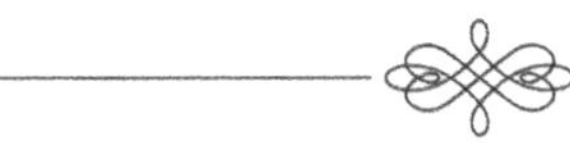

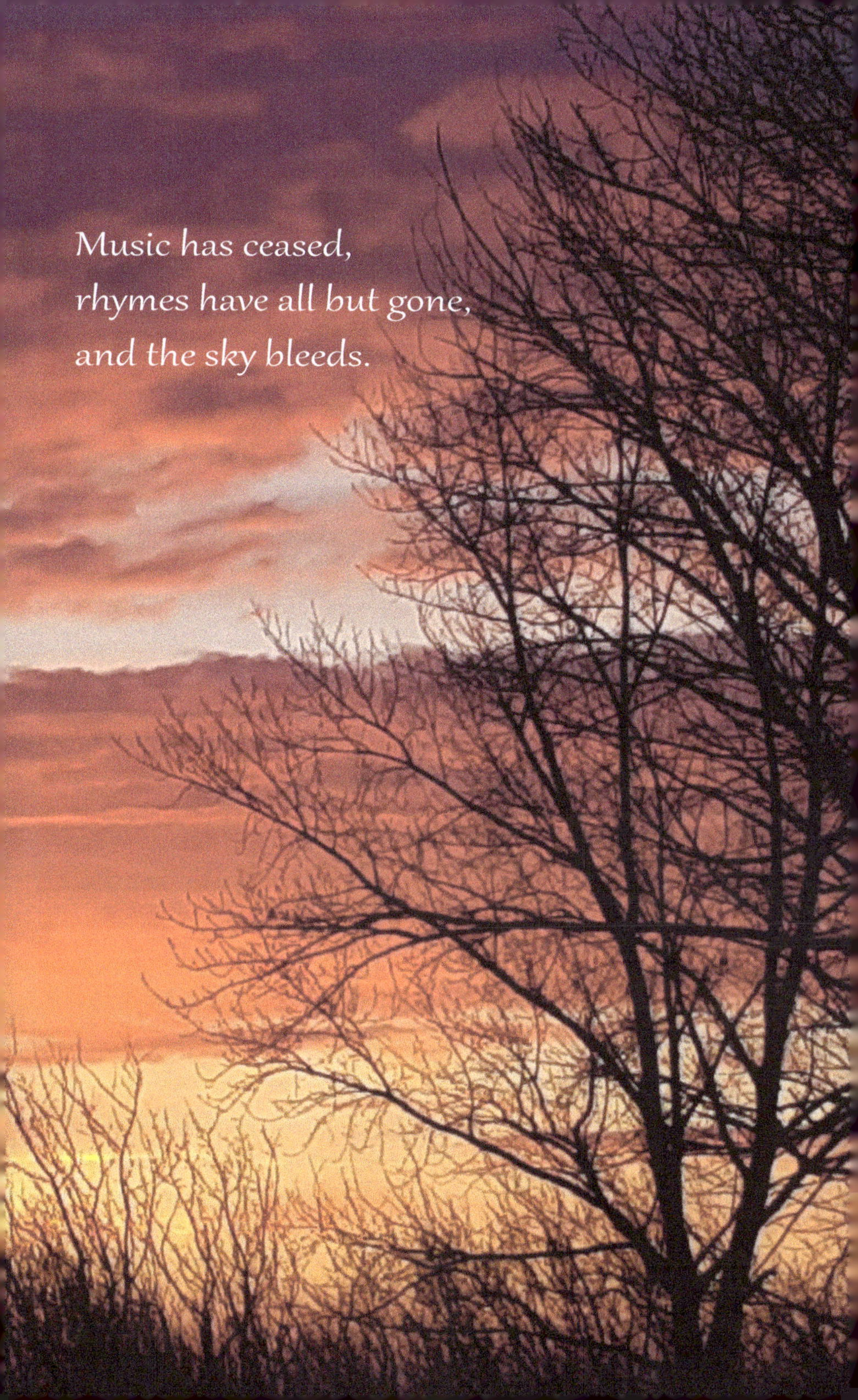
Music has ceased,
rhymes have all but gone,
and the sky bleeds.

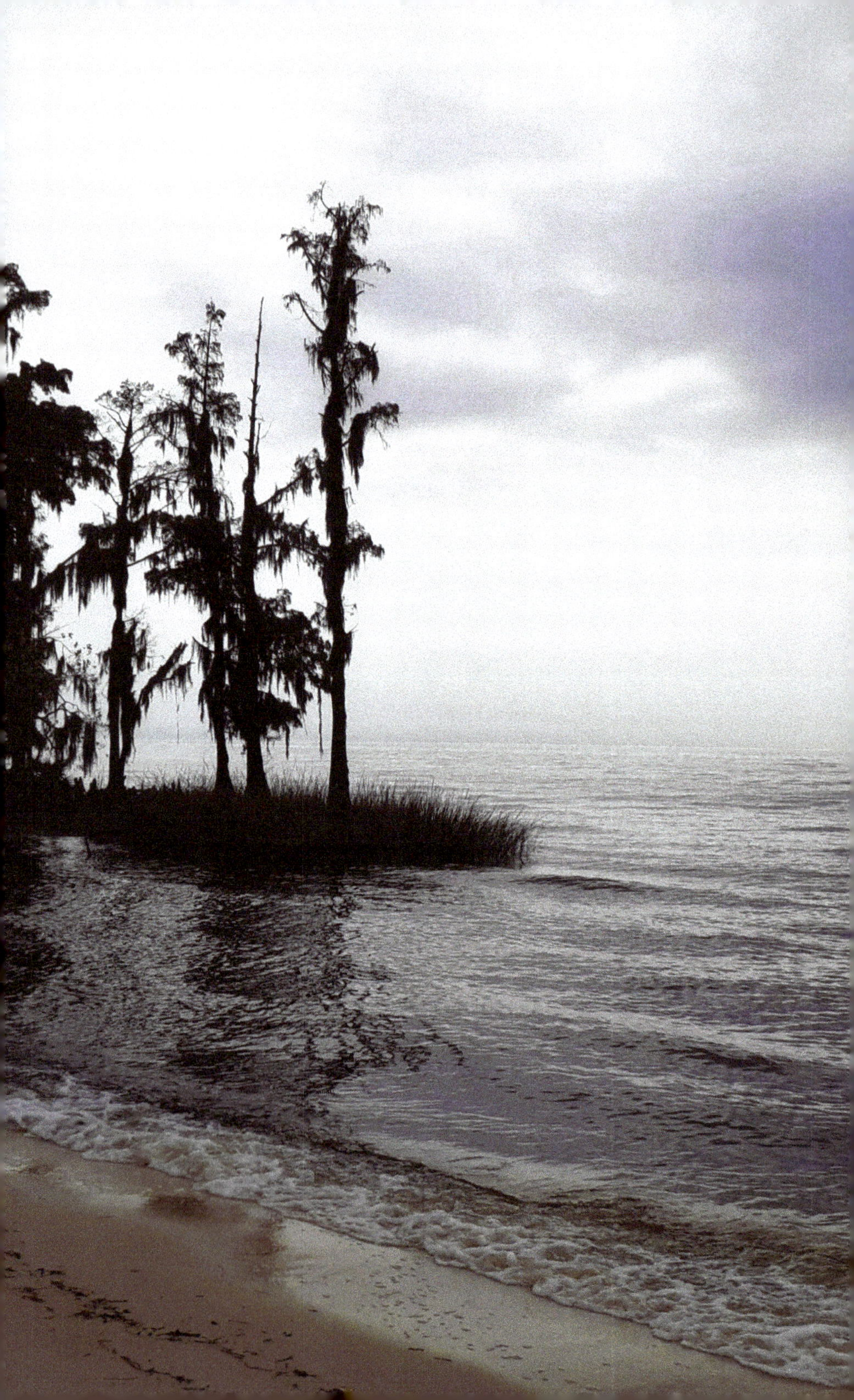

Struggling

Ashamed for my anger,
Bitter for being left,
Unsure of the danger
Of this constant bereft.

I've been left with just me,
Abandoned and confused.
This wasn't supposed to be,
It's not what I choose.

Our path was clear,
Our dreams were strong.
But you are not near,
And gone for so long.

I don't know what to do,
And I'm struggling hard,
With anguish bubbling through,
The hurt I cannot discard.

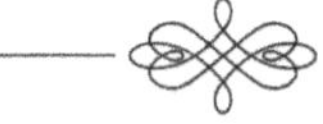

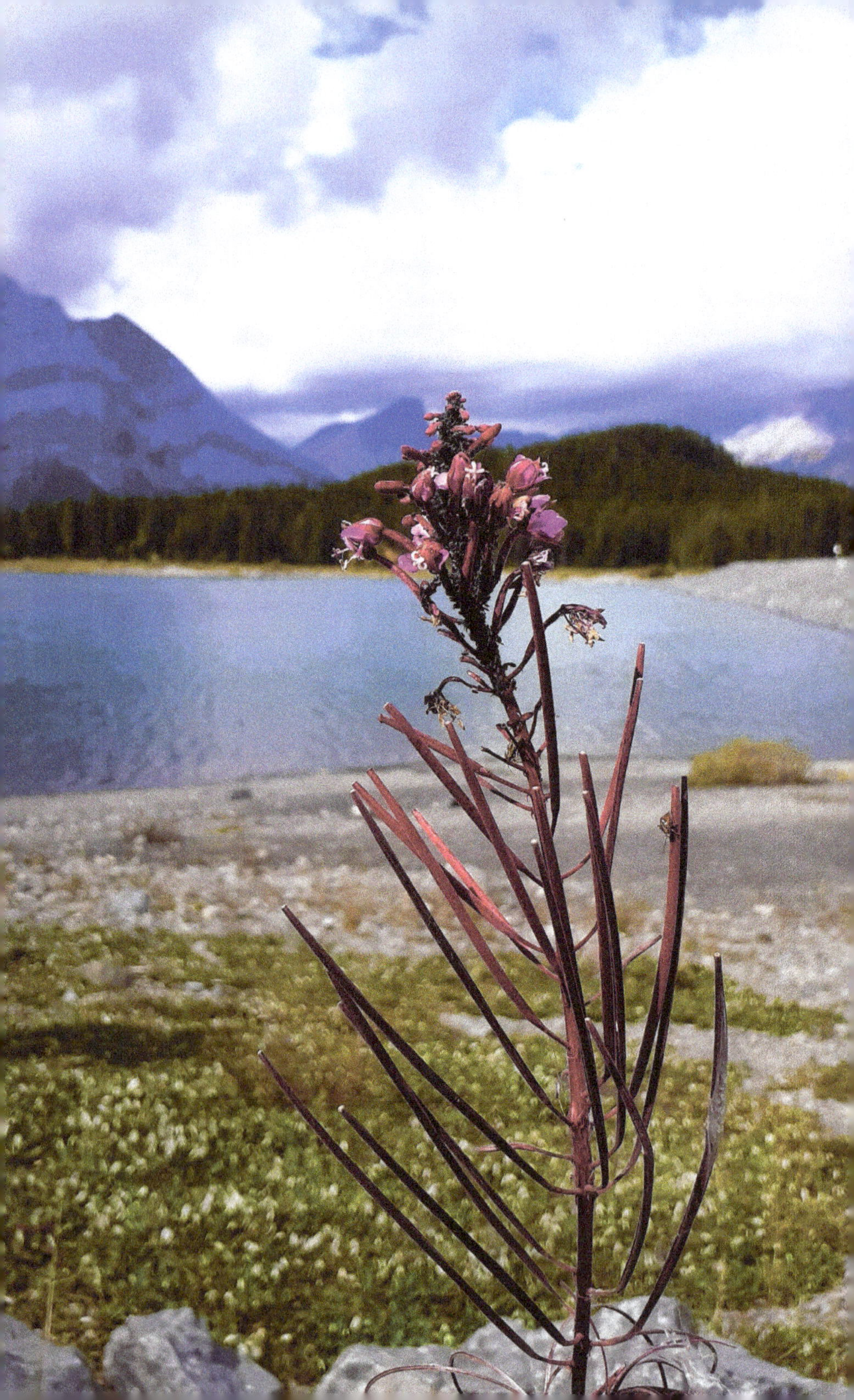

The Emptiness of Me

You see me smile,
But it's nothing but beguile.
It is a lie you see
To hide the emptiness of me.

I fall and fall and fall.
Can't you hear me call?
I'm reeling in pain
Inside of this hurricane.

You see a full life,
Happy and free of strife.
But it is a lie, you see,
To hide the emptiness of me.

I fall and fall and fall.
Can't you hear me call?
I'm stuck in this nightmare
Embittered and full of despair.

You see me as strong
Because I've been doing this for so long.
But darling don't you see?
It is the emptiness of me.

I fall and fall and fall.
Can't you hear me call?
There is nothing for me here.
I just want to disappear.

The truths that I hide
Are because you died,
And all I have is this plea
Screaming from the emptiness of me.

I fall and fall and fall.
Can't you hear me call?
I fall and fall and fall.
My darling, are you there at all?

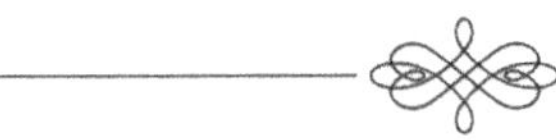

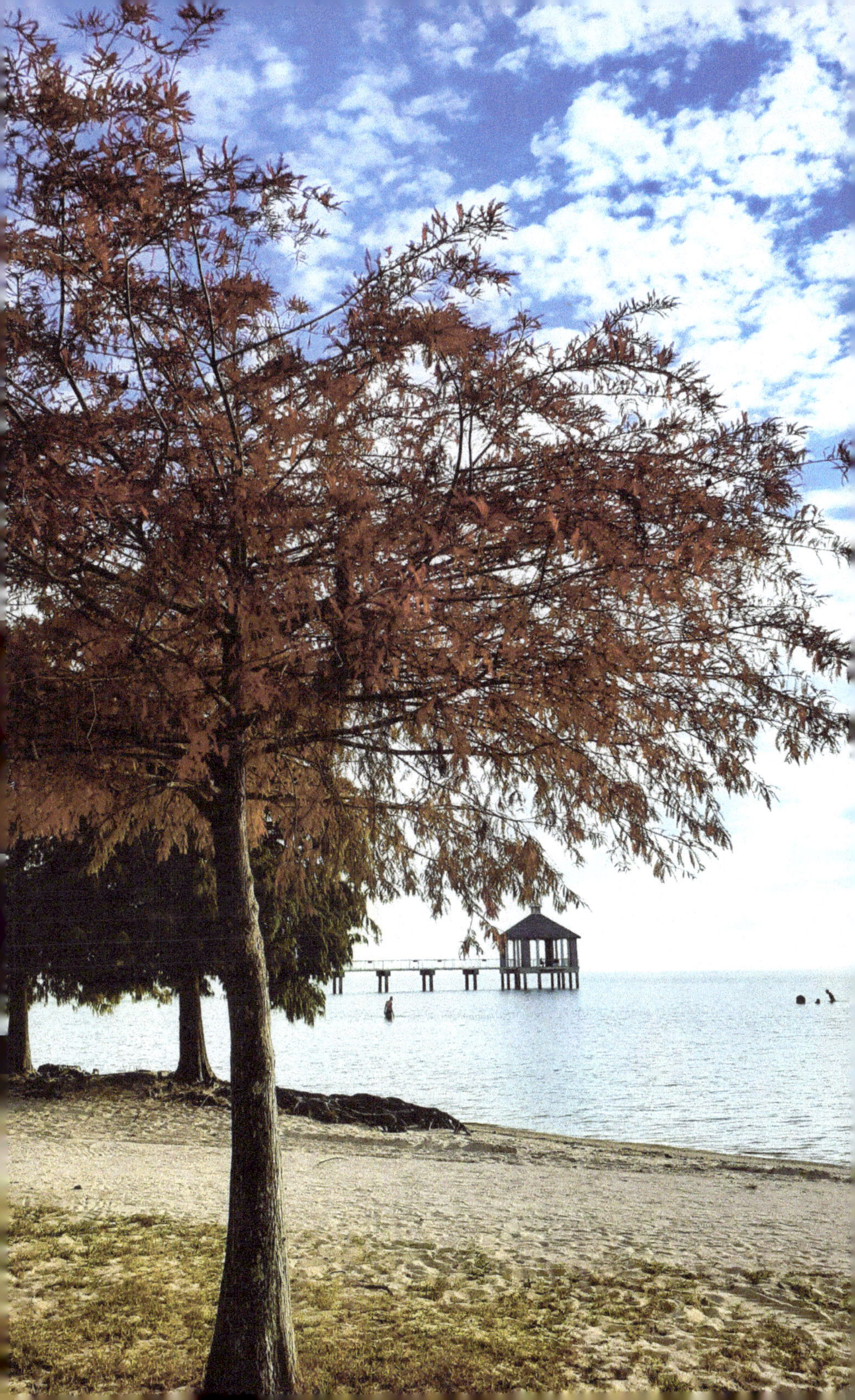

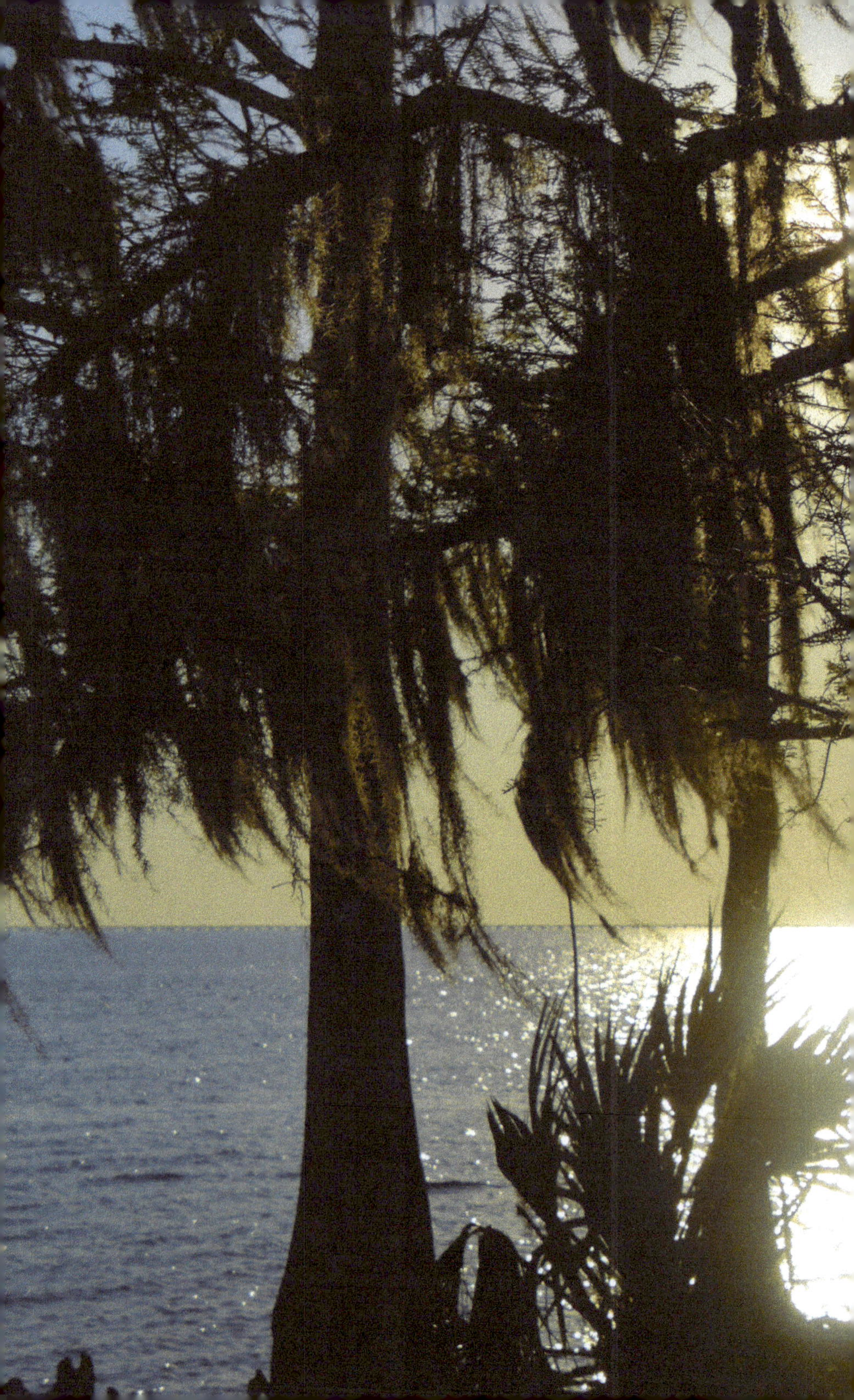

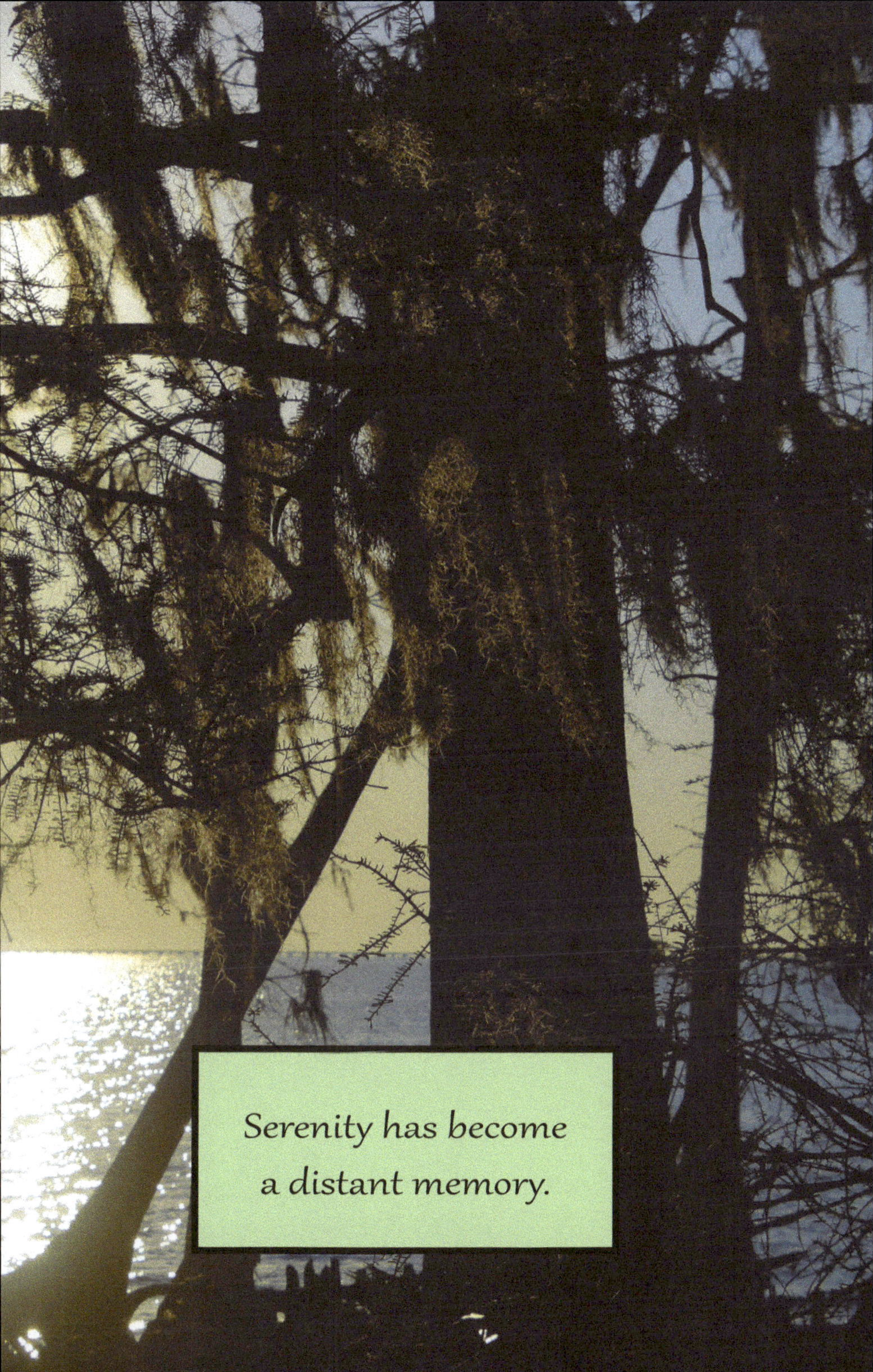

Serenity has become
a distant memory.

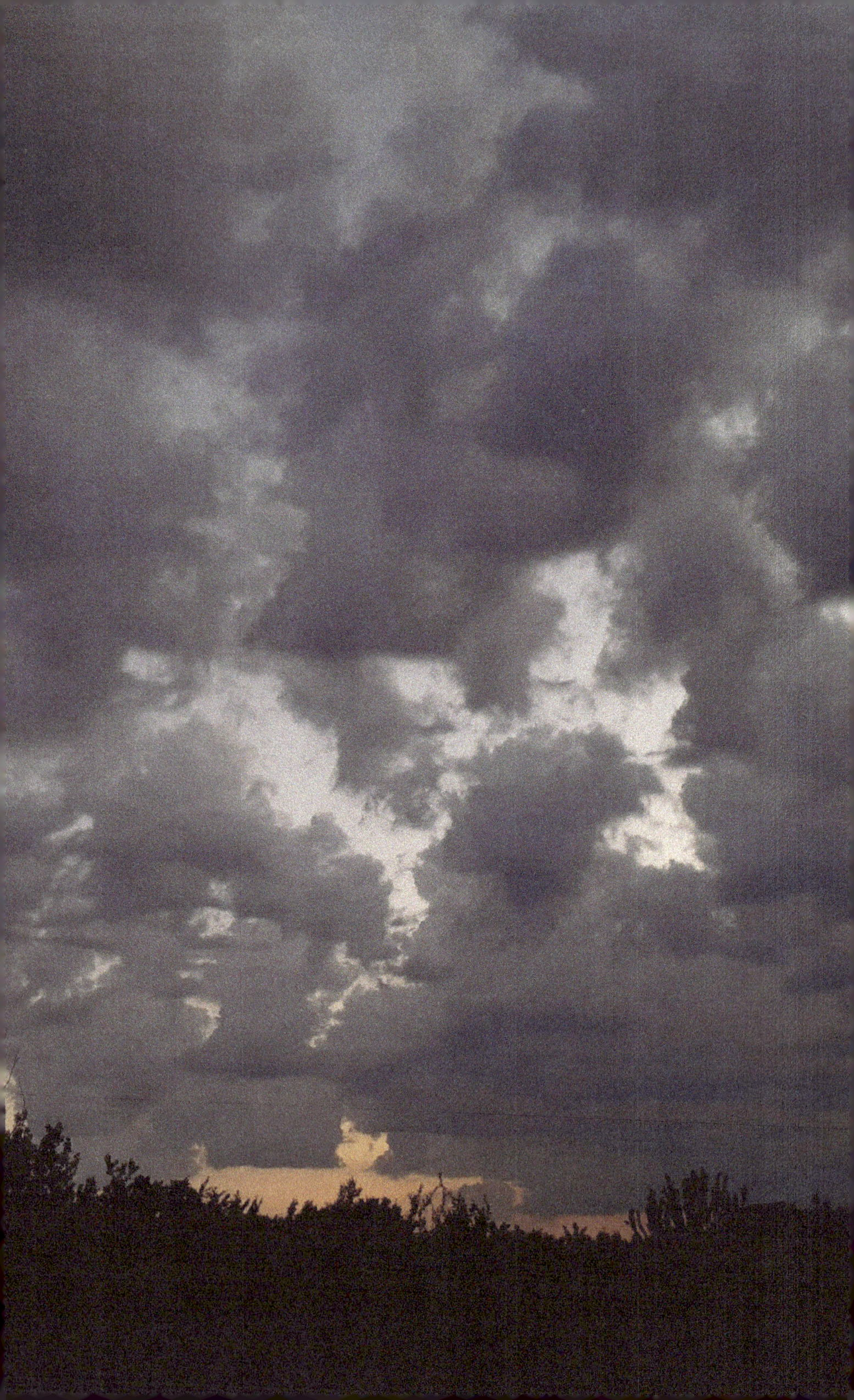

Storms and Rainy Days

There's a fierceness the storm carries,
Black clouds rolling, bellowing, striking
Like an enraged drunk,
With no purpose to his smiting.

And there's a sadness about a rainy day,
Melancholy at best.
Gray clouds quietly seep
Until they surround you to nest.

The gloom of a rainy day hangs heavy,
With barely a break to its tears.
Whether it cries light or hard,
It holds a depressive atmosphere.

I don't know what is better—
The storm or the rain.
One hits me hard,
And the other is constant pain.

I want so much to see the sun,
Where white clouds play about the blue.
But I'm stuck in this despair
Where it is black and gray, and without you.

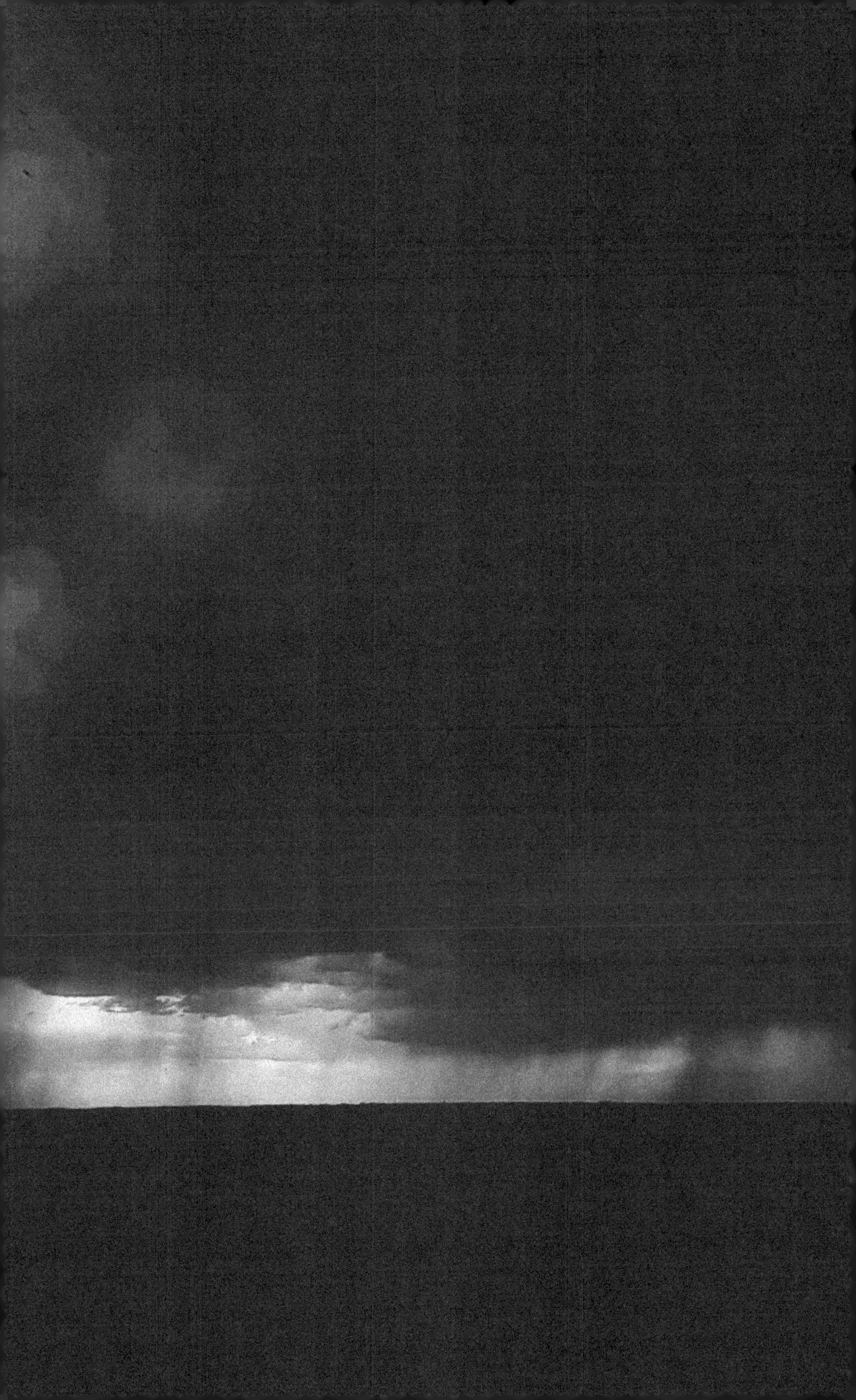

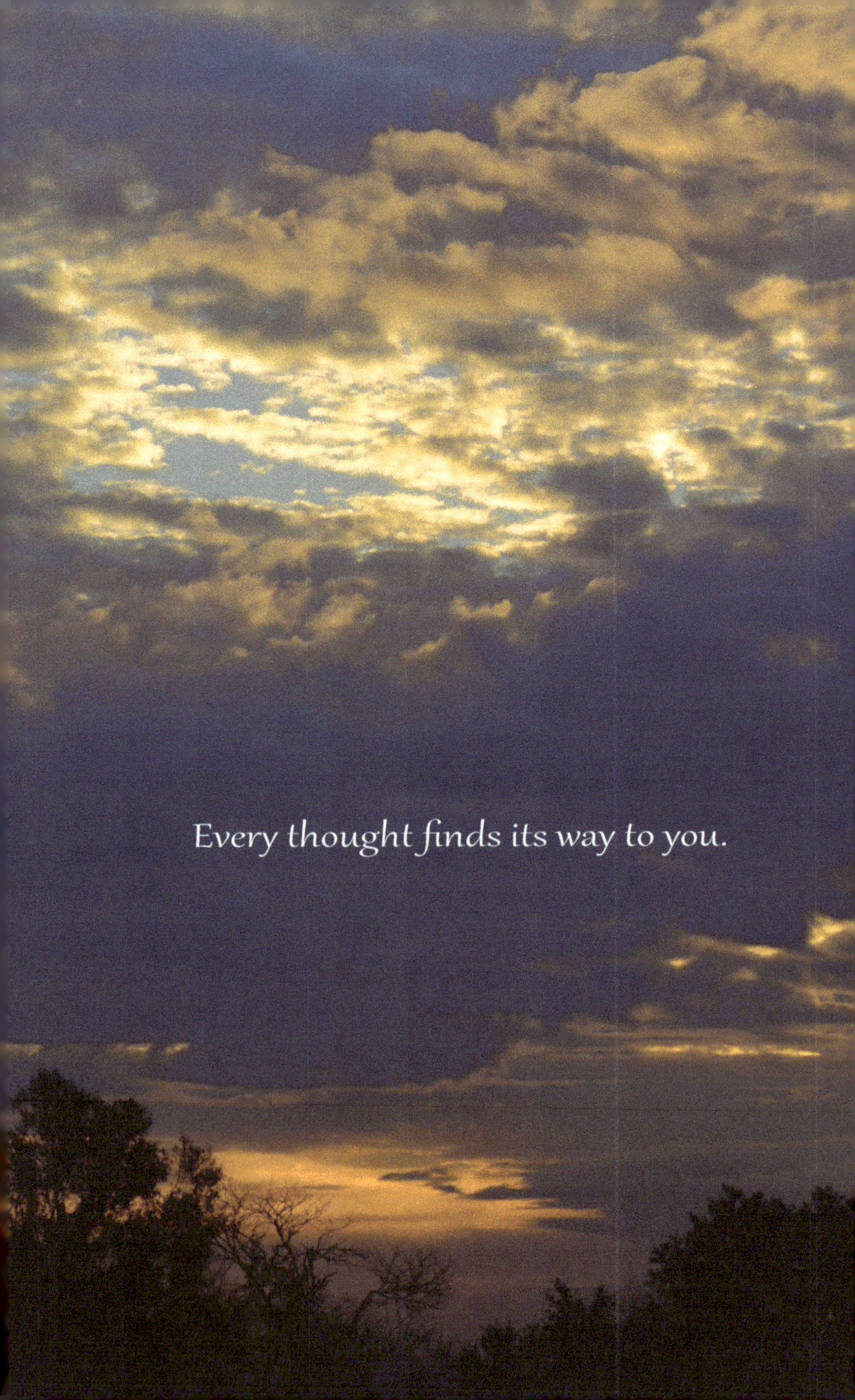
Every thought finds its way to you.

Between Night and Day

There exists a silence between night and day,
A peace of mind that has been far away.
For now I am haunted by a torturing echo
That has long since become my bedfellow.

The ache within my beating heart
Throbs my head since we've been apart,
And robs me of this elusive sleep,
With hours upon hours of constant weep.

I long for your touch when our fingers entwined,
And the feel of your skin connected with mine.
But your place on our bed has turned cold,
And my heavy tears I can no longer hold.

If I could only reach that ethereal place
Where all my sorrows would be erased.
I want so much to drift away,
But the silence is not mine between night and day.

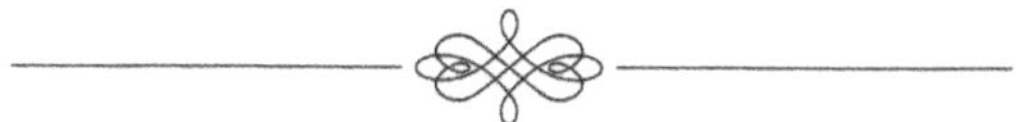

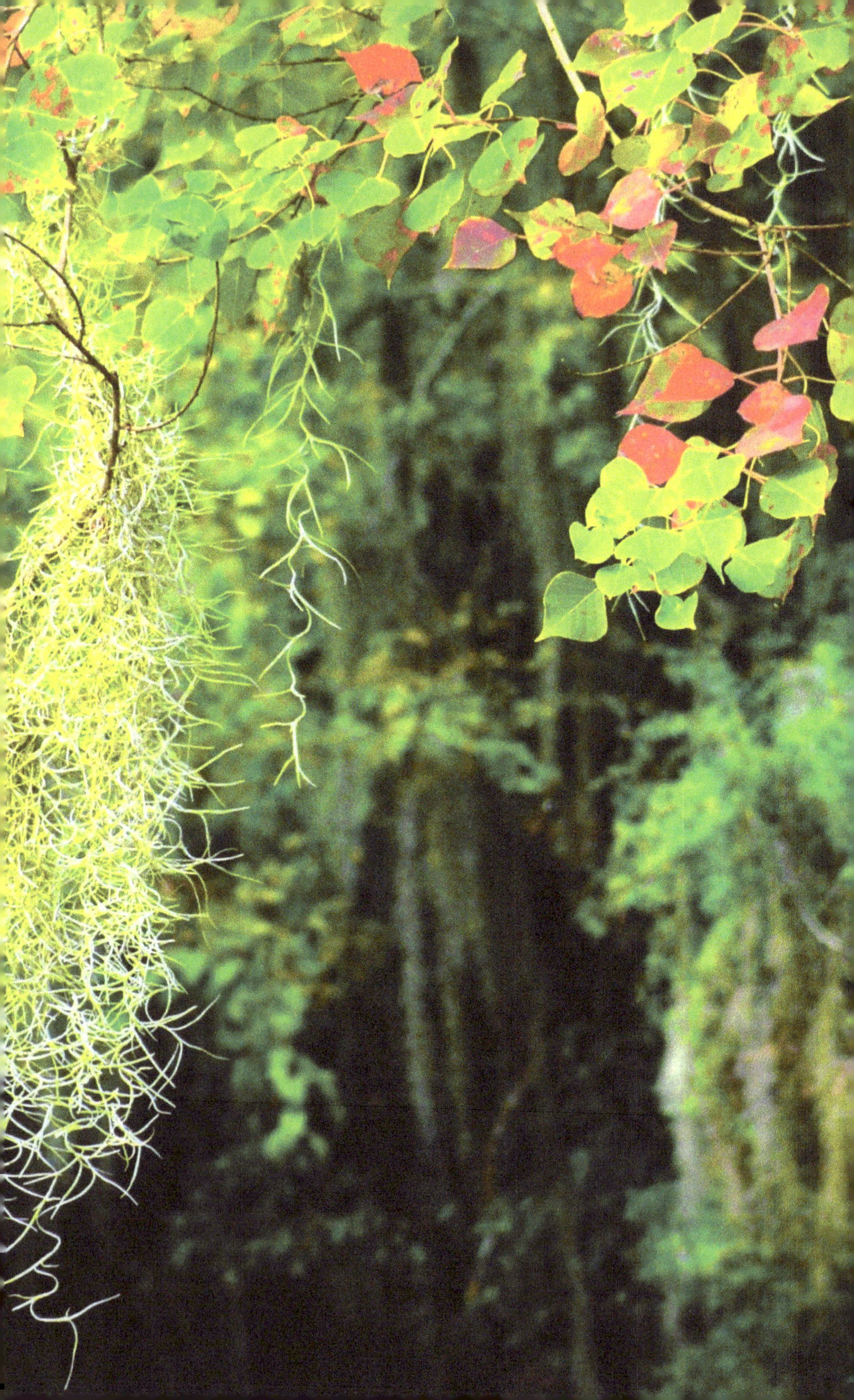

Echoes

Standing where we once danced,
I feel your presence.
Hmm . . . our bodies swaying in time,
I remember your essence.

Music echoes from the piano you played
Far off in the distance.
Each note carries your love,
Your beauty and eloquence.

Your place on our bed is still warm
From our passion and innocence.
I'm held captive in the precious moments
That gave meaning to my existence.

My heart aches from the echo of you,
Overwhelming and intense.
Because standing where you once were,
I feel your absence.

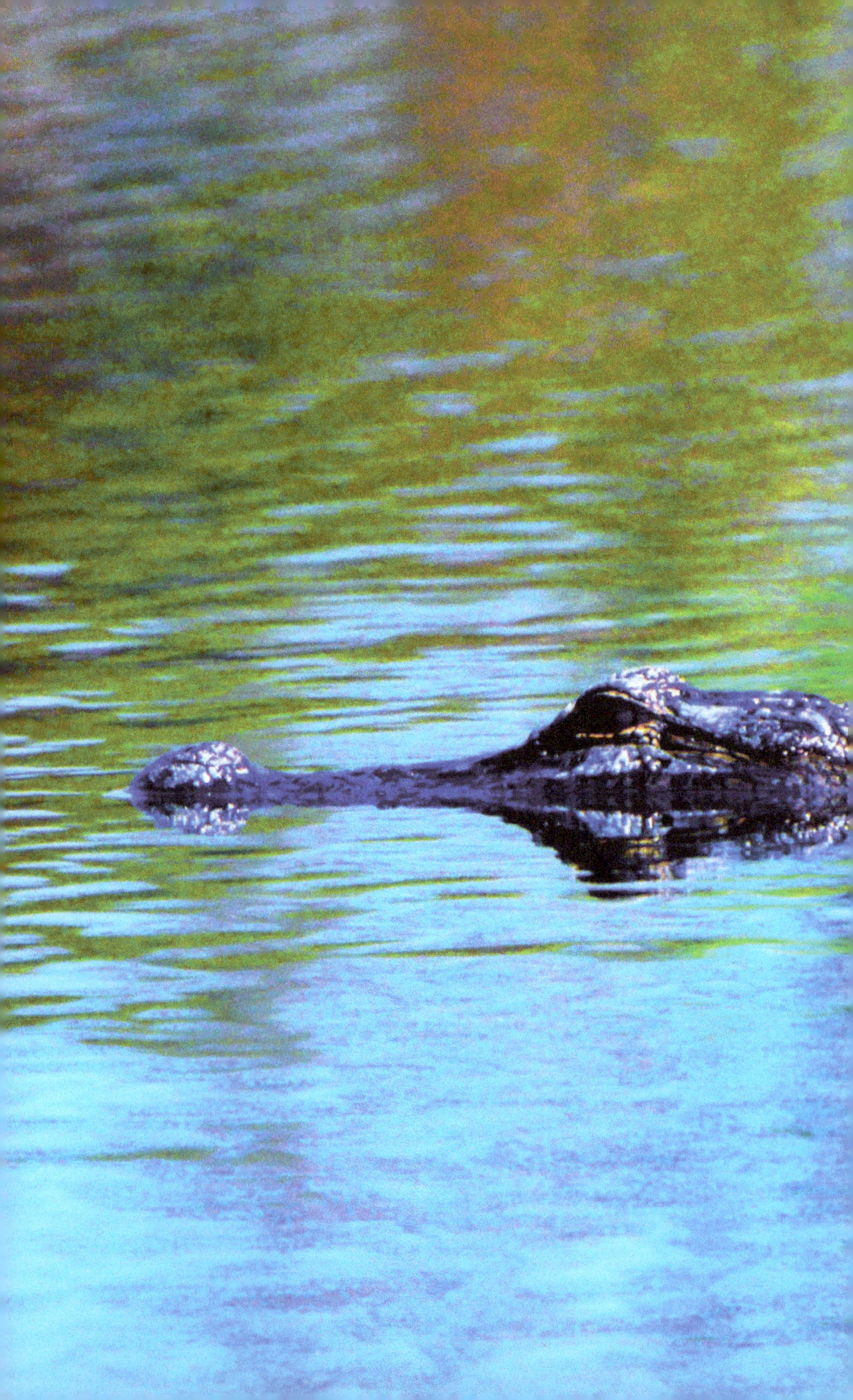

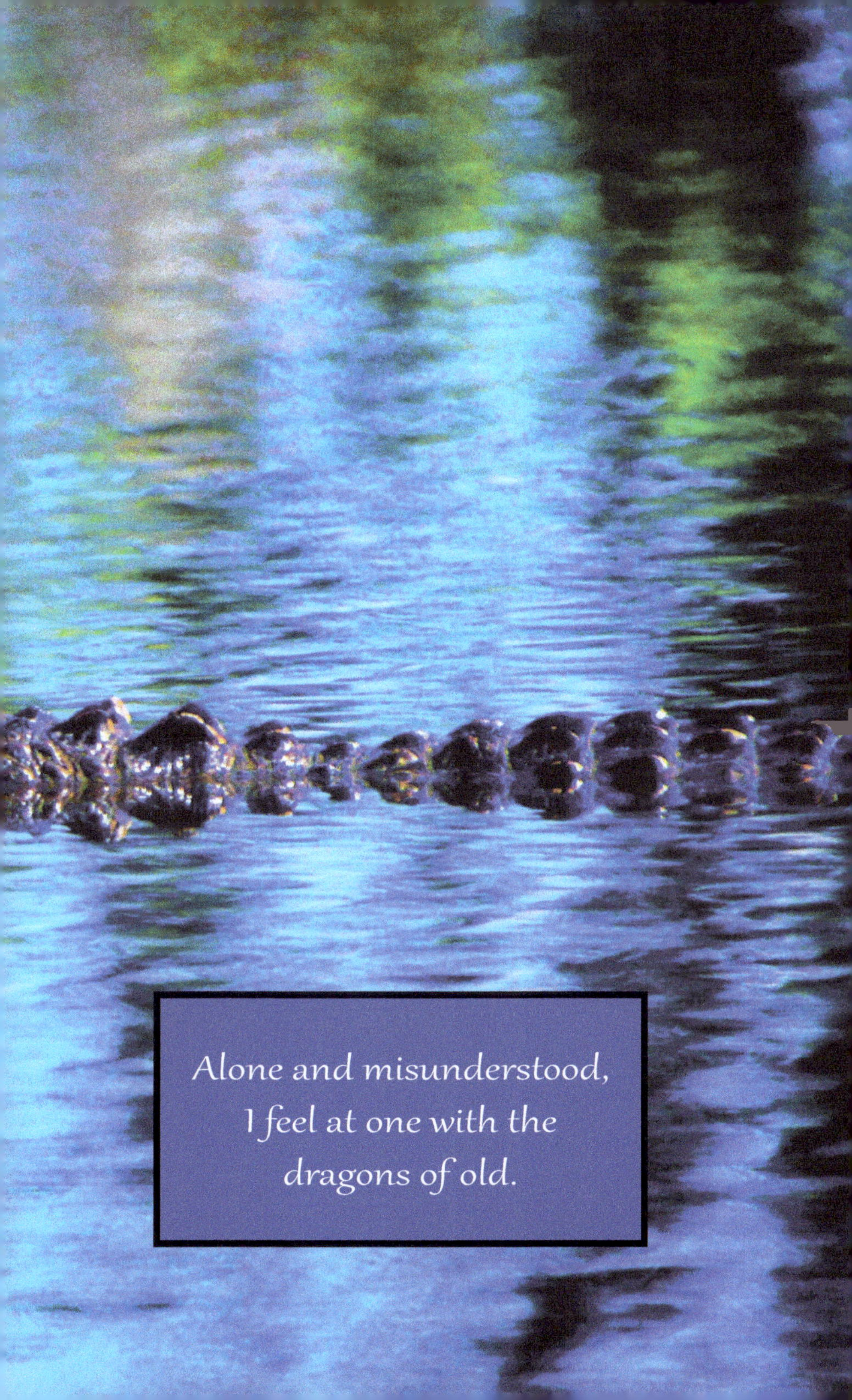
Alone and misunderstood,
I feel at one with the
dragons of old.

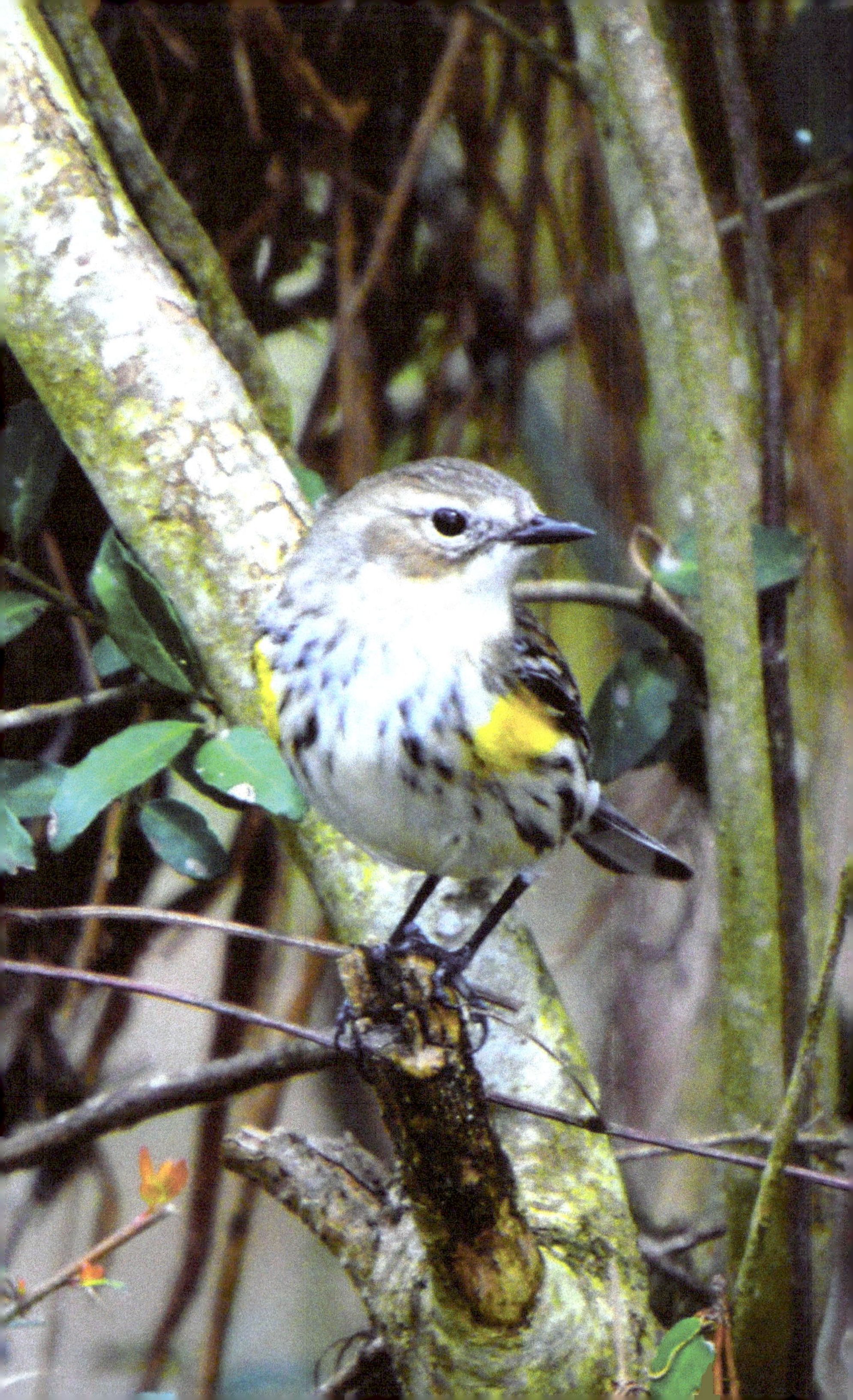

Through My Window

Through my window,
Dusty flecks shimmer through beams of light.
Through my window,
A fat cardinal sits on a sill of white.

In the distance,
Poplars whisper stories under the breeze.
In the distance,
Everything in the forest seems at ease.

Amid the quiet,
Violet flowers yawn their petals.
Amid the quiet,
A yellow bumbler hovers, then settles.

With my heart,
I desperately long to heal my woe.
With my heart,
I sit watching life pass through my window.

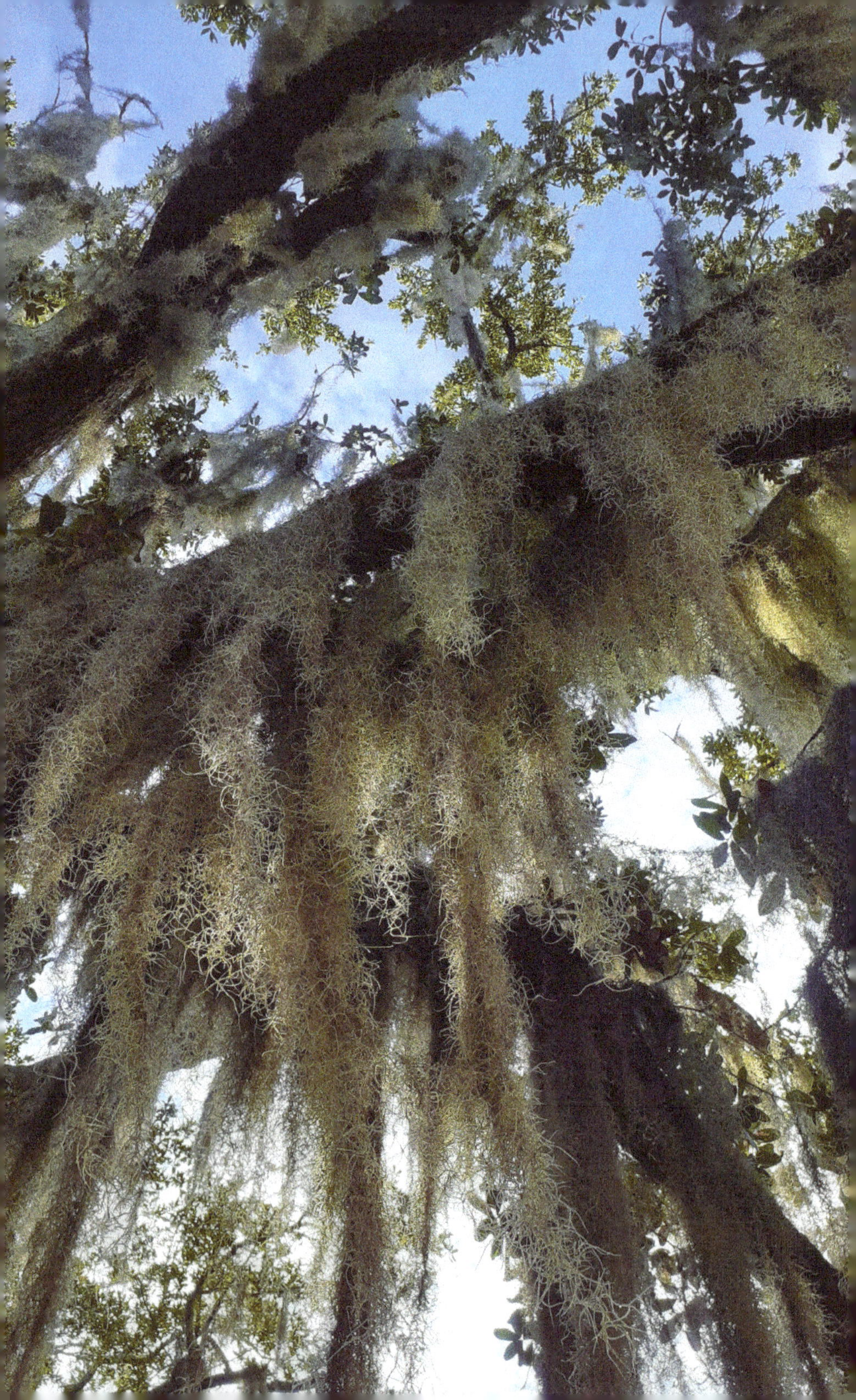

Where the Swamp Dogs Sing

Without you I've been utterly lost,
And needing a healing at any cost.
For all the travels I've had,
South I must go before I am mad.

There's a crying in my heart
That's been tearing me apart,
And the only peace that can bring
Is where the swamp dogs sing.

Serenity lives amongst these trees
That sets my mind at gentle ease.
Their magical whiskers within my reach,
As I sit on the shore of our sandy beach.

There's a crying in my heart
That's been tearing me apart,
And the only peace that can bring
Is where the swamp dogs sing.

Here, I'm not alone,
For all around I've been shown
The memories that keep me fed,
And our echo that has been spread.

There's a crying in my heart
That's been tearing me apart,
And the only peace that can bring
Is where the swamp dogs sing.

Without you I am not whole,
Because we are but one soul.
But for now, I must carry on,
Feeling the beat of our life that has become our song.

There's a crying in my heart
That's been tearing me apart,
And the only peace that can bring
Is where the swamp dogs sing.

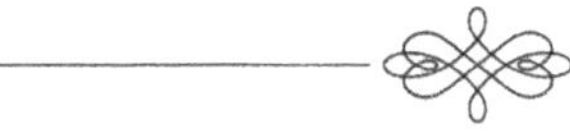

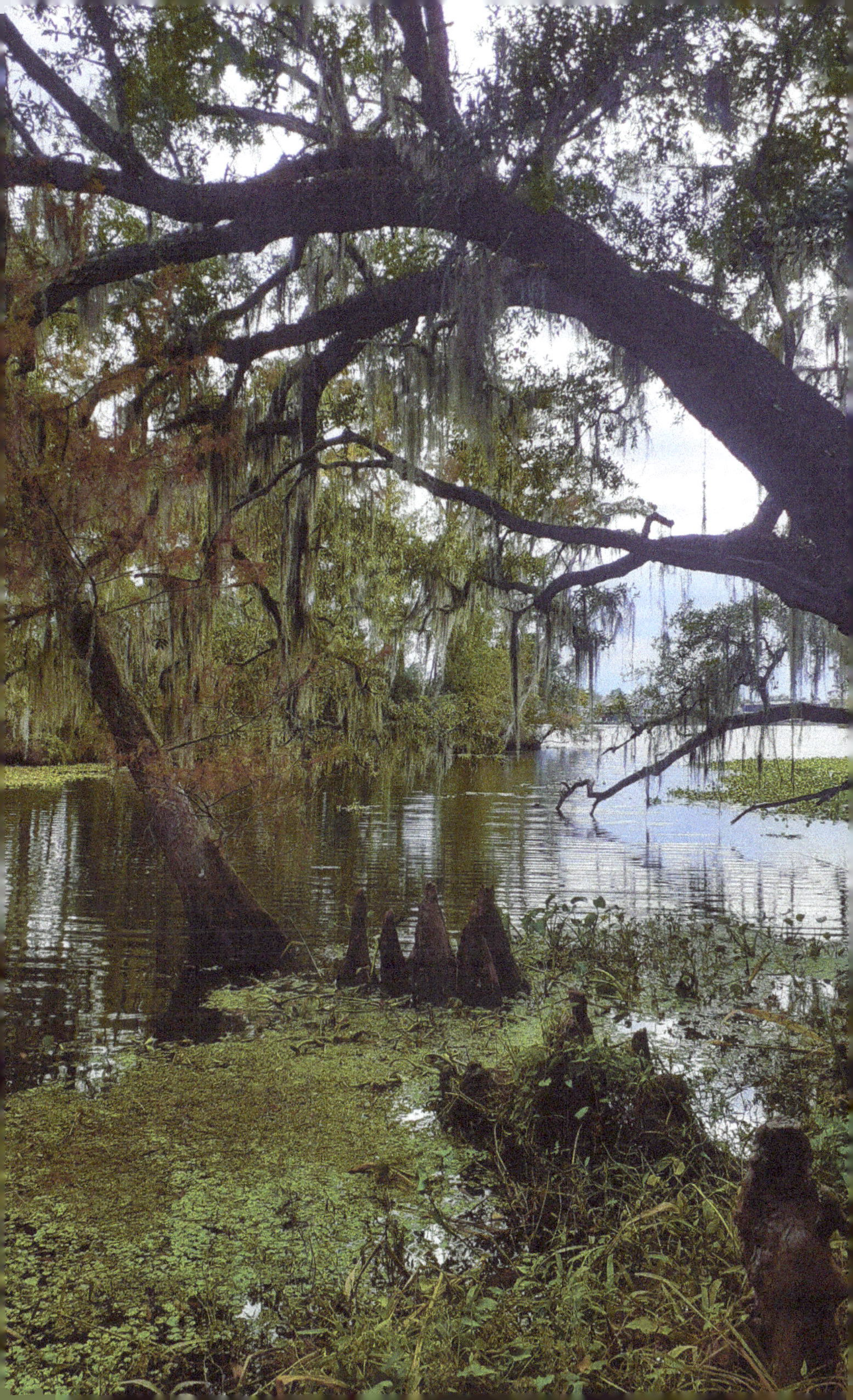

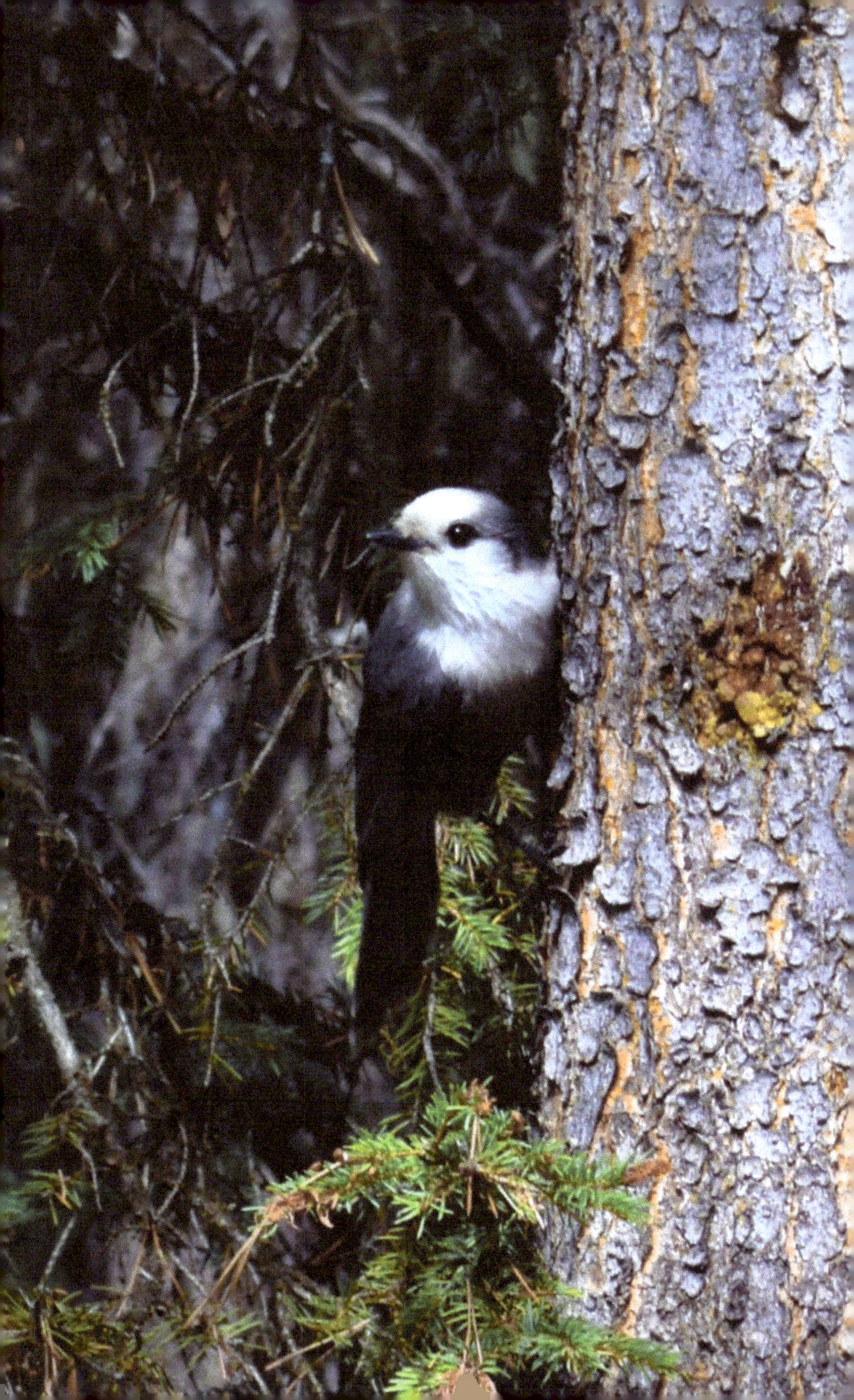

Mountain Bird

Little mountain bird flying in a craze,
From shrub to evergreen, searching.
Seeking for hours on sunlit days,
Hoping its mate is somewhere perching.

He has vanished from her,
And she is filled with strife.
She has nowhere to go,
For they were bound for life.

Resting her weary wings upon my table,
She is replenished with water and seeds.
Then back to the forest when she's able,
To fill her soul from the one she needs.

He has vanished from her,
And she is filled with strife.
She has nowhere to go,
For they were bound for life.

She throws herself upon a thorny tree,
And sings a haunted tune—
A melodic and imploring plea,
Her blood dripping, as though she's immune.

He has vanished from her,
And she is filled with strife.
She has nowhere to go,
For they were bound for life.

Back to me the tortured being comes,
Alone, weakened, and battered
From her failed attempts at martyrdom,
With her whole world having been shattered.

He has vanished from her,
And she is filled with strife.
She has nowhere to go,
For they were bound for life.

I am one with this winged creature,
And take pity on her soul.
Together we mourn, yet endure,
And somehow learn to become whole.

I stand before her,
And she is filled with hope.
She has somewhere to go,
And with her, I will learn to cope.

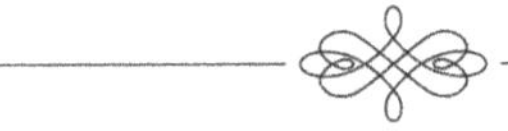

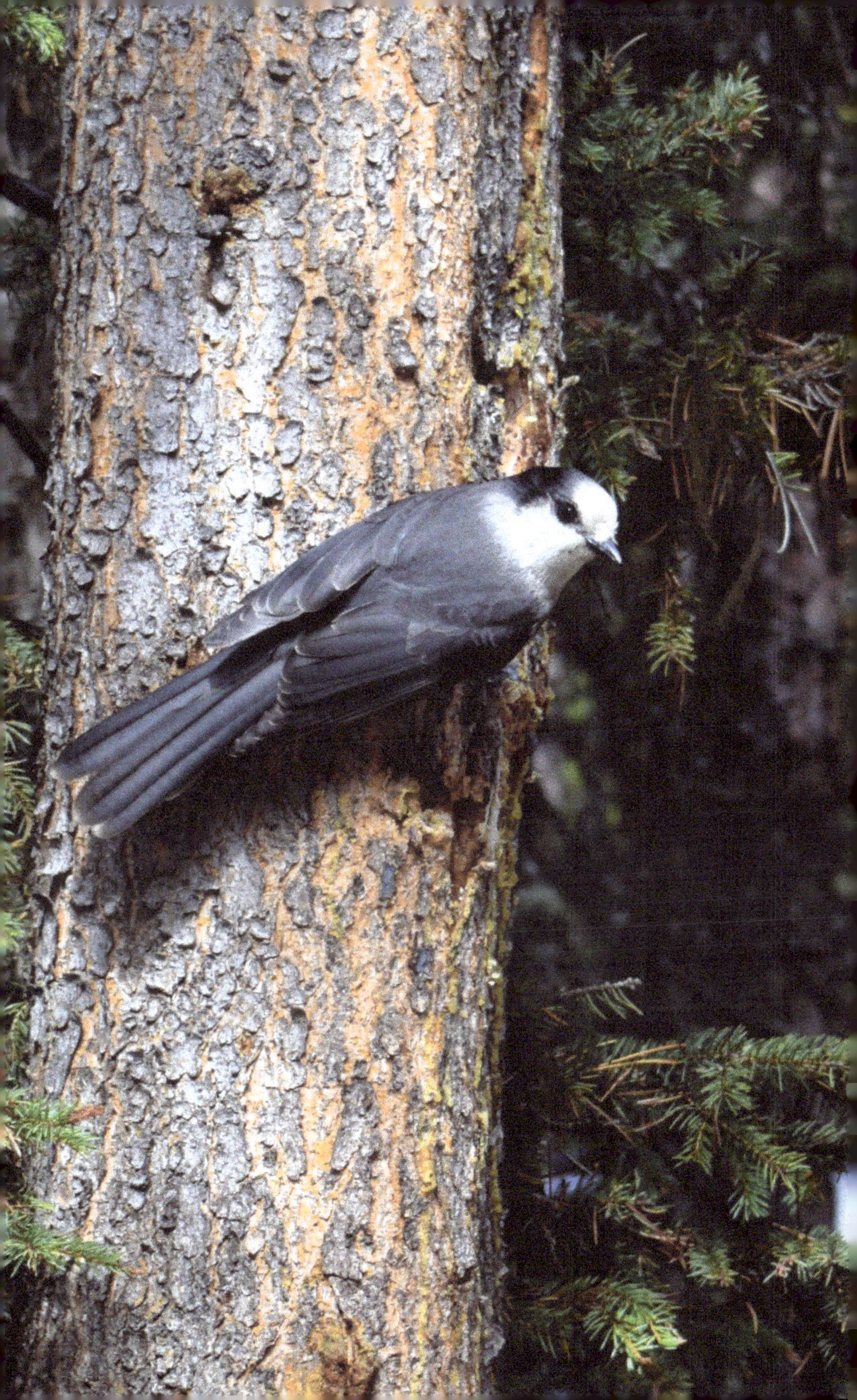

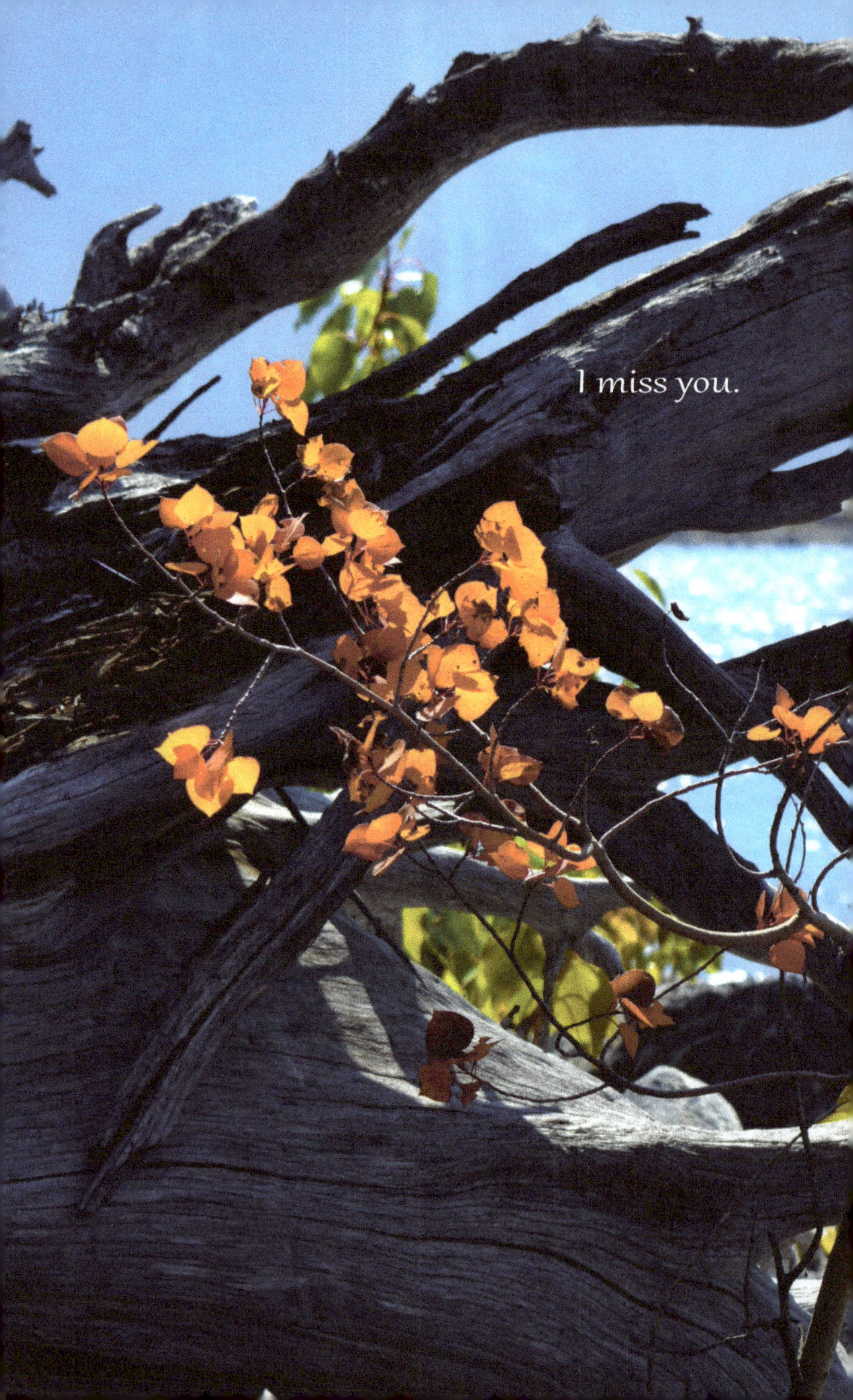
I miss you.

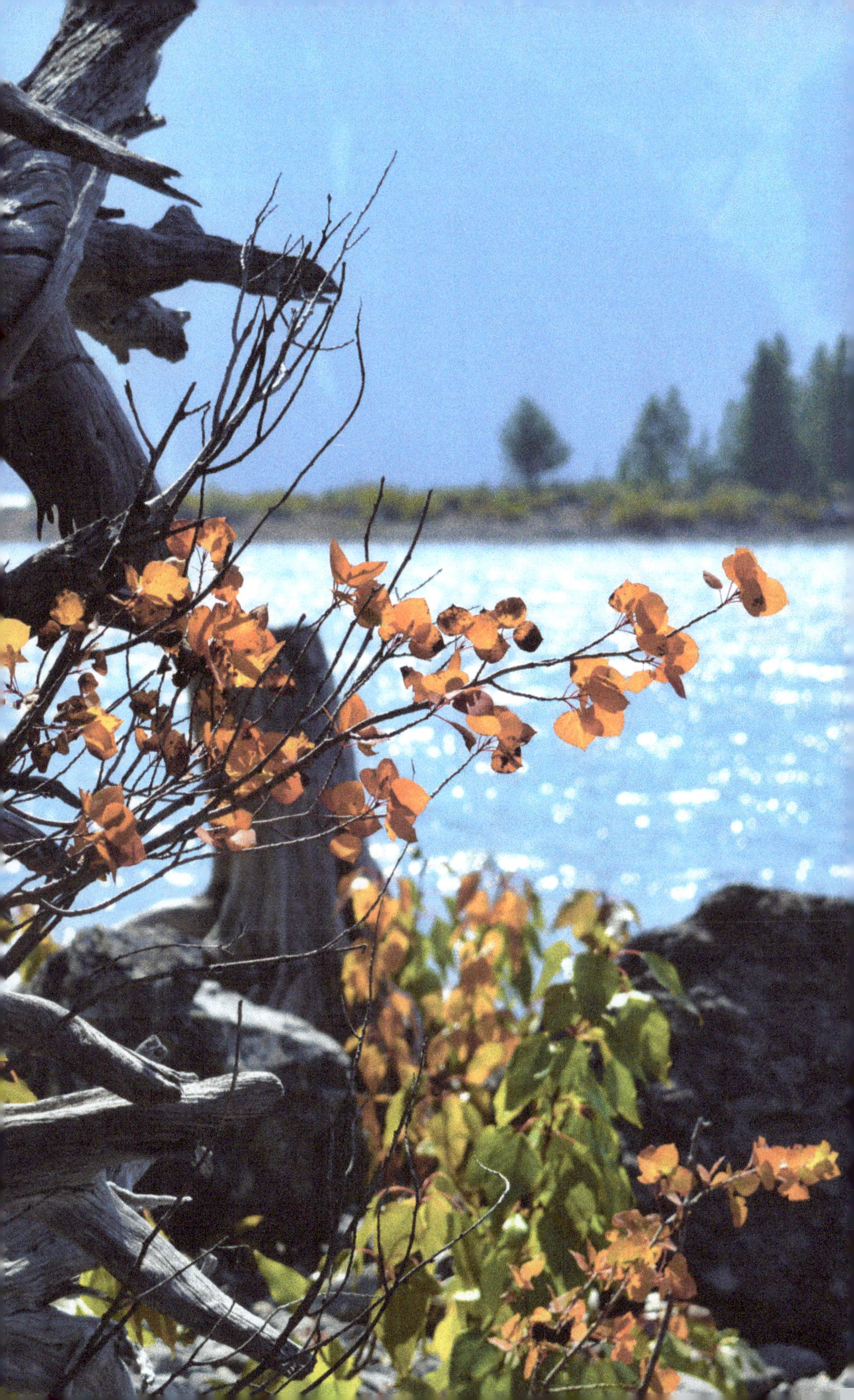

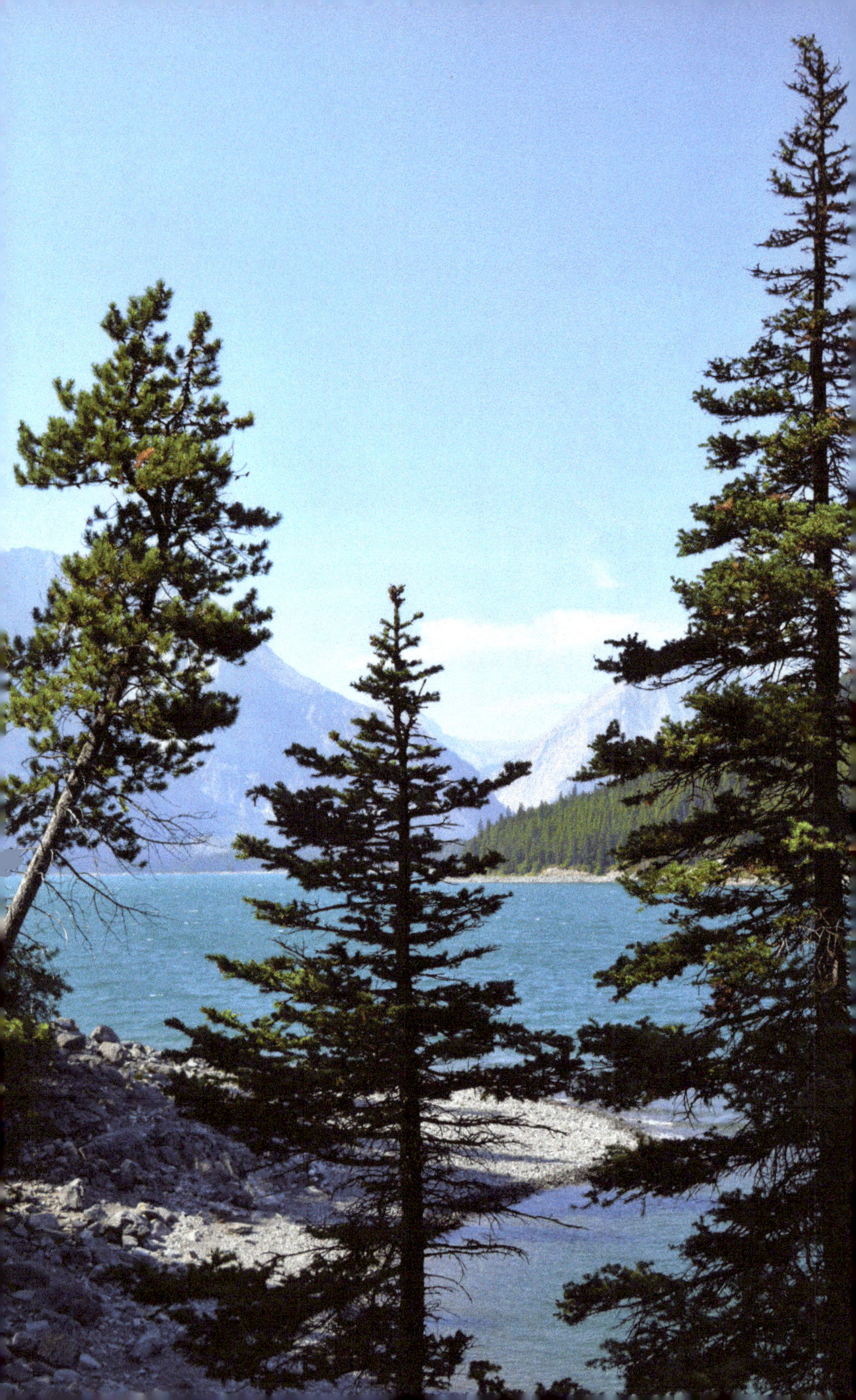

I Remember You Said

I remember you said, "Don't go falling in love with me".
But how could I not? It was my destiny.
The chemistry of us from the moment we met
Was undeniable, and I have not one regret.

I remember you said, "Nothing would ever change."
But as you know, everything has been rearranged.
The presence of you in my life
Has only ever made me want to be your wife.

I remember you said, "I am not the jealous kind."
Yet I know what lurks about inside your mind.
For I feel that same deep ache, too,
When every moment is not spent with you.

I remember you said, "I will heal you."
That is but one thing I believe to be true.
Body and soul, you have more than soothed me,
And I promise I will never doubt your doctoring ability.

There are a lot of things you have said,
With many of them whispered in the quiet of our bed.
And although you've been gone a long while,
I remember every word, and that gives me a great big
smile.

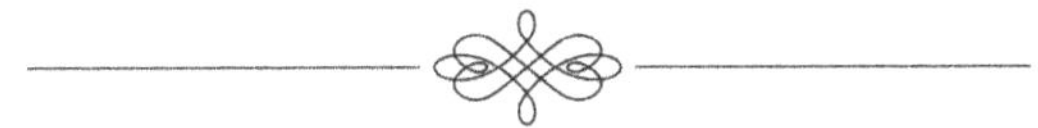

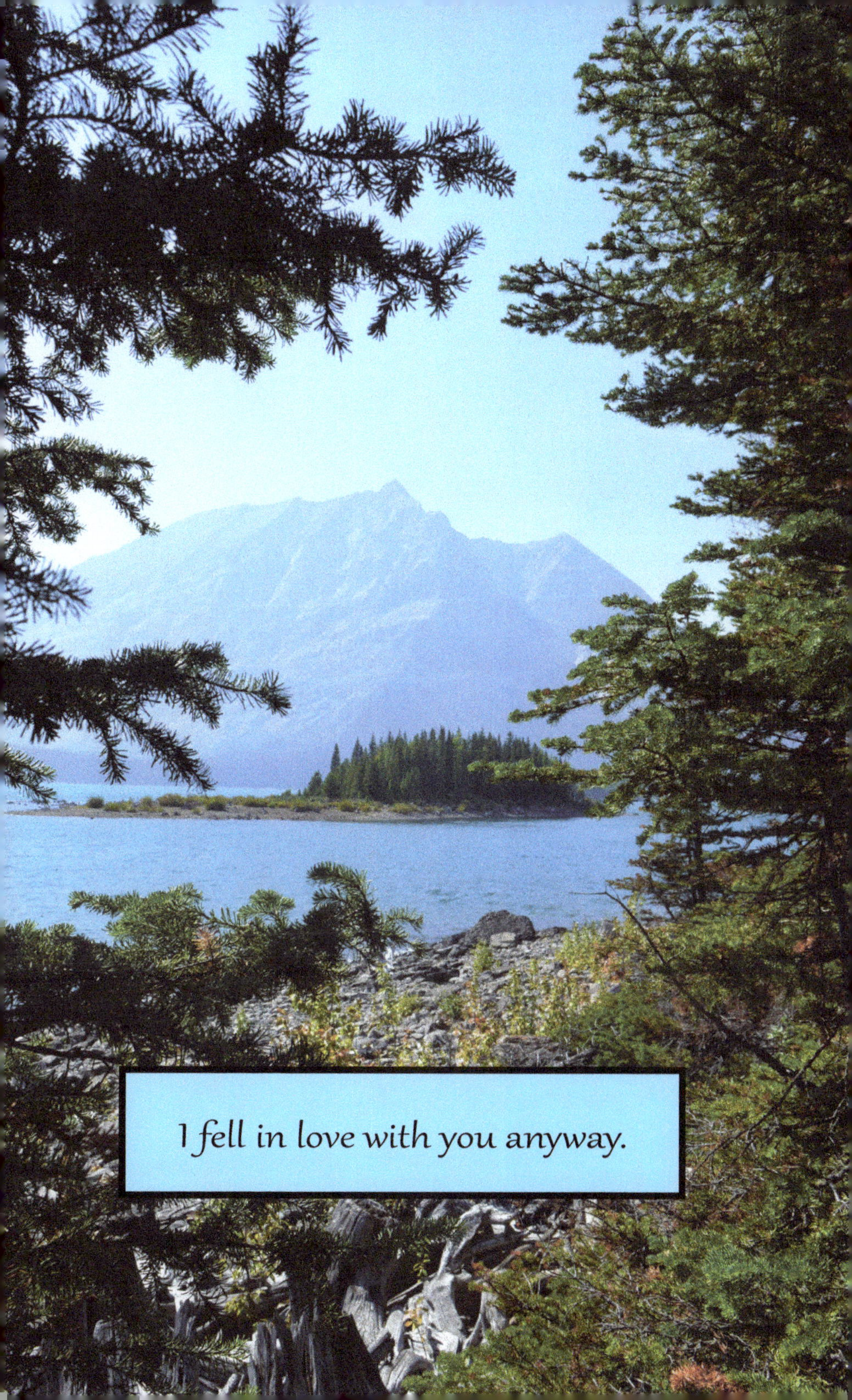
I fell in love with you anyway.

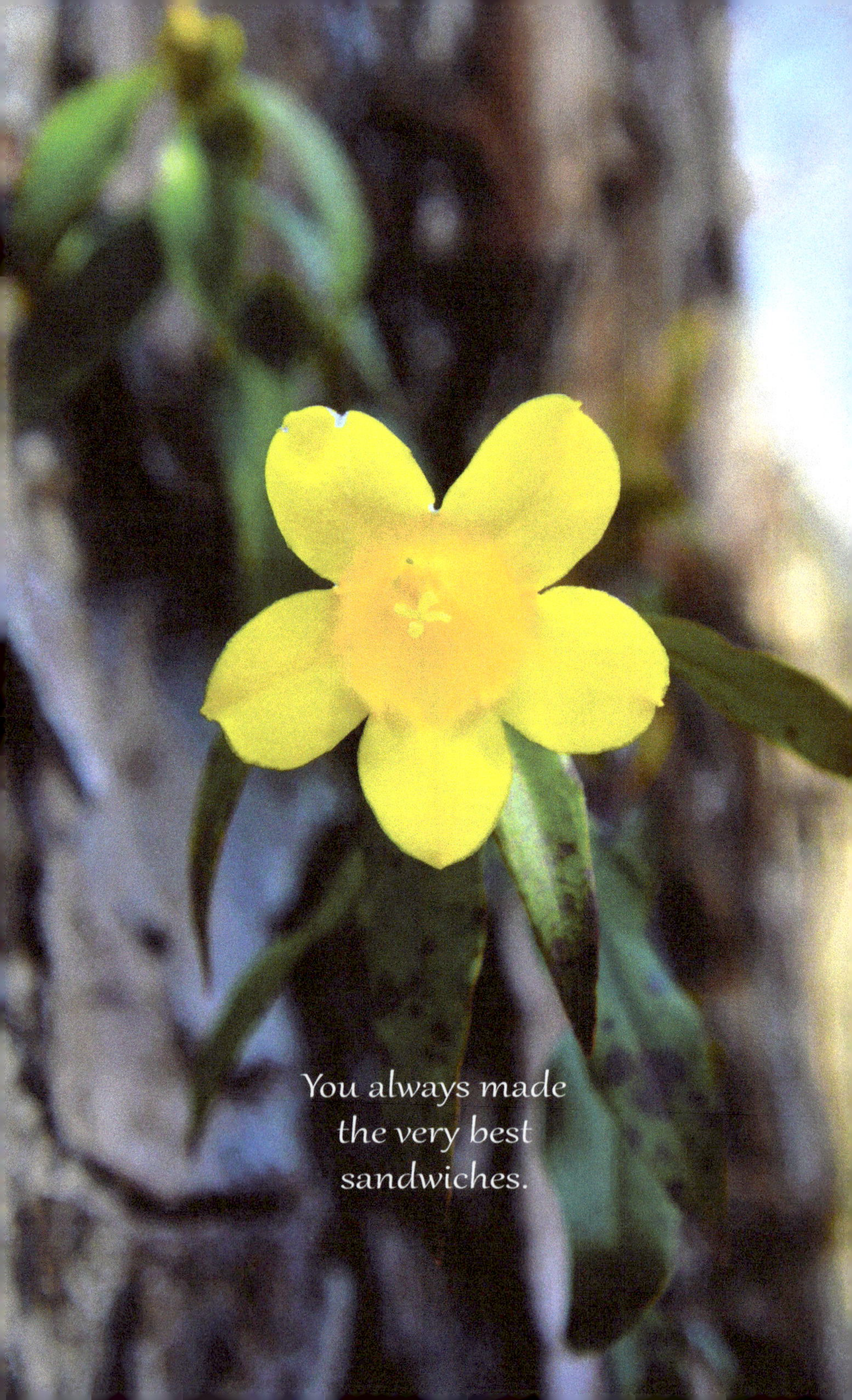
You always made
the very best
sandwiches.

I Miss Your Toes

I miss your toes warming between my legs.
I miss your elbow nudging me to wake.
I miss the sound of your breath as you sleep.
I miss your gentle kisses.
I miss your intense kisses.
I miss the beat of your heart against my ear.
I miss the intensity of your eyes (you know when).
I miss you making me morning coffee.
I miss your pretend shock as I say your nickname.
I miss you laughing at my karaoke.
I miss all of you, all the time,
But mostly, I miss your toes.

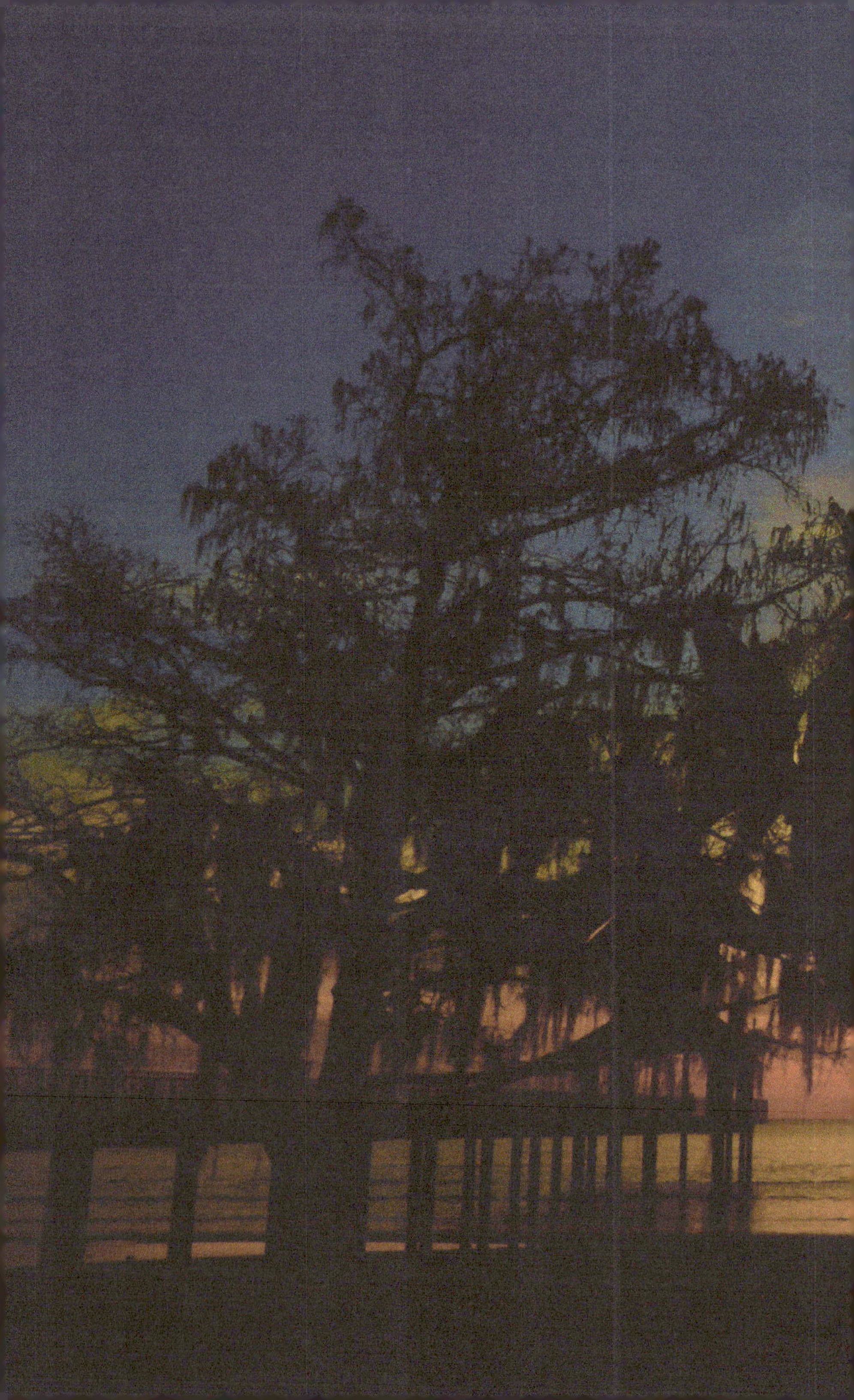

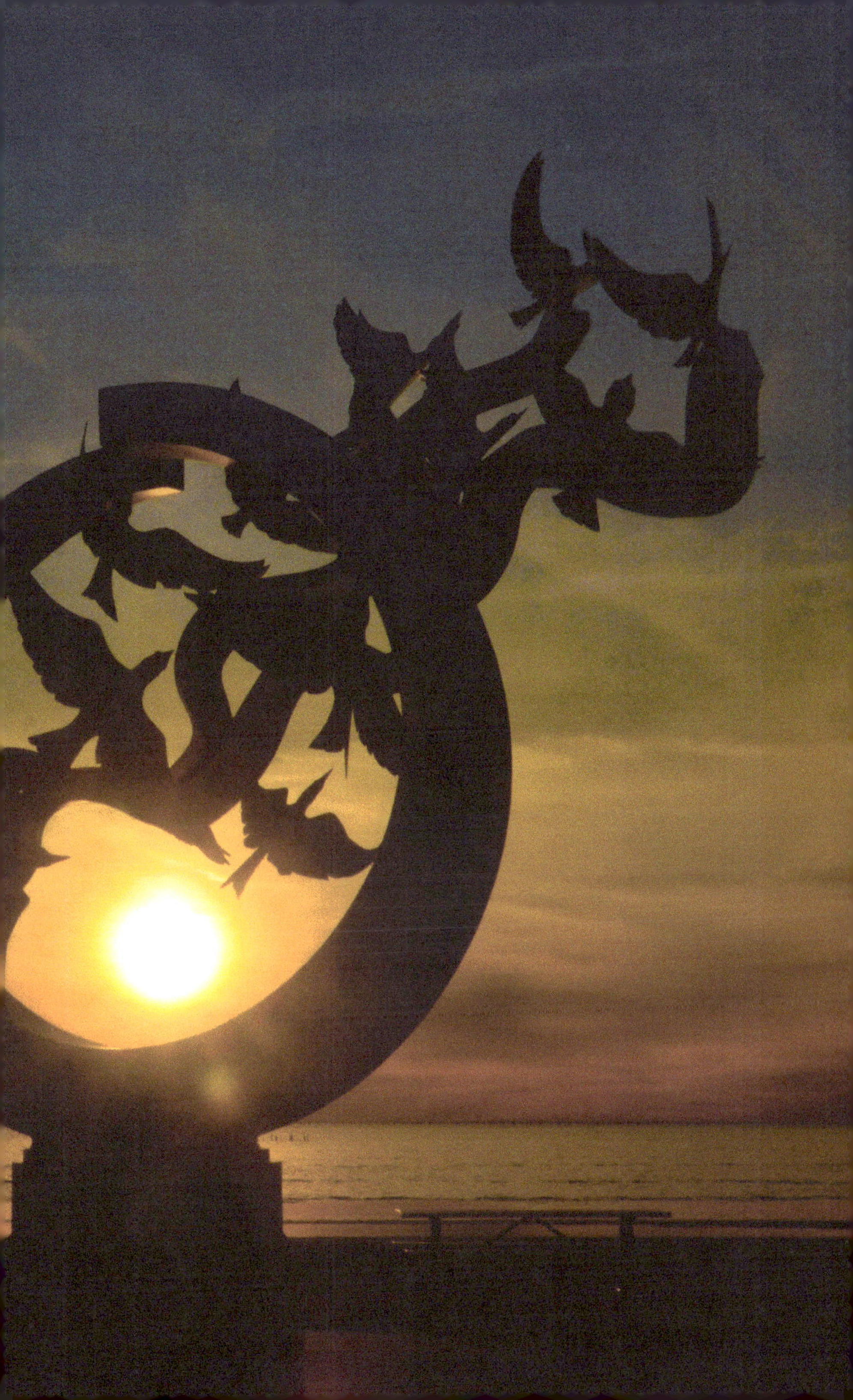

DESTINY

&

FOREVERMORE

An ethereal tether is bound

across time and space,

like two stars caught

in a gravitational swirl

shining their kaleidoscopic

incandescent beauty

for all the universe to marvel.

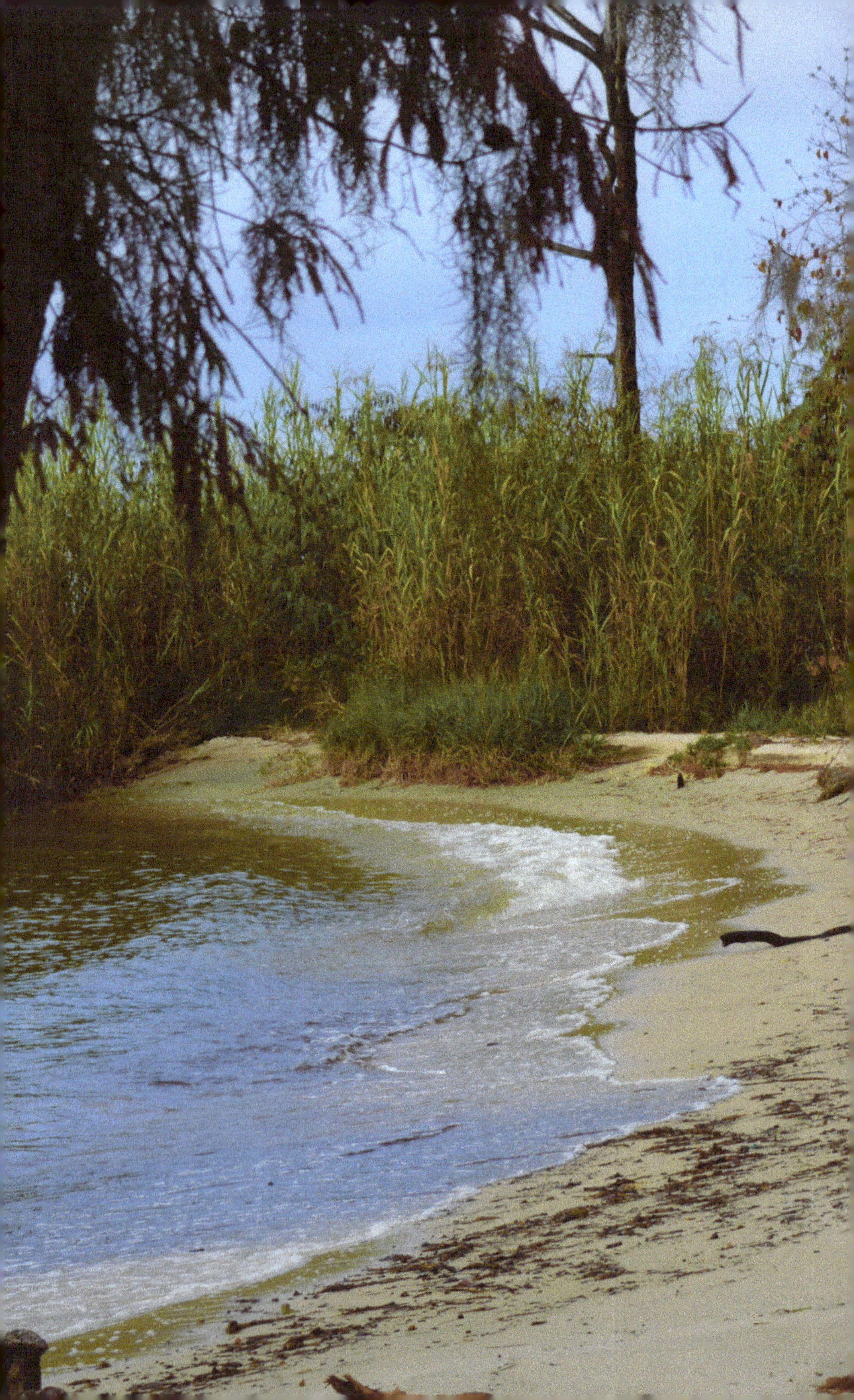

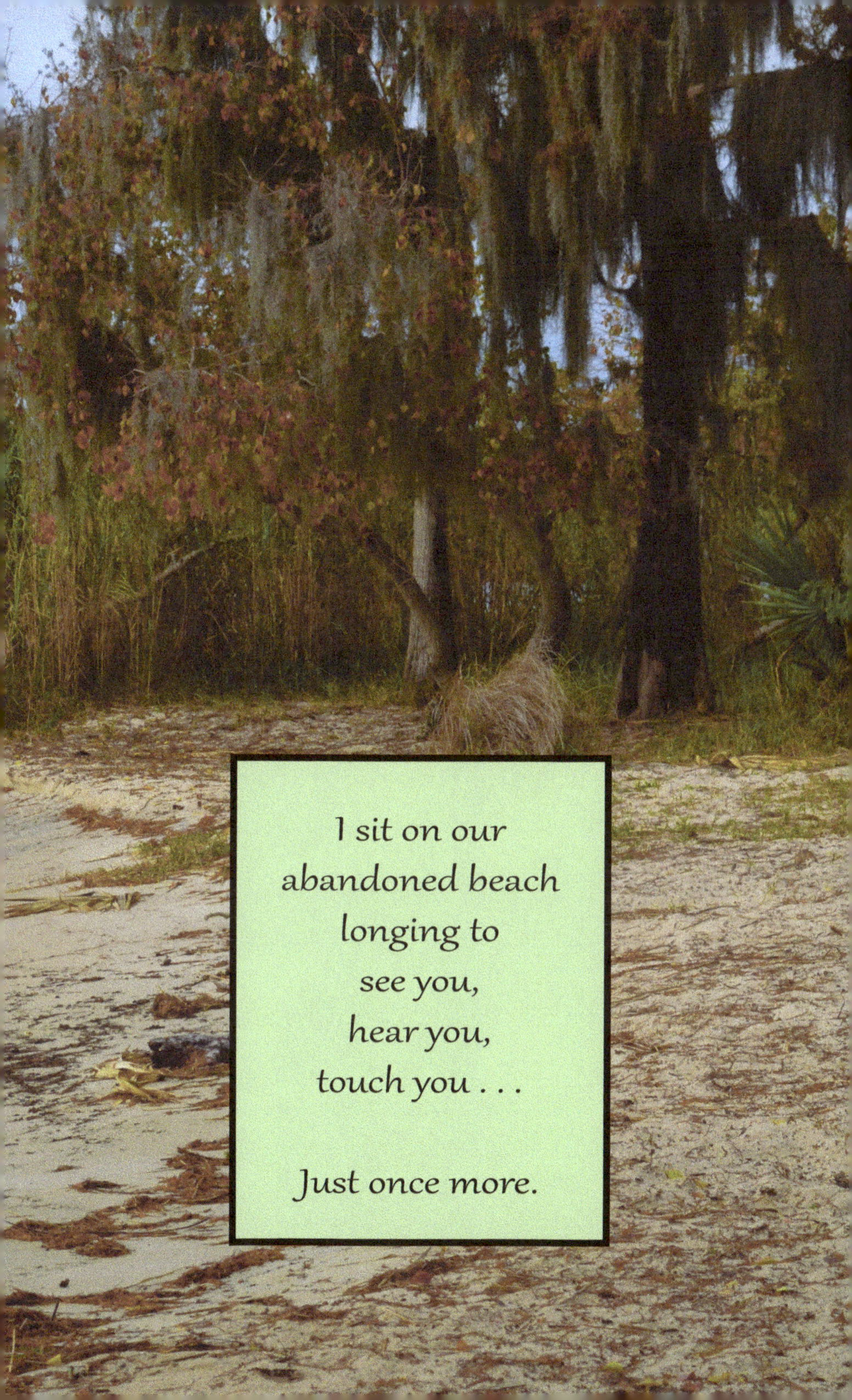
I sit on our
abandoned beach
longing to
see you,
hear you,
touch you . . .

Just once more.

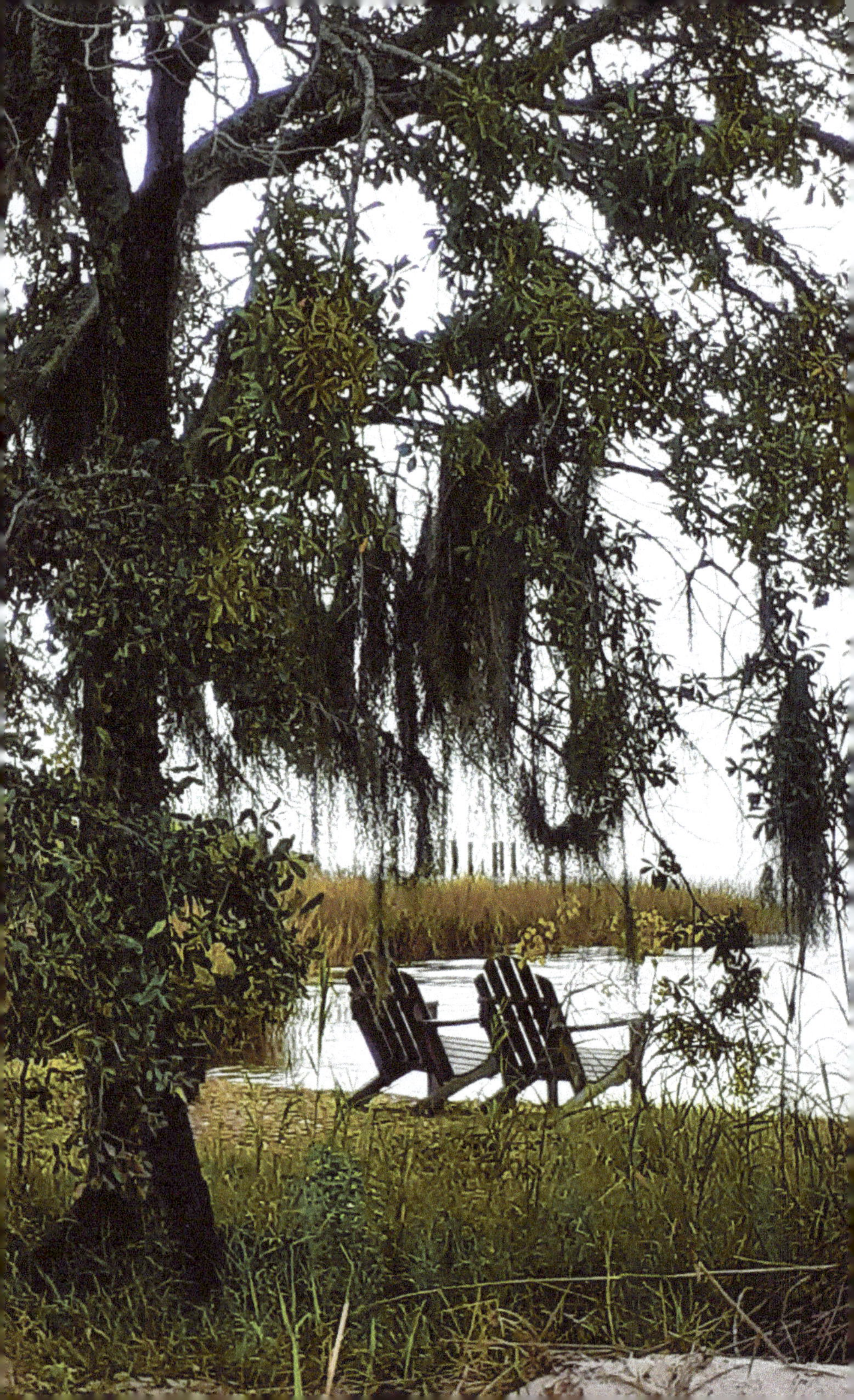

Upon This Shore

Upon this shore we found our love,
And felt our cares drift away
By the moonlit tides that caressed our feet,
Dancing about until dawn's next day.

The far end is our secluded crescent,
Where our passion still echoes upon the sand.
And the other, our sitting chairs,
Where we conjured our dreams and created new plans.

The warm water purified our love,
And quelled many of our fears.
It carries the salt of our bodies
From tenderly licking our crying tears.

Many seasons will come and go,
But our essence will always remain.
As the love of Adonis and Aphrodite
Is within a single red rose, forever sustained.

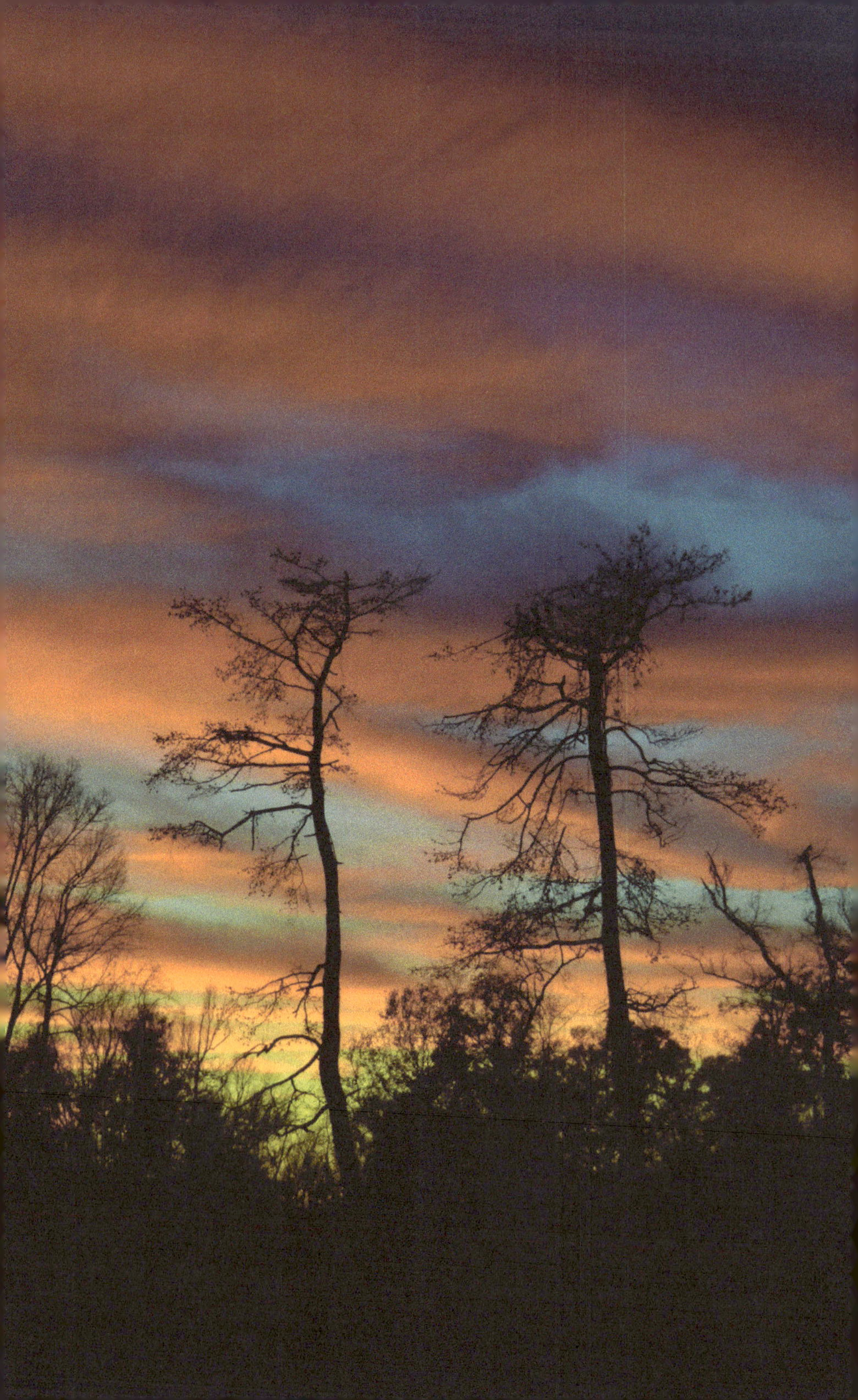

I Imagine

I imagine you beside me as I wake,
Expecting your touch to heal my ache.
My nights are filled with dreams of you,
And in the quiet of my day, you're there, too.

I hear your voice in every melody,
With each note creating its own elegy.
I can still feel your tenderest kiss
Teasing me into . . . hmmm . . . utter bliss.

The love you had when you looked at me
Is forever seared in my memory.
You're the most beautiful man I've ever known,
And even though your gone, I'm never alone.

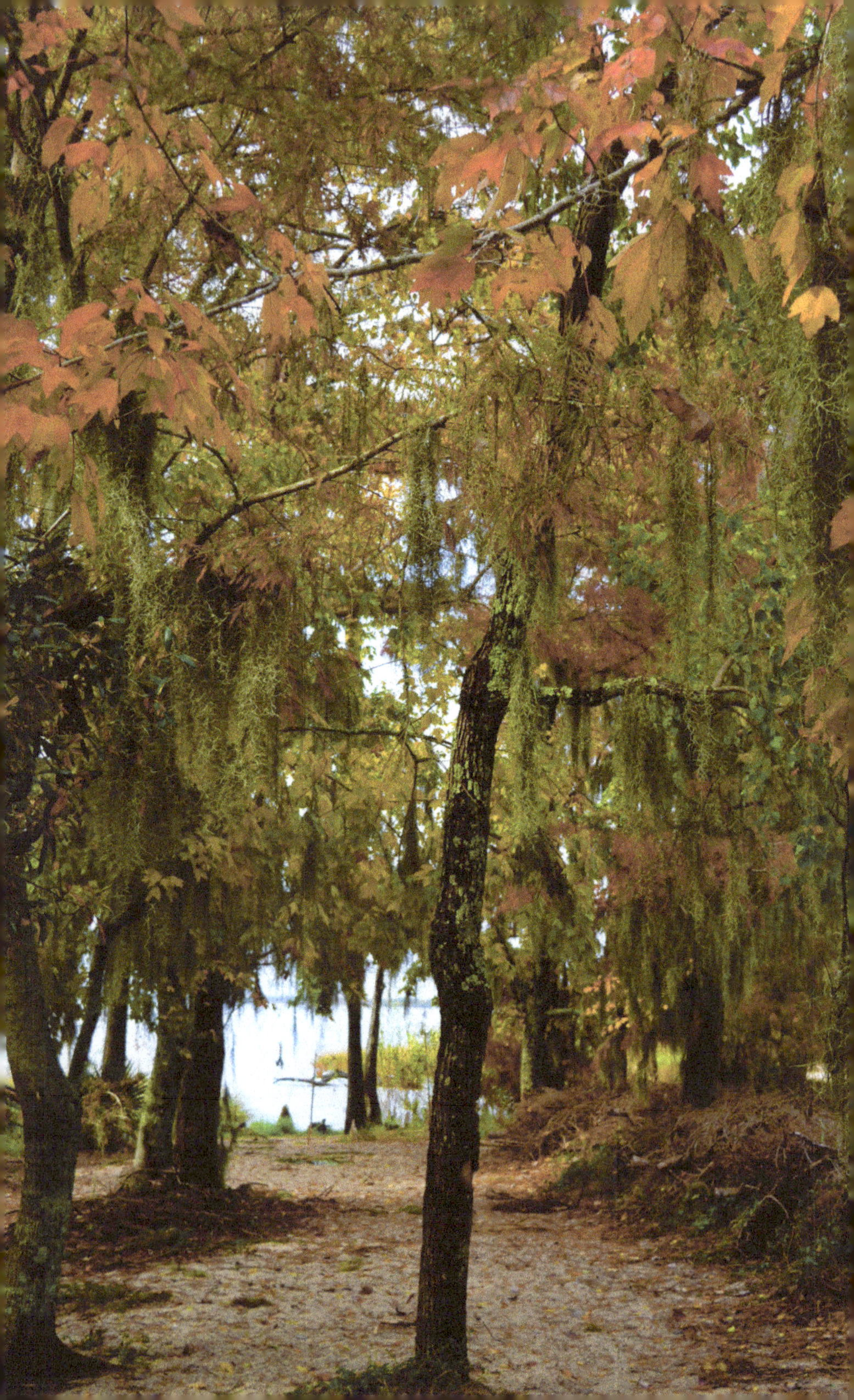

There's a Sweetness About the Air

There's a sweetness about the air.
Like honeysuckle on a hot summer's day,
It drips a palate of candy enticing my senses,
Stirring a moment in memory like no other way.

We had walked about along nature's path,
Not far from the sandy shore of our secluded beach
Where mossy trees told grand old stories,
And painted turtles played within our reach.

The night had stayed warm as the dusky sun set,
And we dipped ourselves in the lake,
Our bodies glistening in the golden aura
As we made love in the water's wake.

Your gentle motion took me back and forth
With the pulsating rhythm against the shore.
A final wave came crashing upon us
With a love I'd not ever known before.

We laid entwined upon the sand,
Its grains sprinkled about our skin.
The warmth of your body and safety of your arms
Was the happiest I had ever been.

There's a sweetness about the air.
It takes me back to that memory
And every moment of bliss we've ever shared.
It drips a love, a forevermore, and is filled with serenity.

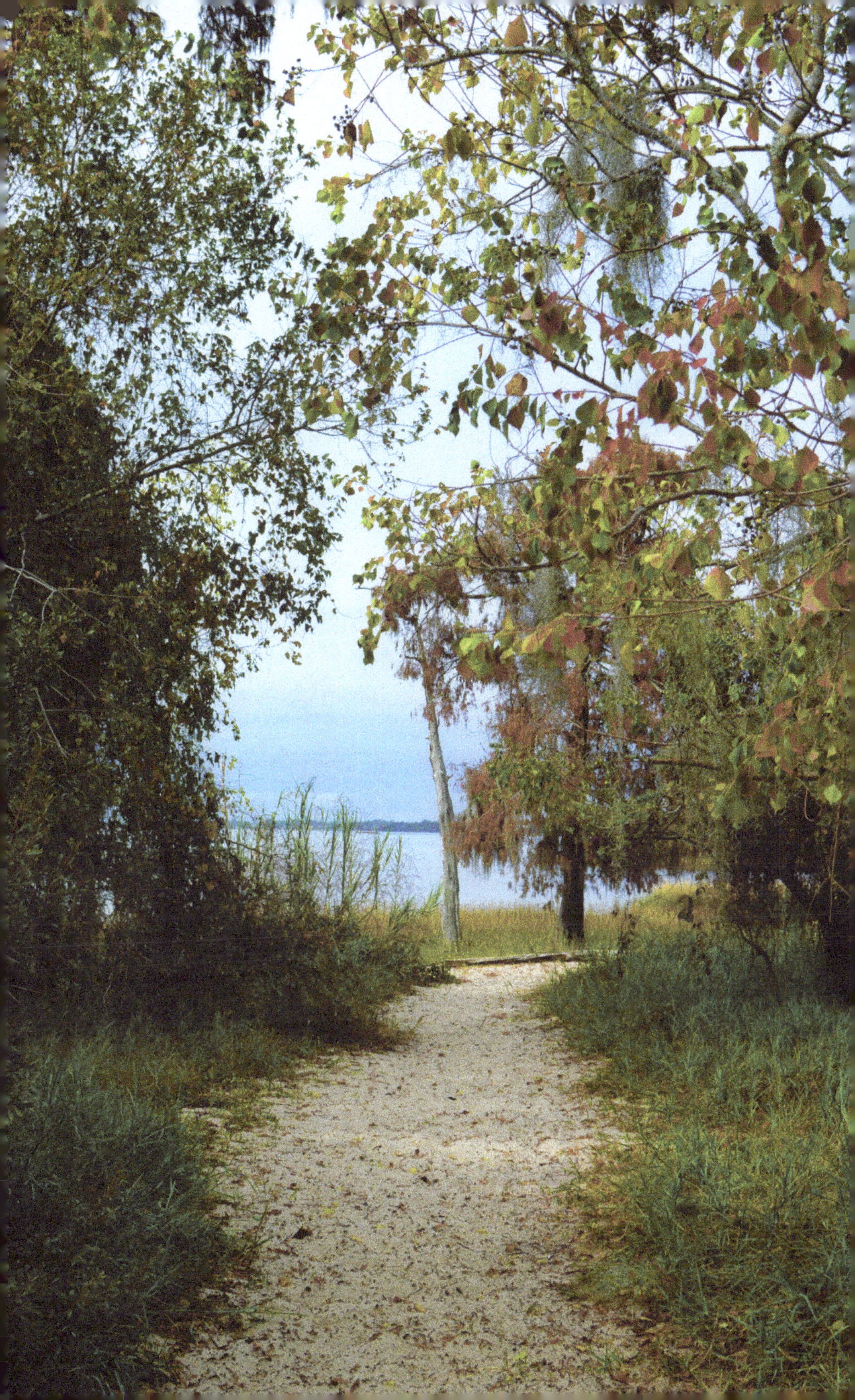

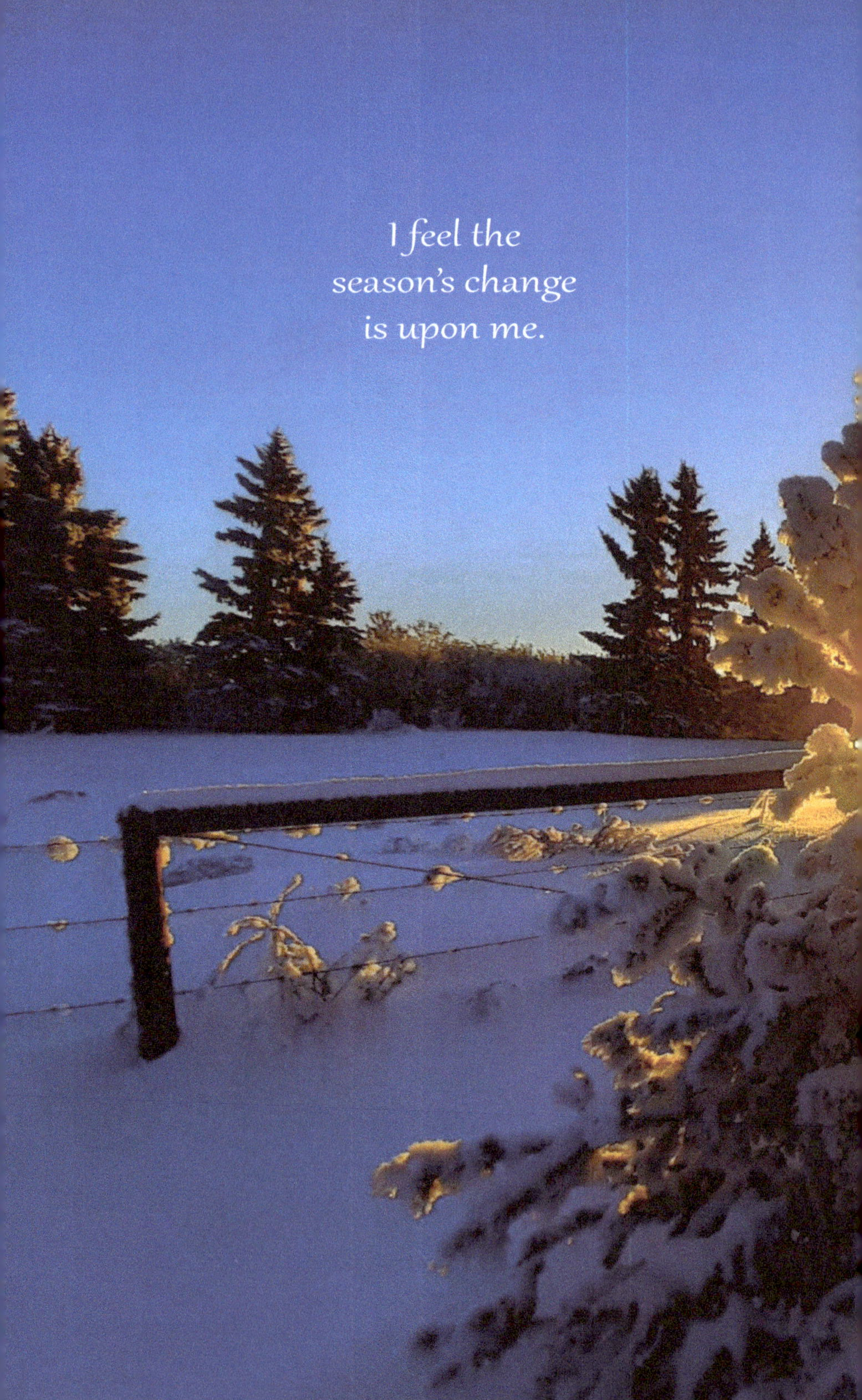
I feel the
season's change
is upon me.

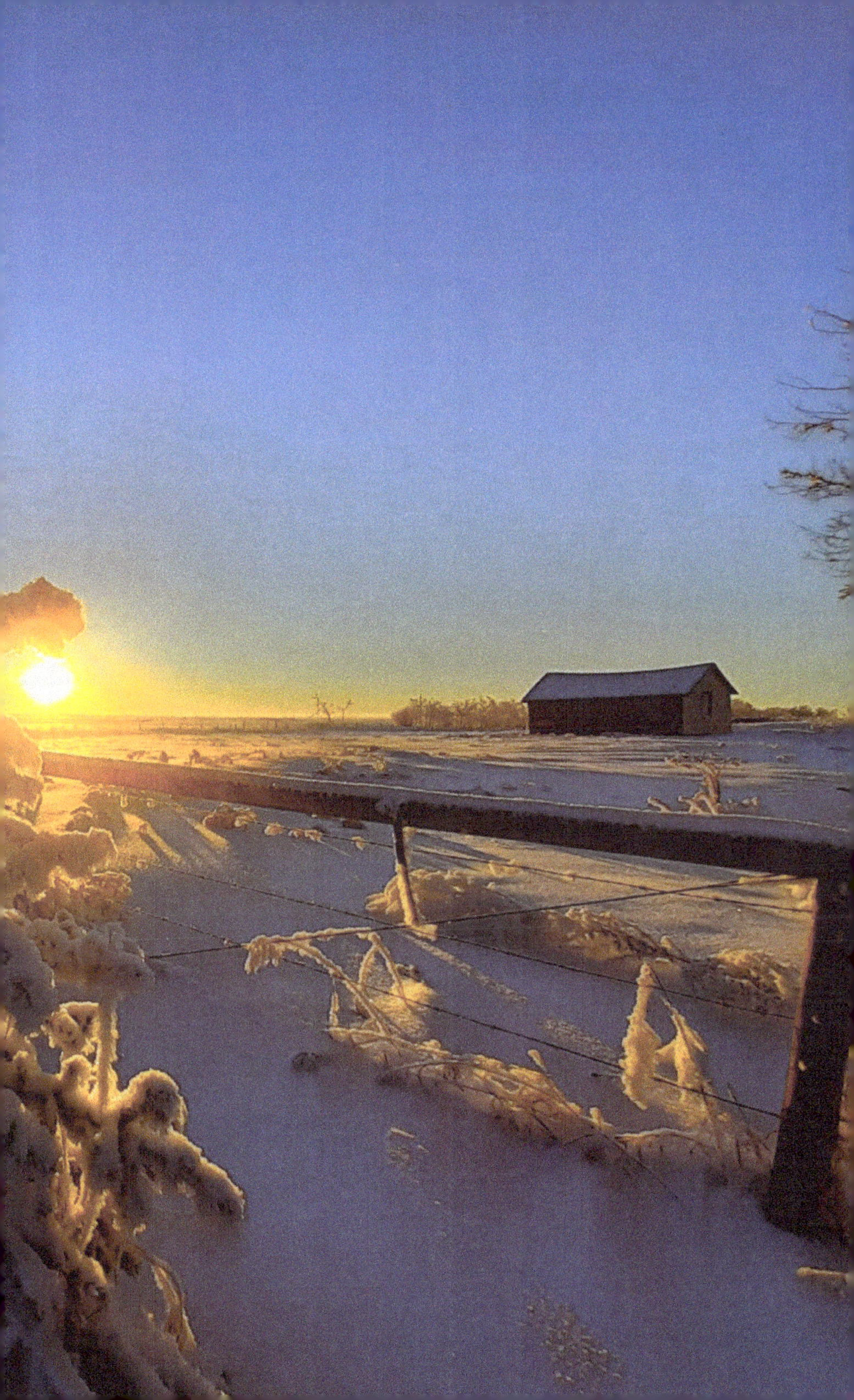

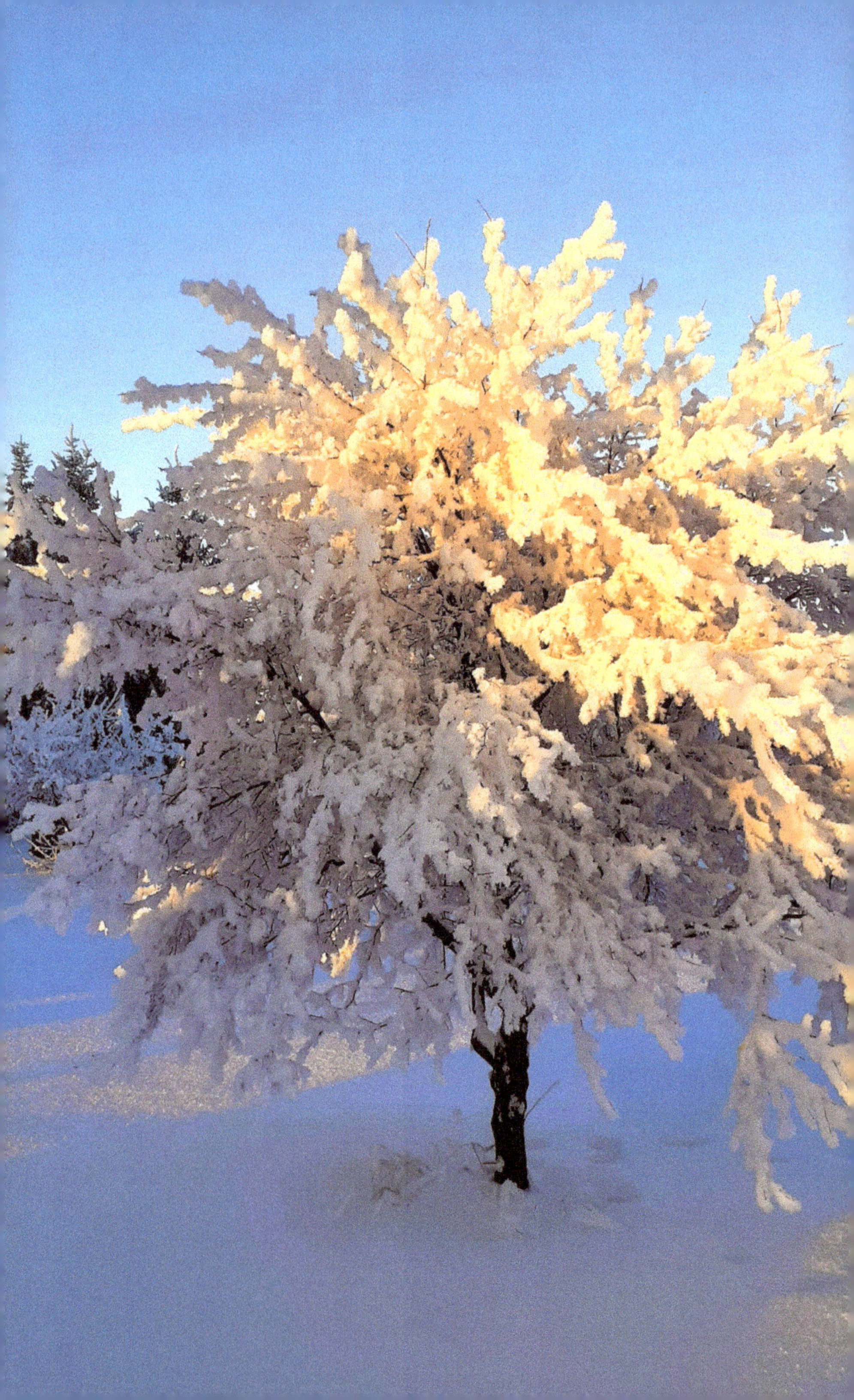

The Winter of My Soul

In the winter of my soul,
I have found a peace that had long since been lost.
It drips with the sweet taste of honey
harvested just before the frost.

I wonder if it had always been there
and why it was so hard to find.
But then, these last years,
so much has lurked and shadowed my mind.

When I was younger,
the sun, the moon, and the stars had guided my way.
I felt their warmth and blissful light
each and every day.

Was it the constellations that had changed?
Or was it me?
Did the sun grow cold?
Did the moon stop breathing along the sea?

I'm older now and well aware of
the machinations of my heart.
Grief had skulked far too long,
and that was largely on my part.

But more than ever,
I'm ready to go forward and live my life.
Even though I've lost,
I will always be a mother and forever your wife.

The sun is rising,
revealing its glory for me to cast my eyes,
And for the first time in a long time,
I've come to realize:

Life is to be lived with all the joy
and love that can be found,
Along with beauty, and music,
and goodness that does abound.

I'm feeling a warm serenity
in the wintery days of my soul.
It's like a lazy Sunday of dreams fulfilled,
making my heart whole,

Or the stillness of a morning pond
where crickets can be heard,
And the cornucopia of melodies
that are sung by a bluebird.

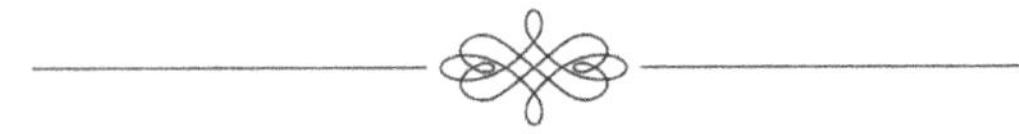

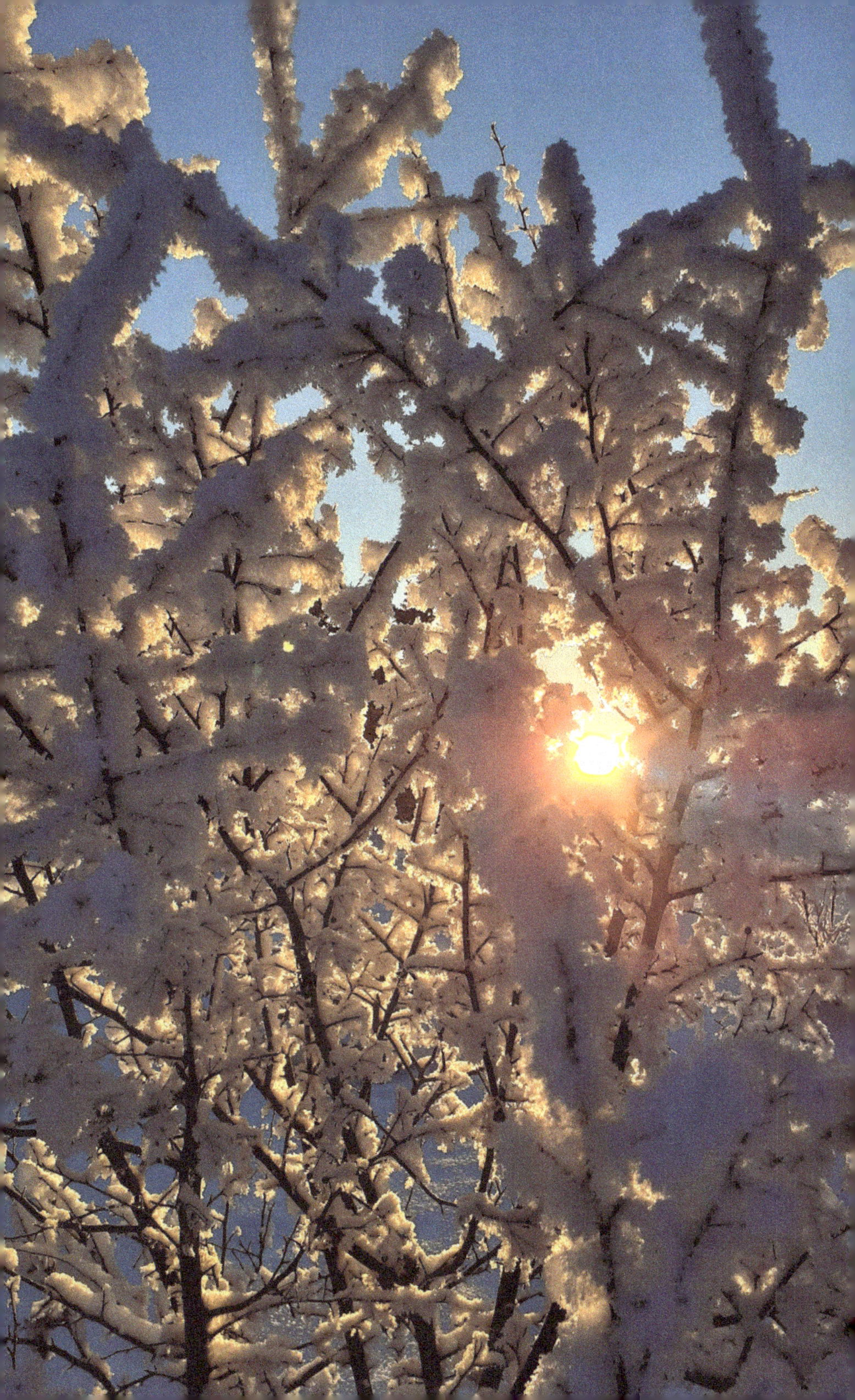

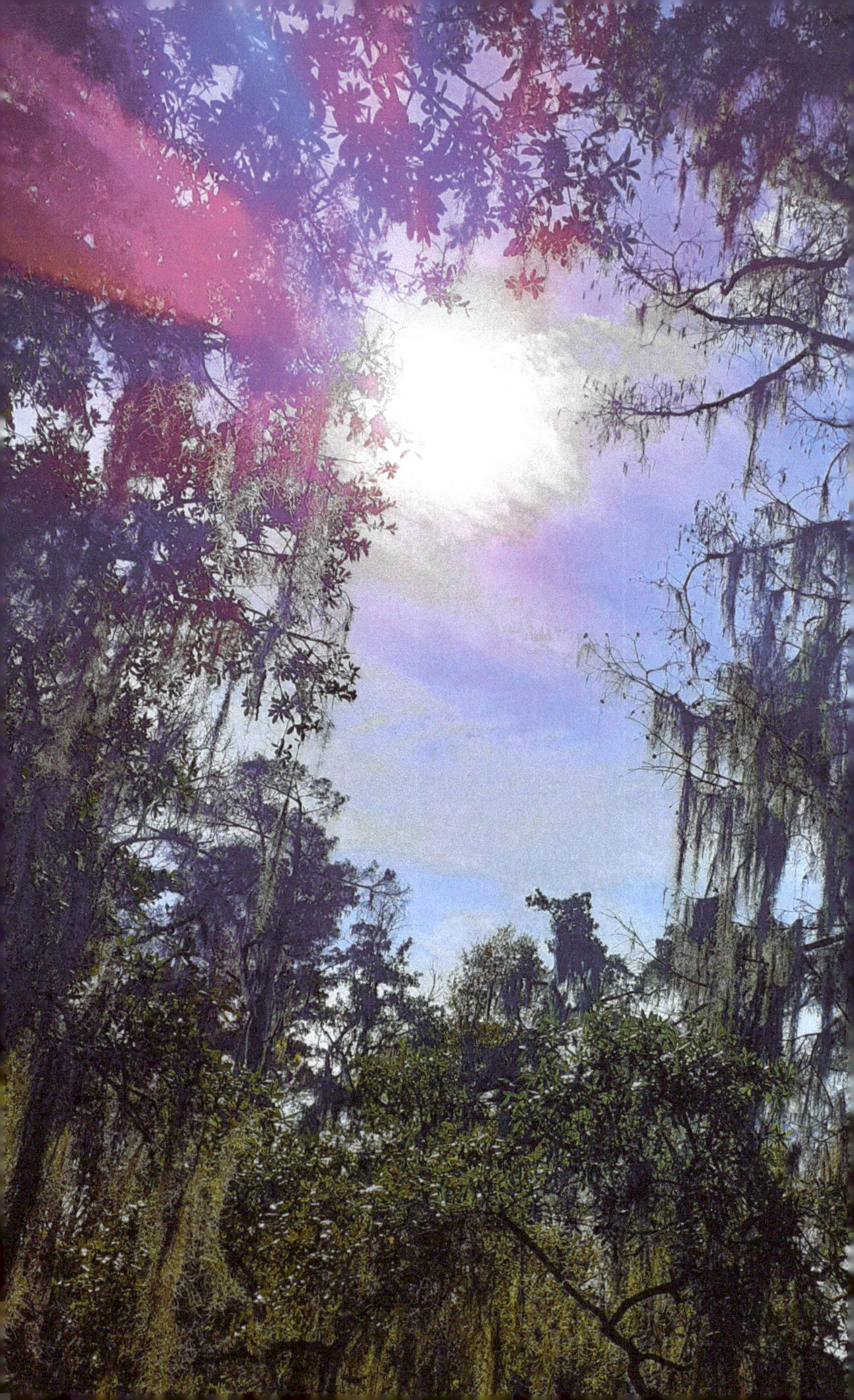

The Legend of Us

The paradise of us is a constant echo
That, after a while, begins to grow
Until time and space can no longer hold,
And the legend of us must be told.

It all began in our dreams—
A place we'd meet, or so it seemed.
Night after night, you were there,
Standing under the crescent's stare.

My heart knew you were the one.
One touch and I was undone.
You were the Adonis to my Aphrodite,
The only soul that would ever complete me.

When you found me on this mortal plane,
Our love nearly drove us both insane.
For our circumstance were beyond control
Until we learned to separately become whole.

Then together we built our life,
And I was honored to become your wife.
But there were lessons we had yet to learn,
For to be parents we so yearned.

I am without words for that kind of pain,
For the many years of hurt and shame.
But we found a way to move on,
And give meaning to what is sadly gone.

Thank you for the time we've had—
The bliss, the carefree, and the mad.
For you, my love, I would do anything,
Because you are my absolute everything.

My earthly life has been beautiful,
But now I feel the heavens pull.
There, I will find you once more,
Patiently waiting on our sandy shore.

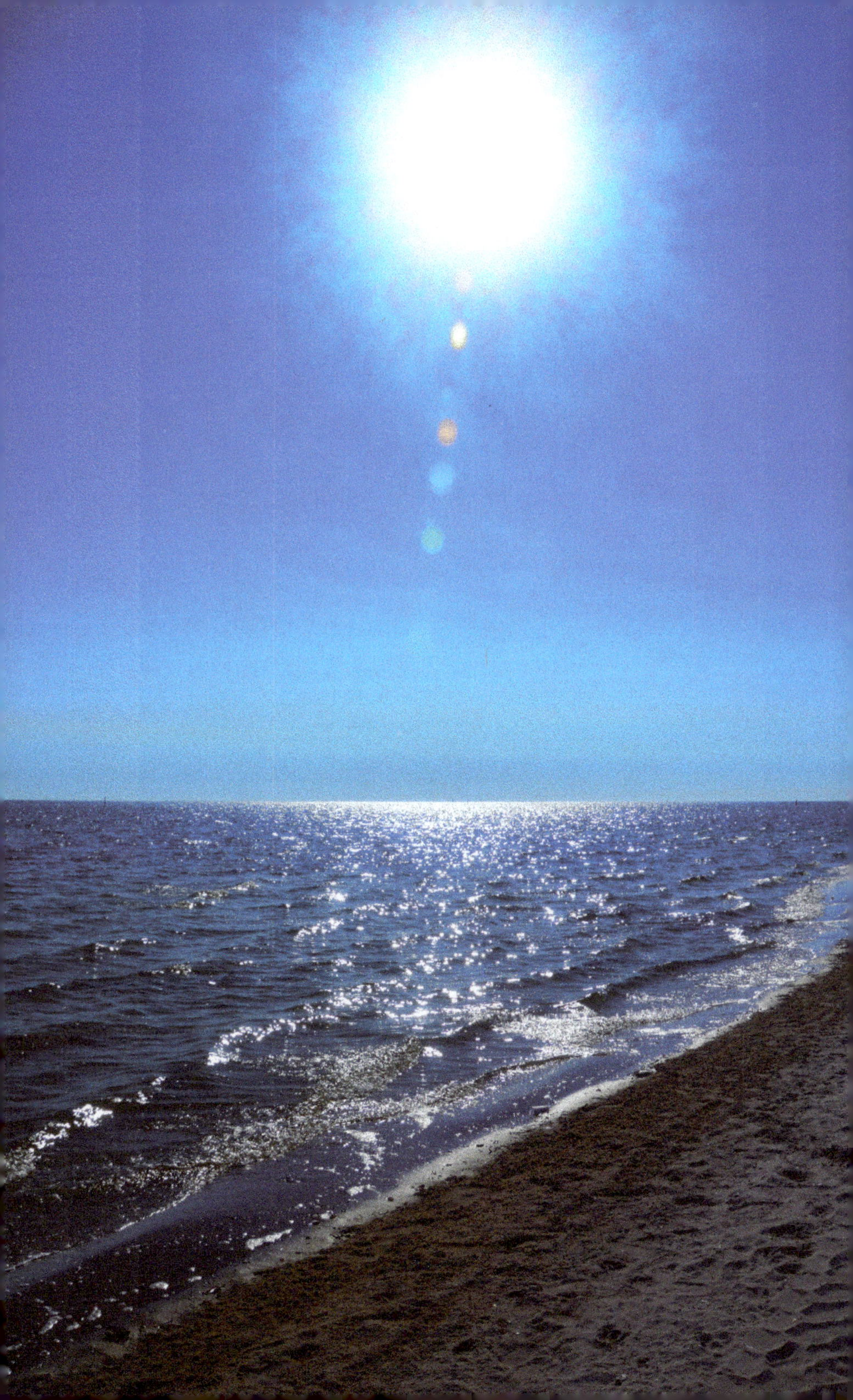

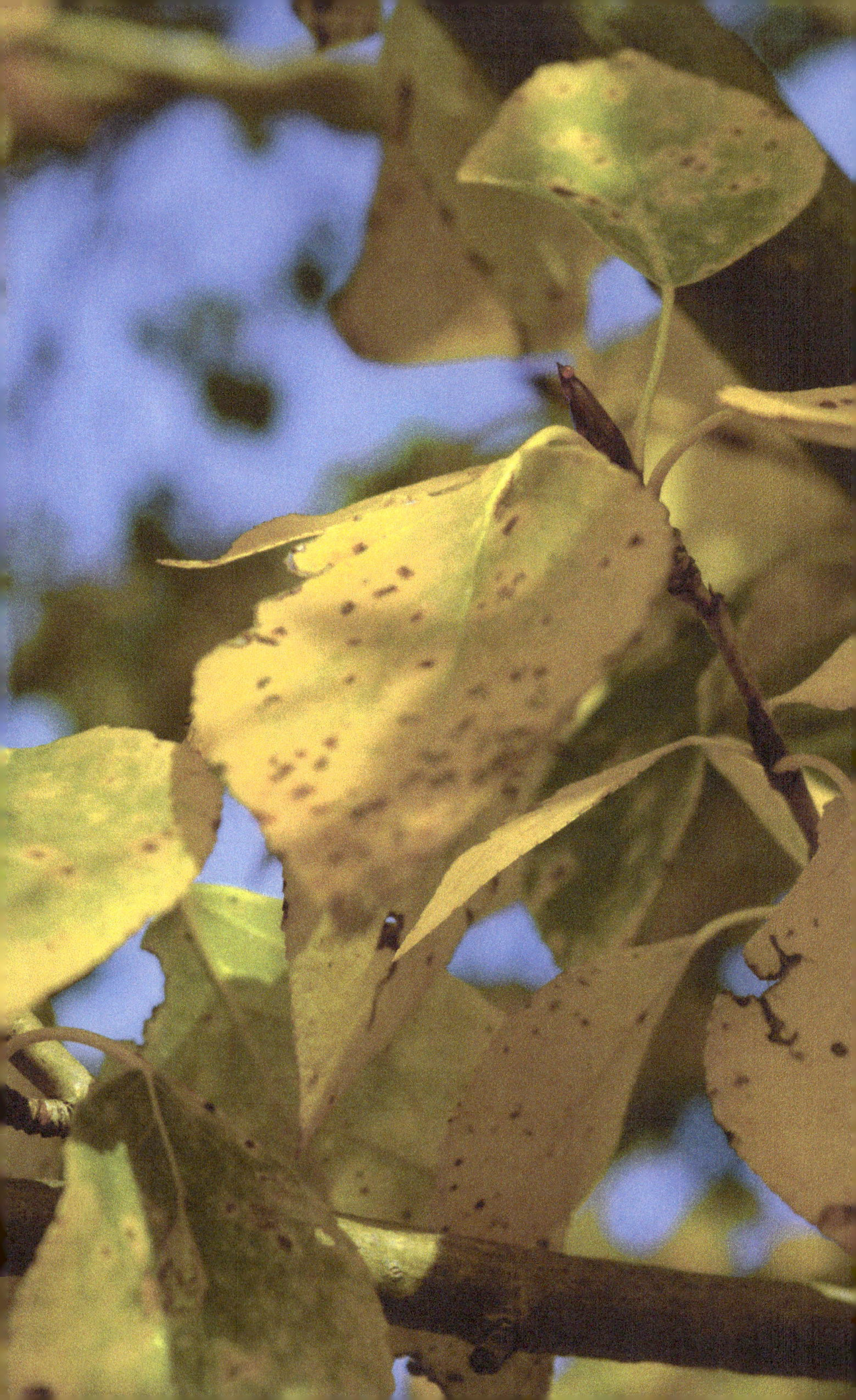

I Am a Leaf

I am a leaf—
Delicate as lace,
Tattered by the wind,
Burned from the heat,
Drenched in the rain,
Fallen to the ground,
Left in the cold,
Soon to die.

I am a leaf.

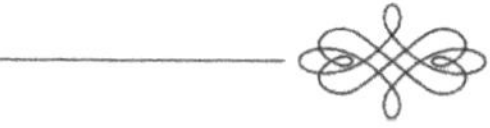

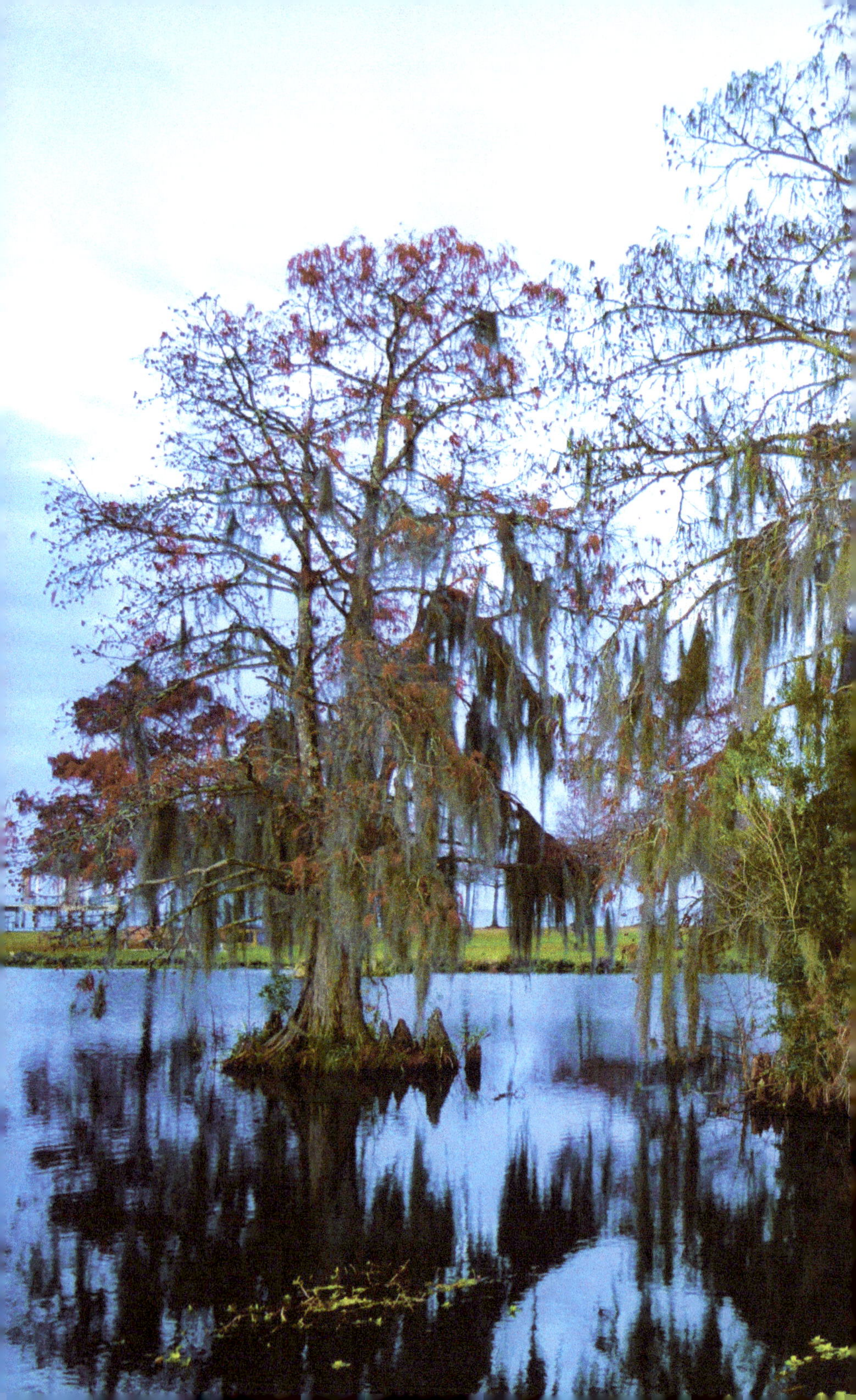

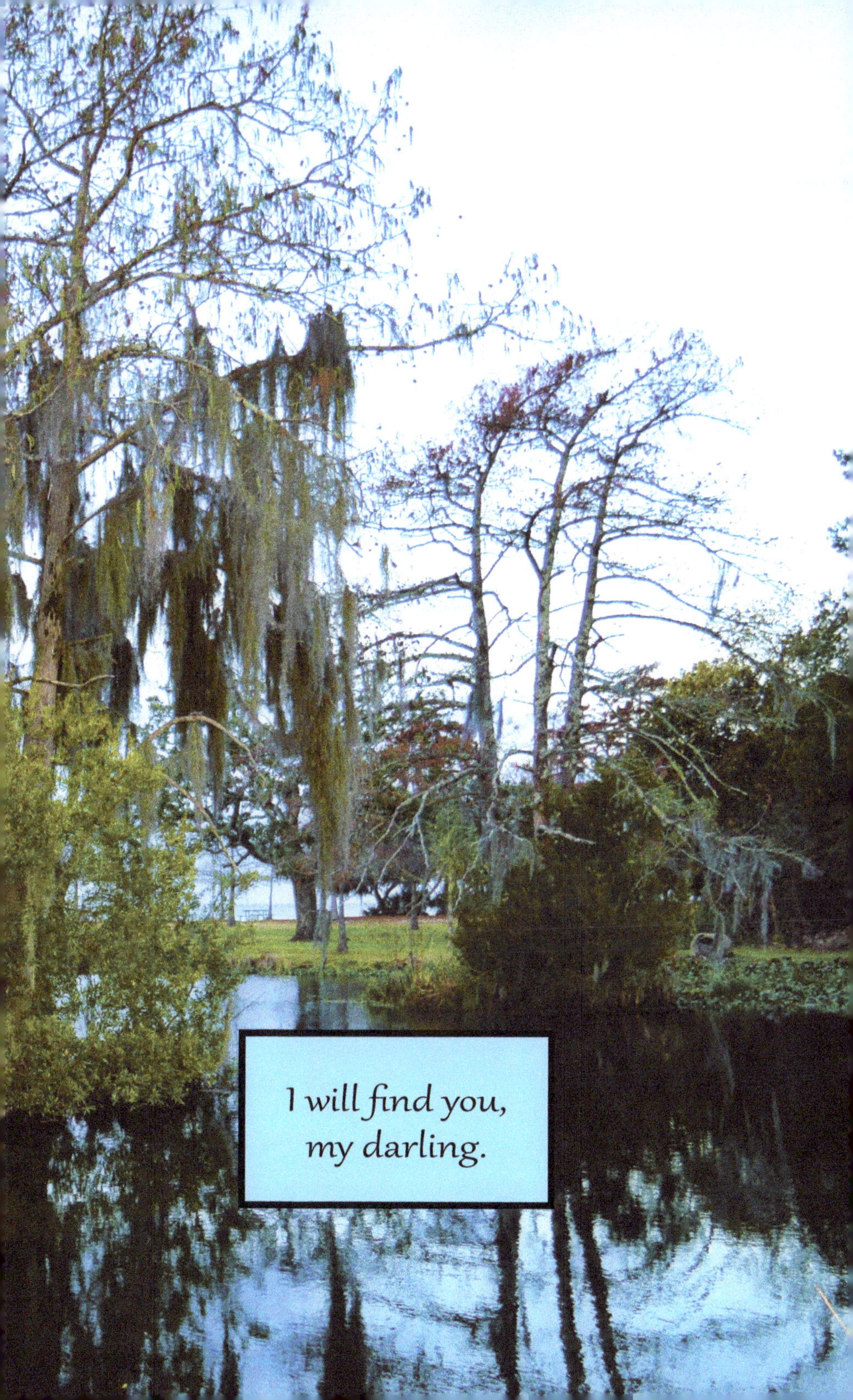
I will find you,
my darling.

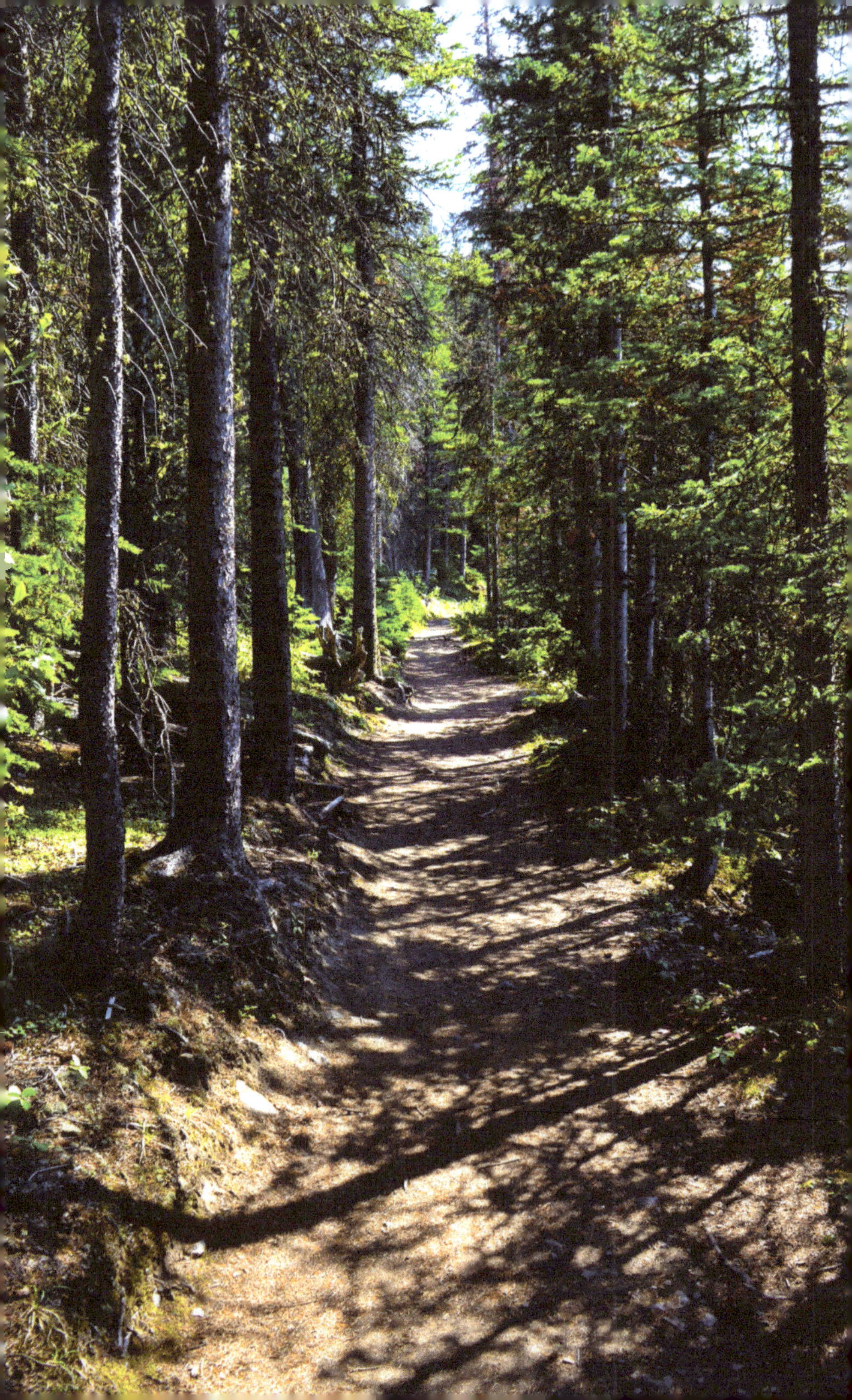

The Path

There exists a path so clear before me,
And although shadows creep across,
The light from above grants my eyes to see
Past what lurks and stones that are tossed.

My soul is filled with all that is good
From the trails that intercept.
They are like little neighborhoods,
But from my path I must not be swept.

I mustn't be lured by a detour,
Because it really has no place to go.
They come enough to be sure,
But they soon pass when the west winds blow.

At times I need more than to face
An obstacle that is in my way.
I've learned that I must embrace,
And wring out what I just can't slay.

Once during a time of dark shadow,
I cried out in my moment of plight.
Then help came in the form of a crow,
And he took me high up on his flight.

Everything below was my life, to be sure,
And what I saw was more than I could believe.
The good, the bad, and all I'd endured,
But the path itself was the trunk of a tree.

I had been traveling for so long,
And the path had seemed endless.
Many times, I felt like I didn't belong,
And yet, I was so very blessed.

The light had never left me.
It always hovered above,
Giving strength as the need may be,
And warmth that wrapped me in gentle love.

My reward was happiness and peace galore,
With a love that is true.
Not just for a little while, but for an evermore.
And besides all of that,

I finally found you.

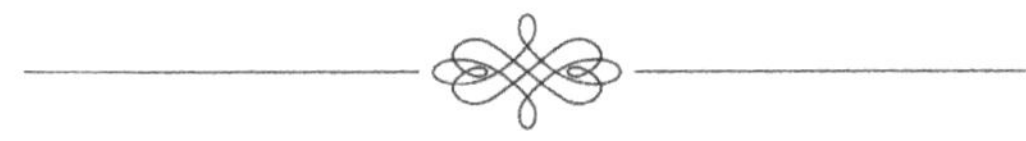

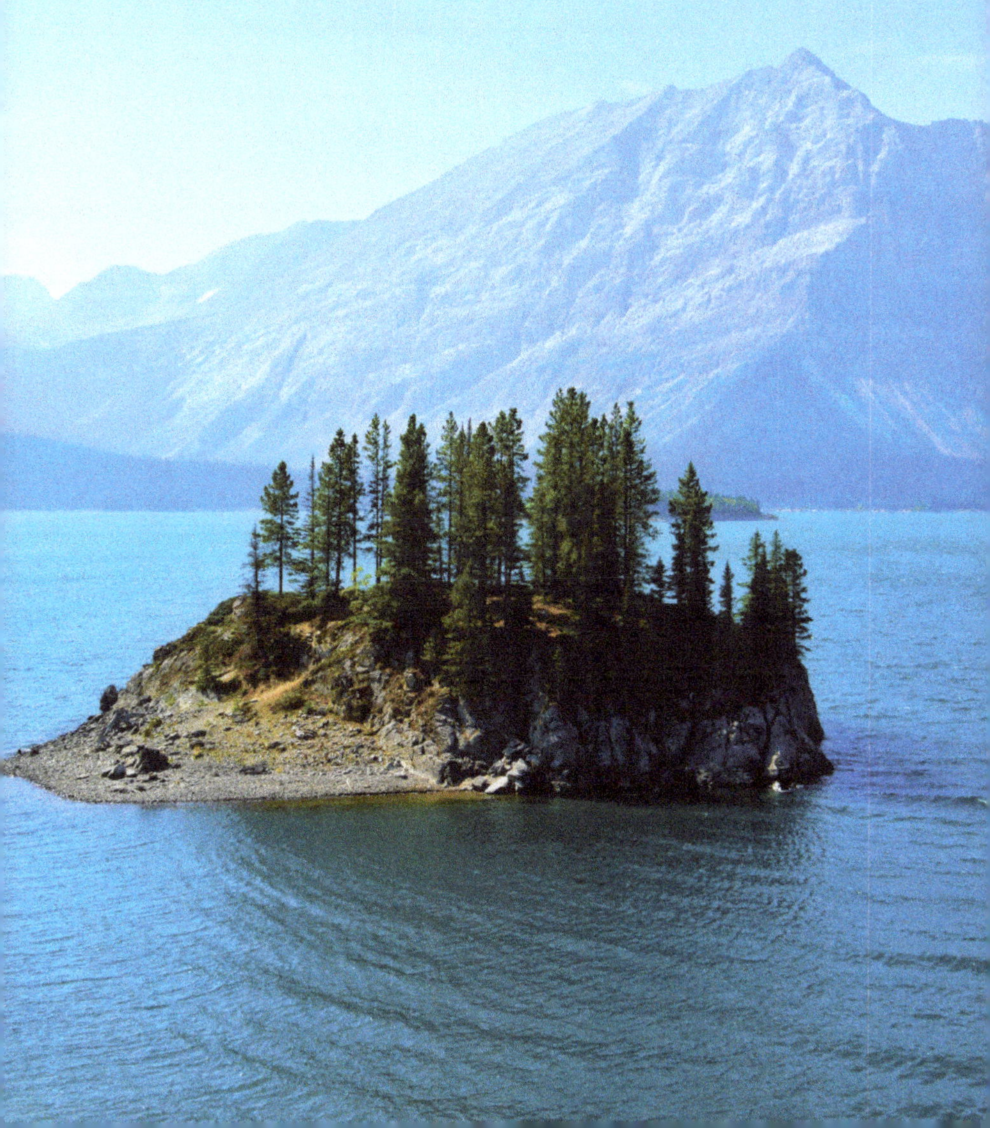
We must begin again,
my love.

Find me.

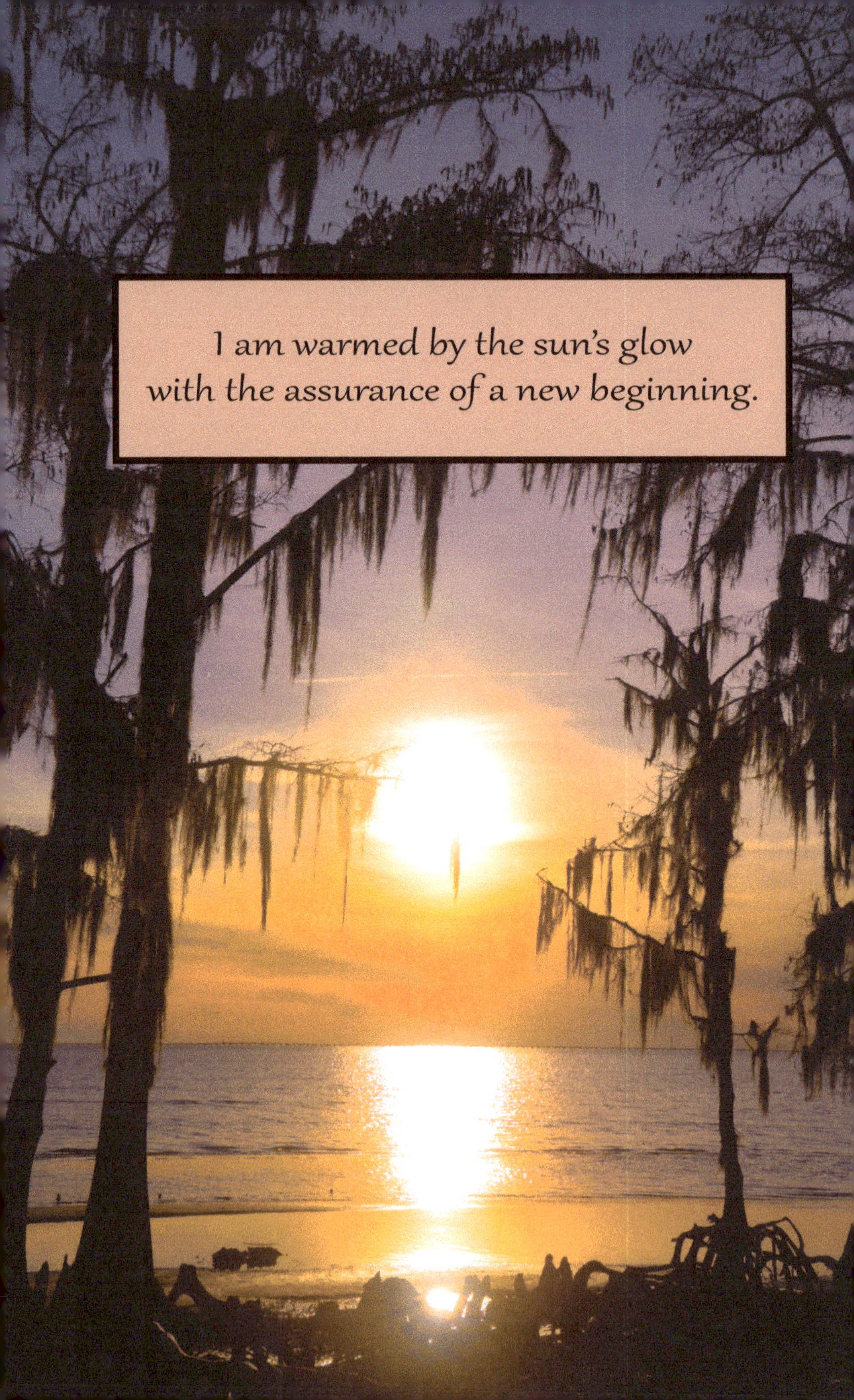

I am warmed by the sun's glow
with the assurance of a new beginning.

By the Light of the Crescent Moon

This place pulls me somehow.
Like the moon tugs at the shore,
It dances and ebbs at me,
And I have to know more.

I'm beckoned this night,
And I don't know why.
But I need to find out,
I need to try.

I feel like I've lived many lives
Because there's so much familiarity.
And this place, this shore,
Has about it an eternity.

From the trees hang mossy beards;
They are wizards of old.
And in these swamps, dragons sleep.
Of stories long ago, they were told.

I'm walking along the beach
With my toes soaking up the sand.
Was this all just by chance?
Or was it somehow planned?

My heart is pounding
With what I will find,
Yet I keep going forward
For fear I will lose my mind.

There's been a wanting in my life,
As though I haven't been whole.
There's someone from my dreams—
He's the other half of my soul.

He comes to me while I sleep,
And brings me to this beach.
I can almost touch him,
And then he's out of reach.

I can see his face so clear,
As though he were a part of me.
Will he be here tonight?
Is he my true destiny?

My heart wells with certainty
As I approach the private lagoon.
And I see my true love standing
By the light of the crescent moon.

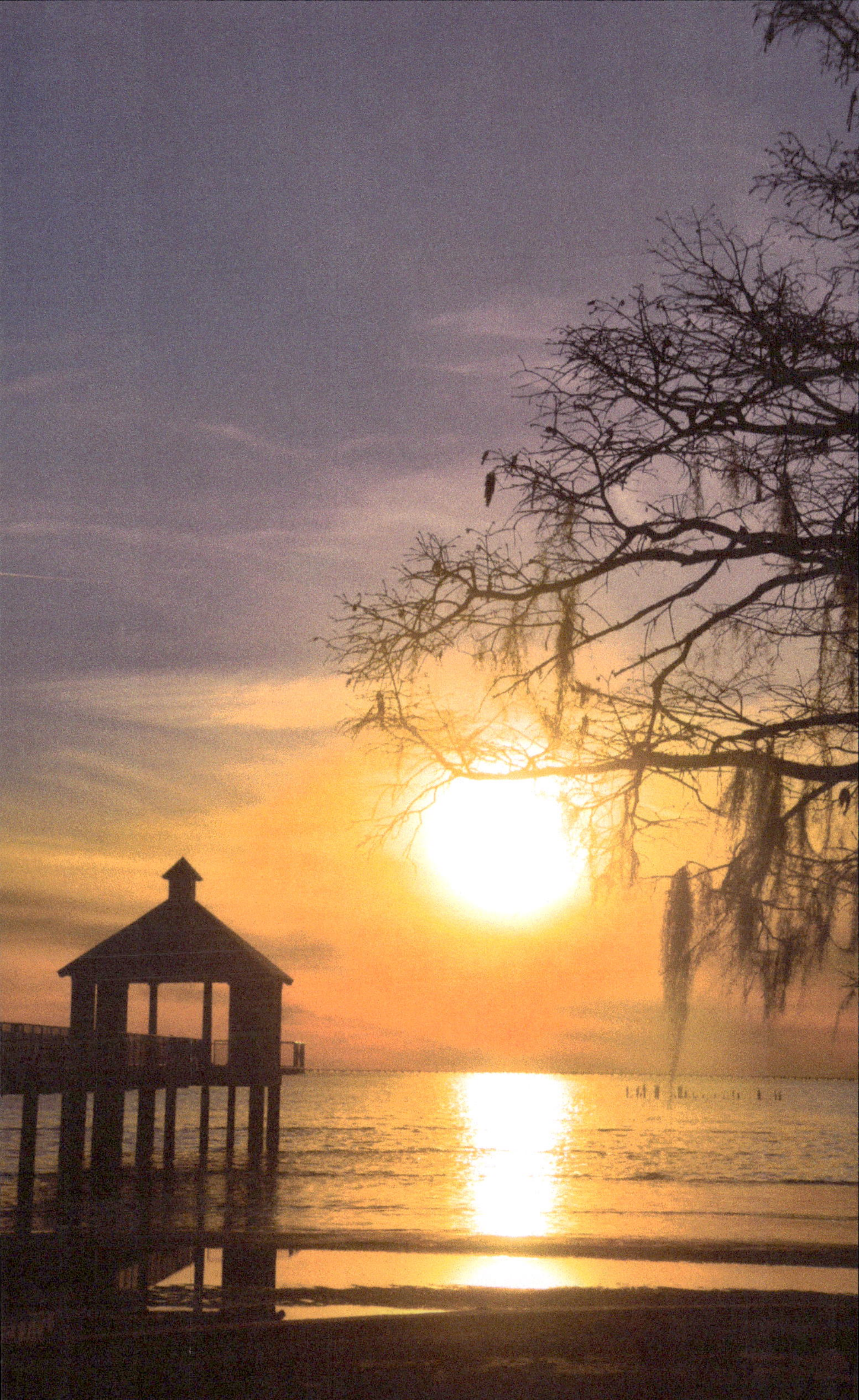

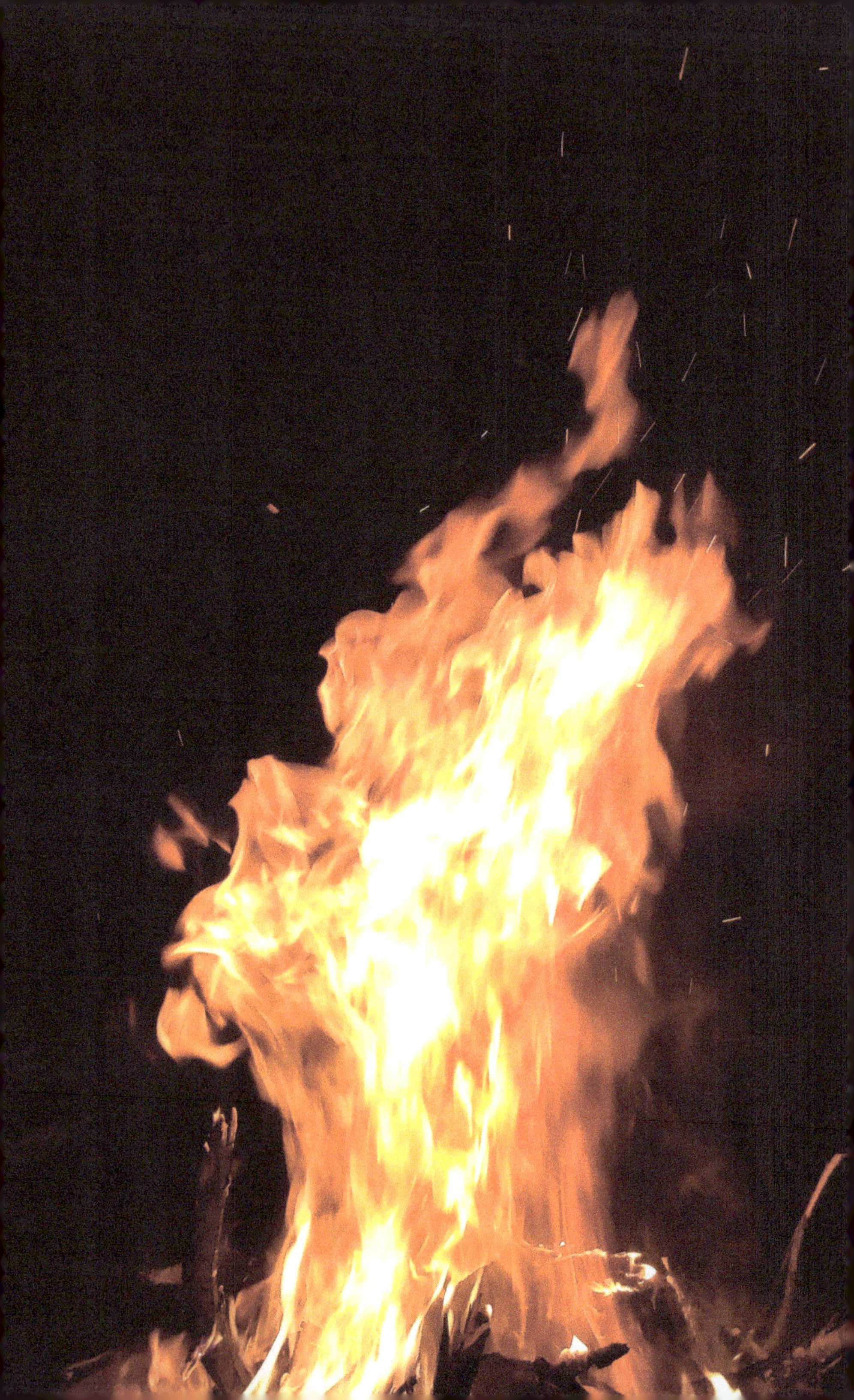

Eternal Flame
Reprise from The Echo of You

There exists a fire calling to me—
A familiarity I've not known.
It burns a path deep in my soul,
Lighting a way for me alone.

In my mind soft whispers echo,
"You know me and my name.
Your heart will find me soon,
For I am your love, your eternal flame."

The path is filled with treachery—
Darkness, angst, deceit, and sorrow.
If it were not for the burning light,
I fear I might not see the morrow.

In my mind soft whispers echo,
"You know me and my name.
Keep enduring my dear one,
For I am your love, your eternal flame."

The longing I feel keeps me going
To find the one that beckons me.
Through turmoil this course I stay,
Coming closer to my destiny.

In my mind soft whispers echo,
"You know me and my name.
Let the fire light your way,
For I am your love, your eternal flame."

His voice is my constant companion,
Reassuring all my fears.
With determination I continue on,
Searching for him through my tears.

In my mind soft whispers echo,
"You know me and my name.
Look to me as your strength,
For I am your love, your eternal flame."

As the path comes to its end,
The fire burns out of control.
Weakly, I fall to the ground,
For the journey has taken its toll.

In my mind soft whispers echo,
"You know me and my name.
I'm right here in front of you,
For I am your love, your eternal flame."

From the midst of its hot center
Emerges the one I am destined for.

Kneeling down, he holds me close,
Vowing to never let go forevermore.

In his ear I softly whisper,
"I know you and your name.
Our hearts are beating as one,
For I am your love, your eternal flame."

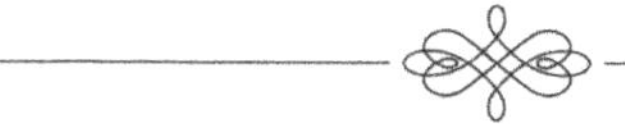

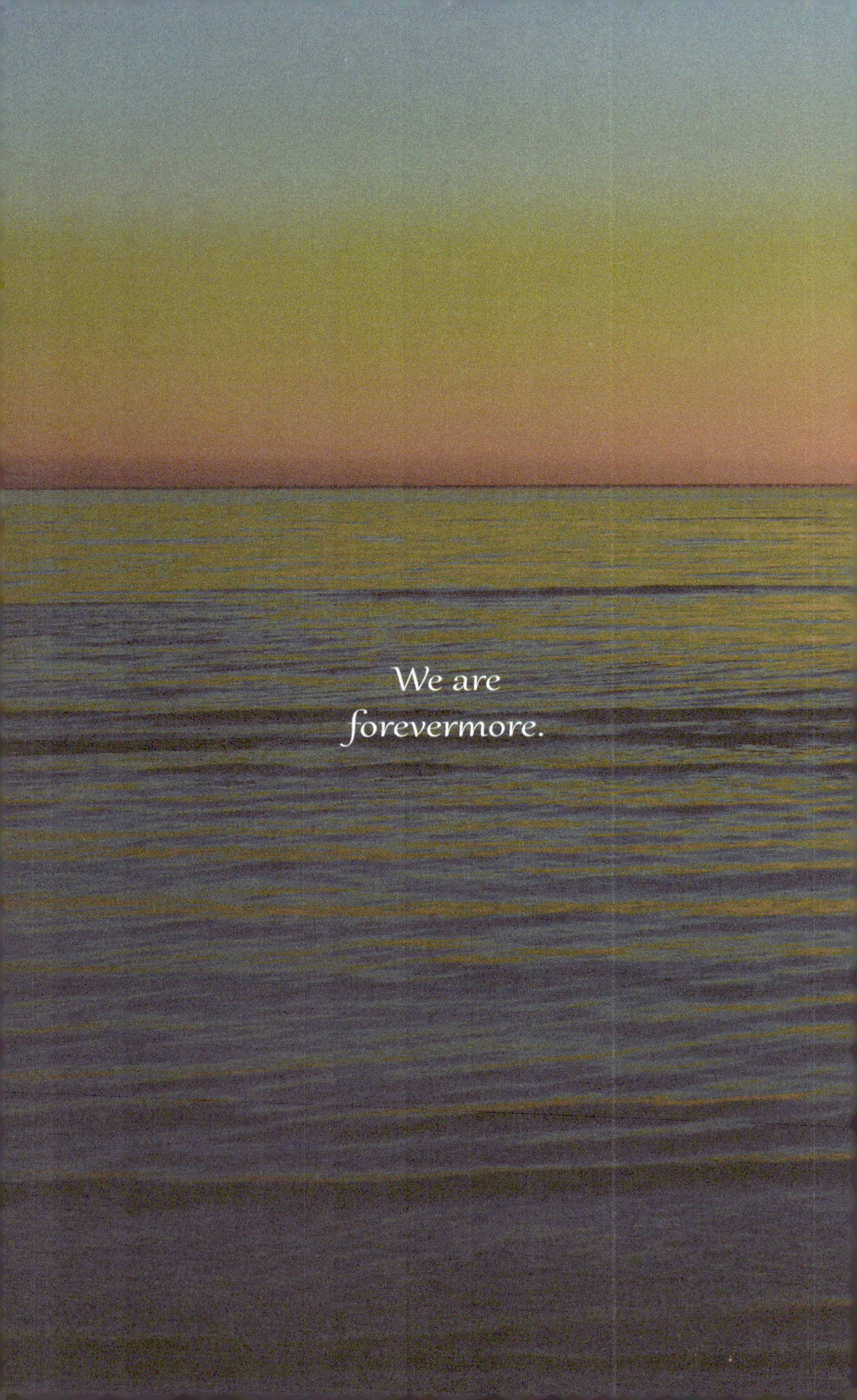

We are
forevermore.

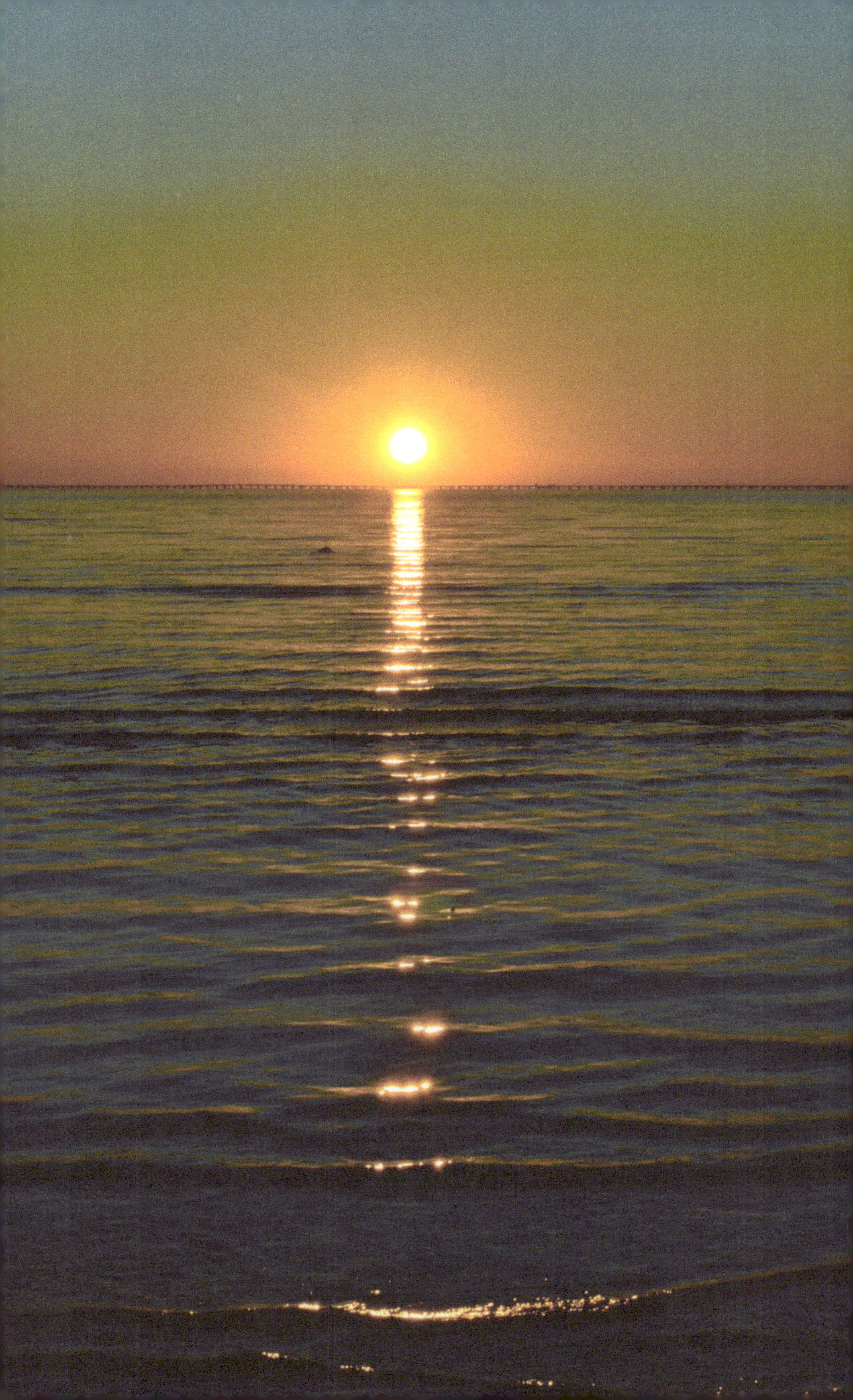

As each life ends,

memories of all

the previous ones return,

only but for an instant.

Then, I am reborn

to find you once again.

I would live a thousand lives

and cross a thousand worlds

to be with you, my darling,

for I am in love with you,

body and soul.

Forevermore.

ACKNOWLEDGMENTS

It wasn't long after *The Echo of You* was published that I found myself waking in the wee hours of the morning flooded with emotions that needed to be transformed into poems. Then, during the day, I couldn't seem to take enough photos to satisfy the calling in my soul. I clearly wasn't done telling the story of this destined couple! Several months later, after much travel and living a reclusive lifestyle, *The Echo of Us* was born.

This book truly would not have seen the light of day had it not be for the support of three very key people in my life:

Glenn, my husband of over twenty-five years, thank you for painstakingly supporting my travel to far away places and providing me with all the camera equipment I could possibly need. Thank you for encouraging me into photography all those years ago, even when I thought I didn't want to at the time. Now, I can't think of anything

I love more than to sit in the solitude of nature and capture the art of creation.

Christian, I am beyond words for the gratitude I have for you. You came into my life when I thought I'd never find the heart to write again. But there you were, the constant bright spot in every project we've ever worked on together! Whether it be mentoring, editing, partnering, or just listening to me, you have been a source of enlightenment and an example of perseverance. I hope I give more than I take.

Charlene, you have been the best friend I could ever hope to have. Thank you for listening to all the words I've ever written! You have cried with me, and laughed with me, and talked with me through all the feels a poet like me has. And that's a lot! I appreciate you more than you know.

In addition to the aforementioned, I am grateful for Peter Lougheed Provincial Park in Alberta, Canada, Fontainebleau State Park, Fairview-Riverside State Park, and Fireside RV Resort in Louisiana, United States, where I spent a considerable amount of my time capturing the rise and fall of the sun, the lush landscape, and the profuse wildlife.

And most importantly, thank you, dear reader, for without you, there would be no books. Keep reading! Keep imagining! And like the couple in this book, keep following your heart!